LIBRARY

Teaching, Learning and Assessment
in Science Education

Teaching, Learning and Assessment in Science Education

*Edited by Dee Edwards,
Eileen Scanlon and Dick West
at The Open University*

Published in association with
The Open University

Paul Chapman Publishing Ltd
144 Liverpool Road
London
N1 1LA

British Library Cataloguing in Publication Data

Teaching Learning and Assessment in
Science Education
I. Edwards, Dee
507

Edwards D., Scanlon E. and West D.

ISBN 1 85396 245 7

Typeset by Inforum, Rowlands Castle, Hants
Printed and bound by Athenaeum Press Ltd., Newcastle-upon-Tyne

B C D E F G H 9 8 7

Contents

Acknowledgements   vii
Contributors' details   ix
Preface: *Dee Edwards*   xi

PART 1: Science Education and Teaching
   Introduction
   Dee Edwards   3
1.1 Teaching and learning about science: considerations in the
   philosophy and sociology of science
   Derek Hodson   5
1.2 Three decades of science education reform in the USA
   Senta A. Raizen   33
1.3 Science education in Japan and the United States: are the
   Japanese beating us at our own game?
   Anton E. Lawson   58
1.4 International comparisons in science education
   Elaine Brown   66
1.5 Laboratory practice in further and higher education:
   developments in the design of practical work
   Mark Atlay and Dee Edwards   79
1.6 Exemplary practice in science classrooms
   Kenneth Tobin and Patrick Garnett   98

PART 2: Learning Science
   Introduction
   Eileen Scanlon   113
2.1 Why is science difficult to learn? Things are seldom what
   they seem
   Alex H. Johnstone   115
2.2 Research and the development of science in the primary school
   Wynne Harlen   124

2.3 Cognitive and conceptual change in adolescence
    Marcia C. Linn and Nancy Butler Songer   139
2.4 Twenty-nine children, five computers and a teacher
    Tim O'Shea, Eileen Scanlon, Malcolm Byard, Steve Draper,
    Rosalind Driver, Sara Hennessy, Roger Hartley, Claire O'Malley,
    Conroy Mallen, Geoff Mohamed and Daz Twigger   171
2.5 An exploration of long-term far-transfer effects following
    an extended intervention programme in the high-school
    science curriculum
    Philip Adey and Michael Shayer   190

PART 3: Issues in Assessment
    Introduction
    Dick West   223
3.1 Diagnostic assessment and its contribution to pupils' learning
    Mary Simpson   225
3.2 Problems in the assessment of scientific skills
    Bob Fairbrother   237
3.3 Reflections: accountability, the pressures and the opportunities
    Neill Patterson and George Walker   250

Author Index   265
Subject Index   271

Acknowledgements

1.1 Hodson, D. Teaching and learning about science: considerations in the philosophy and sociology of science. © The Open University.

1.2 Raizen, S. A. (1993) Three decades of science education reform in the USA, from Raizen, S. A. (1991) The reform of science education in the USA: *déjà vu* or *de novo? Studies in Science Education*, Vol. 19, pp. 1–41. © The Open University.

1.3 Lawson, A. E. (1990) Science education in Japan and the United States: are the Japanese beating us at our own game? *Science Education*, Vol. 74, no. 4, pp. 495–501. Reprinted by permission of John Wiley & Sons, Inc.

1.4 Brown, M. E. International comparisons in science education. © The Open University.

1.5 Atlay, M. and Edwards, D. Laboratory practice in further and higher education: developments in the design of practical work. © The Open University. Based on extracts from Boud, D., Dunn, J. and Hegarty-Hazel, E. (1986) *Teaching in Laboratories*, SRHE and NFER-Nelson, London, pp. 13–18, 19–22, 32–3, and from *Science: Core and Option Unit Specifications and Sample Learning Activities*, BTEC Publications, London, pp. 15–19.

1.6 Tobin, K. and Garnett, P. (1988) Exemplary practice in science classrooms, *Science Education*, Vol. 72, no. 2, pp. 197–208. Reprinted by permission of John Wiley & Sons, Inc.

2.1 Johnstone, A. H. (1991) Why is science difficult to learn? Things are seldom what they seem, *Journal of Computer Assisted Learning*, Vol. 7, pp. 75–83. Reprinted by permission of Blackwell Scientific Publications Ltd.

2.2 Harlen, W. (1992) Research and the development of science in the primary school, *International Journal of Science Education*, Vol. 14, no. 5, pp. 491–503. Reprinted by permission of the author and Taylor & Francis.

2.3 Linn, M. C. and Songer, N. B. (1991) Cognitive and conceptual change in adolescence, *American Journal of Education*, Vol. 99, no. 4, pp. 379–417. Reprinted by permission of The University of Chicago Press.

2.4 O'Shea, T. *et al.* Twenty-nine children, five computers and a teacher. © The Open University.

2.5 Adey, P. and Shayer, M. (1993) An exploration of long-term far-transfer effects following an extended intervention programme in the high-school science curriculum, *Cognition and Instruction*, Vol. II, no. 1, pp. 1–29. Reprinted by permission of the authors.

3.1 Simpson, M. Diagnostic assessment and its contribution to pupils' learning. From Brown, S. and Munn, P. (eds.) (1985) *The Changing Face of Education 14 to 16: Curriculum and Assessment*, NFER-Nelson, London, pp. 69–81.

3.2 Fairbrother, B. Problems in the assessment of scientific skills. From Wellington, J. (ed.) (1989) *Skills and Processes in Science Education*, Routledge, London, pp. 99–114.
3.3 Patterson, N. and Walker, G. (1990) Reflections: accountability, the pressures and the opportunities. From Fairbrother, R., Foden, West, D. and Wilson, C. (eds.) *Assessment and Accountability*, ASE Occasional Papers, 57–71.

Contributors' details

Derek Hodson is a Professor of Science Education at the Ontario Institute for Science Education. He has previously held posts at the universities of Manchester, England, and Auckland, New Zealand.

Senta Raizen is Director of the Center for the Improvement of Science Education, Washington DC.

Anton Lawson is in the Department of Zoology, University of Arizona, Tempe, Arizona, USA.

Elaine Brown is Lecturer in Science Education at The Open University, Milton Keynes, England.

Mark Atlay was a chemistry lecturer and works at the Centre for Science Education at The Open University.

Dee Edwards is a Lecturer in Science Education and is Director of the MA module in Science Education at The Open University.

Kenneth Tobin is Professor of Science Education at Florida State University, Tallahassee, USA.

Patrick Garnett is Associate Professor and Head of the Science Department at Edith Cowan University, Mt Lawley, Western Australia.

Alex Johnstone is a chemist and is Professor at the Centre for Science Education, University of Glasgow, Scotland.

Wynne Harlen is Director of the Scottish Council for Research in Education. She was formerly Professor of Science Education at the University of Liverpool.

Marcia Linn is Professor of Mathematics, Science and Technology Education and Director of the Instructional Technology Program at the University of California, Berkeley, USA.

Nancy Butler Songer is Assistant Professor of Science Education at the University of Colorado, Boulder, USA.

Tim O'Shea is Professor of Information Technology in Education at The Open University. He was co-investigator of the Conceptual Change in Science project, funded as part of the ESRC Information Technology in Educational Research Initiative.

Philip Adey was originally a chemistry teacher and is now a Senior Lecturer at King's College, London University.

Michael Shayer was responsible for the science wing of the Concepts in Secondary Mathematics and Science Programme at Chelsea College, London, in the 1970s and was Director of the two CASE (Cognitive Acceleration through Science Education) projects at King's College, London University.

Mary Simpson is Director of Research at Northern College, Aberdeen Campus, Scotland.

Bob Fairbrother is Senior Lecturer in Science Education at King's College, London University. He was formerly Chair of the Association for Science Education's Committee on Assessment and Examinations.

Neill Patterson is Headteacher of Boxmoor School, Hemel Hempstead, England.

George Walker is now Headteacher of the International School, Geneva, Switzerland. He was formerly Headteacher of Cavendish School, Hemel Hempstead, England.

Preface

Two companion volumes of readings have been prepared for the course entitled Science Education (ES821); these are *Teaching, Learning and Assessment in Science Education* and *Challenges and Opportunities for Science Education*. ES821 Science Education is a module in the MA in Education offered by The Open University. The Readers have been prepared by members of the Centre for Science Education and the Institute of Educational Technology at The Open University.

The Readers are one component of the course, which includes distance teaching and learning materials, personal tuition and prescribed texts.

Teaching, Learning and Assessment in Science Education is in three parts: 'Science Education and Teaching'; 'Learning Science'; 'Issues in Assessment'. Each part has a more detailed Introduction that will give the reader a clear idea of the topic coverage. The editors have endeavoured to ensure that both books take a broad, international view on the subject matter and are not tightly focused on recent developments in England and Wales.

Some of the material in this Reader is totally new, commissioned by the editors for use in ES821 Science Education; some has been adapted and edited from previously published papers. As a consequence students of ES821 Science Education may notice that some of the references do not conform to the course style.

The editors would like to thank the other members of the ES821 Course Team for their help in selecting the articles and especially Elaine Brown and Mark Atlay for their considerable assistance during the compilation of the manuscript.

Opinions expressed in the articles are not necessarily those of the Course Team nor of The Open University.

Dee Edwards

PART 1: Science Education and Teaching

Introduction

Dee Edwards

This part of the book is about issues in science education and teaching in a broad sense, in order to give the reader an international perspective. The authors are science education professionals from the USA, Canada, Australia and Britain. After engaging with this part the reader should be aware of the similarity between the science curriculum development schemes in these countries in the years since the Second World War.

The articles start with a consideration of ideas in the philosophy of science and science education, including some of the theoretical models of student learning that guide teaching approaches. The author, Derek Hodson, has experience of science education in Britain and New Zealand and is now Professor of Science Education in Ontario, Canada.

The author of the second article, Senta Raizen, is Director of the National Center for the Improvement of Science Education in Washington, DC. She details the development of science education reform in the USA, since the 1950s, including the reasons why most of the curriculum projects were not successful.

The third article provides a little light relief as Anton Lawson declares a commonly held feeling that the Japanese are 'beating us at our own game', or appear to be ahead in the fields of technology that are based on science education, quoting international surveys that 'prove' this superiority. He hypothesizes why this should be so; could it be inherent higher intelligence, or should it be attributed to the greater involvement of parents in children's education?

As the issue of international comparisons has been raised, the fourth article, by Elaine Brown of the Centre for Science Education at The Open University, synthesizes some of the data from international surveys and the bases from which these were derived. Are such comparisons valid, or what constraints should we place on the interpretation of international league tables?

Mark Atlay and I then look at the development of laboratory practical work in higher and further education over the past twenty years, by examining the frameworks common in the 1970s and comparing these with the more skill-based criteria of BTEC.

The last article in this section introduces an analysis of science teaching in the classroom, as Kenneth Tobin and Patrick Garnett compare the teaching of two primary teachers and two secondary teachers. This article concludes with the implications their work has for the education and training of teachers.

Together these articles survey a range of issues and concerns that effect science teaching in the classroom and laboratory at many levels.

Teaching and learning about science: considerations in the philosophy and sociology of science

Derek Hodson

INTRODUCTION

It seems reasonable to suppose that an individual student's understanding of the nature of science and scientific activity results from the interaction of curriculum experiences with informal learning experiences, including television, films, books, advertising, museum visits, and so on. In general terms, curriculum influences are of two kinds: those that are explicitly planned and those that are not. There are explicit messages about science and the nature of science in some school textbooks and, on occasions, teachers take steps to emphasize particular features of scientific method during laboratory work and class discussions. More frequently, however, messages about the nature of science are conveyed implicitly, through such things as instructional language, biographical material and design features of learning experiences – particularly laboratory work and writing tasks. Such messages collectively comprise a powerful 'hidden' science curriculum.

It seems likely that an individual teacher's views about science and scientific inquiry will constitute a major factor in determining the 'hidden' curriculum which, in turn, will impact substantially on students' views. Benson's (1986) finding that views about science held by children *within* a class are often remarkably consistent, while those of children in *different* classes can be substantially different, lends support to the contention that children's views are strongly influenced by curriculum experiences and that these are determined by teachers' own views about science. In addition, Duschl (1983) found that teachers' beliefs about science influenced their choice of curriculum activities and materials. Lantz and Kass (1987) found that three high-school chemistry teachers taught the same content in significantly different ways because of differences in their understanding about the nature of chemistry, and Lederman (1986) concluded that pupils' conceptions of the nature of science are positively influenced by science teachers who model an inquiry or problem-solving approach. Further evidence is provided by Wolfe's (1989) study of teachers' practices with gifted children and by Zeidler and Lederman's (1987) finding that teacher language (realist or instrumentalist – discussed later) had a significant effect on students' views about the nature of science. In an experimental study, Dibbs (1982) found that he could impact quite markedly on children's views about scientific method by basing his teaching unambiguously on inductivist, verificationist or hypothetico-deductivist conceptions of the nature of scientific experiments. More recently, Carey *et al.* (1989) have shown that a purpose-built 'nature of science' teaching unit can effect a shift in the understanding of Grade 7 students on matters relating to the construction of scientific knowledge.

Such research is not without problems. For example, it seems that teachers working with streamed groups change not only their teaching methods to accommodate differences in perceived abilities, but also, to an extent, their 'philosophical stance', in so far as they engage different ability groups in different kinds of experiments, investigations and problems. Teachers who might adopt a hypothetico-deductive approach with high-ability children may adopt an inductivist stance with those they consider to be less able (Hodson, 1992a). The matter is further complicated by the tendency for teachers to devote considerably more attention to the design of learning tasks intended to bring about the acquisition and understanding of scientific knowledge than to goals related to an understanding of the nature of science and scientific method (Schibeci, 1981). Consequently, it is likely that the relatively unplanned aspects of the science curriculum carry the principal 'philosophical messages' and may be the major factor influencing children's understanding of science and attitudes to science which are reflected in the recruitment to optional science courses.

Such a state of affairs is regrettable. If children are to acquire a proper understanding and appreciation of such matters, it is necessary that philosophical considerations are afforded a more prominent role in the design of learning experiences. In this article an attempt is made to focus attention more sharply on issues in the philosophy of science that have a direct bearing on science curriculum design, in the hope that 'curriculum messages' about the nature of science and the activities of scientists will become more faithful to actual scientific practice.

MAKING THE IMPLICIT EXPLICIT

In recent years teachers have grown used to the principles of what Ralph Tyler (1949) called 'rational curriculum planning' (often referred to as the 'objectives model'). Tyler urged teachers to focus their attention, sequentially, on aims and objectives, content, teaching/learning methods, and assessment and evaluation procedures (Figure 1a). With a little imagination this model can be adapted to describe scientific practice. Scientists study and investigate phenomena, attempt to solve problems, and so on; they have aims and objectives for the pursuit of science. In conducting their activities, they make use of various facts and theories, adopt particular methods, and conform to certain standards. However, knowledge generated by a particular scientist is only admitted to the body of accepted scientific knowledge if it survives a series of assessment

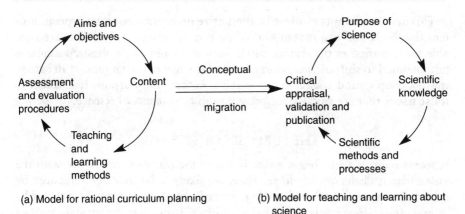

Figure I Adapting a model from curriculum planning. (a) Model for rational curriculum planning; (b) Model for teaching and learning about science.

and evaluation procedures designed, approved and monitored by the scientific community.

An account of scientific practice perceived in this way provides teachers with a model (Figure 1b) for planning a science curriculum that teaches more directly *about* science and teacher educators with a structure for planning pre-service and in-service courses on curriculum matters related to the philosophy and sociology of science. It also provides students with a useful means of thinking about science, in particular about the relationships between the purposes of science, the processes and theories of science, and the mechanisms adopted by practitioners for evaluating the work of others.

In general, contemporary science curricula transmit the following views: science is the pursuit of 'truth' about the physical world; its knowledge content represents secure, reliable and fixed knowledge; it generates knowledge by means of all-powerful, objective, inductivist methods; this knowledge is confirmed by means of (simple) unambiguous experimental tests. Nadeau and Désautels (1984) describe the curriculum image of science in terms of five major characteristics, which they collectively refer to as 'scientism':

- naive realism (science gives access to true knowledge of the universe);
- blissful empiricism (science is the meticulous, orderly and exhaustive gathering of 'facts');
- credulous experimentation (experiments are decisive and make possible conclusive verification of hypotheses);
- excessive rationalism (scientists utilize only logic and objective appraisal of data); and
- blind idealism (scientists are completely disinterested, objective beings, with no subjective biases, engaged in the search for 'truth').

As Nadeau and Désautels argue, none of these views represents a faithful or suitable description of science or scientific practice.

This article attempts to identify alternative perceptions of the purpose, content, methods and assessment/evaluation procedures of science that are suitable for inclusion in the science curriculum. It should be emphasized that it is not intended to shift discussion to the 'cutting edge' of contemporary debate in the philosophy and sociology of science. Rather, the purpose is to identify those issues that are suitable for presentation to students of science.

THE PURPOSES OF SCIENCE

It seems reasonable to begin a discussion of the purposes of science with the views that students already have. These are likely to be strongly influenced by informal sources (mentioned earlier), by early curriculum experiences, and by elementary science textbooks. The latter often assert that the primary goal of science is the generation of scientific knowledge. Of course, this immediately raises questions about the status of that knowledge and the reliability of the methods employed in reaching it, and serves to illustrate the interrelatedness of the four elements in Figure 1b. In elementary school textbooks, science is often regarded as analogous to detective work, a view which implies that scientists discover objective truth about the physical world by means of a series of well-characterized processes. It is also common for textbooks to assert that science is the pursuit of knowledge about the physical world *for its own sake*. Indeed, the disinterested accumulation of knowledge is often regarded as an essential condition, and guarantee, of the highly valued objectivity of science. There are some points raised in such descriptions of science that warrant immediate challenge through discussion and there are others that provide useful orientations around which teachers can structure a series of lessons that gradually build towards an alternative view.

Children's naive views will incline them to the belief that science as 'the pursuit of knowledge' means that scientists simply accumulate information, somewhat in the style of an indiscriminate stamp collector. Thus, it may be necessary, especially with younger children, to draw attention to the existence of different *kinds* of knowledge. Gardner's (1972, 1975) view that scientific knowledge comprises five different classes of 'statements' – definition statements, direct observation statements, instrumental observation statements, law statements and theory statements – may have some value for teachers, and for older students, but is much too complex for presentation to young children. For them, it may be sufficient to point out some differences between *descriptive* knowledge and *explanatory* knowledge. Descriptive knowledge becomes explanatory when patterns and trends in observed behaviour are rationalized by means of conceptual frameworks and relationships. Making this distinction does not imply support for an inductivist model of science (in which science proceeds from naive observations, through generalizations, to theories) nor for the spurious distinction between observation statements and theory statements (or between 'facts' and 'theories'). Superficially, this distinction sounds fine and seems to relate to what we usually consider to be a major aspect of good scientific inquiry – namely, that scientists should have respect for the evidence and not claim more from their investigation than the facts will support. I do not believe that such a distinction exists in any absolute sense. When a new theory appears, or when new instrumentation is developed, our notion of what is a theoretical statement and what is an observation statement may change. As Feyerabend (1962) argues, observation statements are not distinguished from theoretical ones by the fact that they contain special observation terms; rather, they are distinguished *pragmatically*, in that they are statements to which we may assent quickly, relatively reliably and without calculation or inference, because we all accept, without question, the theories on which they are based. Thus, where individuals draw the distinction depends on their knowledge, experience and familiarity with the phenomena or events under observation and discussion. In practice, we have theories that are part of everyone's every-day experience and observational language, theories that are part of scientists' everyday observational language (but are not used by non-scientists), theories that are only the common property of researchers in a particular field, and theories that are still under development and, therefore, not part of common usage for anyone.

When theories are taken for granted, they provide an observation language. So that with the general acceptance of a theory of solubility, we see things *dissolve*, where previously we saw them *disappear*. Both scientists and non-scientists observe *eclipses* or *craters* on the Moon (rather than 'dark patches') because certain theories underpinning our view of the solar system and the cause of lunar features are not in dispute.

In simple terms, what we regard as 'facts' are data obtainable from experience by using, in their collection and interpretation, only those concepts and theories that are universally accepted. In science, when theories change, the facts change. In learning science, when we acquire new theories, or more sophisticated ones, our demarcation between facts and theories changes (Hodson, 1992b).

As students gain experience in science, it may be possible for a more sophisticated view of scientific knowledge to emerge in response to their reflections on the various motives for seeking further knowledge during laboratory activities. For example, some laboratory exercises are designed simply to provide a knowledge base for speculation and hypothesis generation, others to provide opportunities to apply a theory in a new situation, or to test a hypothesis. By getting children to reflect on such matters, it should be possible to provide a stimulus for them to replace their existing naive view that scientists discover absolute truth about the physical world by the more sophisticated view that they construct conceptual schemes that attempt to organize, explain and predict. In other words, scientists have the express purpose of rendering the world logical, comprehensible and predictable, and scientific knowledge is sought and constructed not 'for its own sake' (as in the stereotypical textbook image of science), but for its value in solving problems. Problems may arise with respect to insufficient data, conflict between theory and observational evidence, dispute between rival theories, failure of an otherwise promising theory to generate predictive knowledge, and so on. The precise nature of the problems depends on the current stage of theoretical development of the science or, in Kuhn's (1970) terms, on whether the science is in a *pre-paradigmic, normal, extraordinary or revolutionary* phase.

Problems in the science *classroom* come in a variety of forms. In simple terms, there are 'closed' problems and 'open' problems. They may be closed in the sense of having a single solution and, possibly, a single route to it; they may be open in the sense of having several routes to the solution, several solutions, or both. While open-ended problem-solving is currently very fashionable in science education, it would be a mistake to jump too hastily to the view that closed problems are necessarily dull, boring and educationally trivial. Much depends on the way the teacher frames the problems. Problems that children encounter in class may be further classified as 'practical', in the sense that they have a concrete outcome (a practical procedure, a device, or whatever), or 'cognitive', in the sense that their outcome is the explanation or clarification of some phenomenon or event. By the time children have experienced a range of problems, their understanding of science as 'the pursuit of knowledge' will have shifted quite considerably, from a concern with the discovery of 'truth' about the world to a focus on the construction of explanations, the solving of theoretical problems and the achievement of a degree of control through the construction of technological artefacts (Figure 2). Reflection on such matters serves to illustrate the changing concerns of science itself (an important point) and the relationships between science, technology and society.

It has been argued by Smolicz and Nunan (1975) that much of the rhetoric of science education assumes that the purpose of science is to gain control of

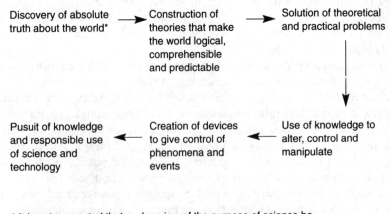

* It is not suggested that such a view of the purpose of science be presented in the curriculum. However, it is the position from which the formal curriculum may have to start, because it is a view that many children will already hold.

Figure 2   Developing the notion of science as the pursuit of knowledge.

the environment and, therefore, that the aims of science education should be to give students confidence in the capacity of science and technology to manipulate, alter and control events. The extent to which this essentially Western (or Northern) view of science is any longer an acceptable (let alone desirable) view for those engaged in the practice of science is discussed at length by Maxwell (1984). He argues that many urgent social problems, including poverty, disease and malnutrition, are not caused by lack of scientific knowledge or technological expertise, but by a misunderstanding or misappropriation of the purpose of science. While he believes that individual scientists cannot be blamed, he insists that the scientific community should be held collectively accountable for the fact that science is pursued in a way that is dissociated from a concern with sound human values. He urges a radical shift from a 'philosophy of knowledge', with its emphasis on the disinterested search for knowledge, to what he calls a 'philosophy of wisdom', which prioritizes what is personally and socially desirable and worth while.

Unfortunately, far from the community of scientists being united in a search for wisdom and environmentally sustainable technology, it is fragmented and disparate in its purposes. This is not to say, however, that science education should ignore the desirability of seeking to establish a social climate that will promote and sustain such unity (see Hodson, 1992c, d, e).

SCIENTIFIC KNOWLEDGE

Teachers are accustomed to selecting scientific knowledge for inclusion in the curriculum on the basis of its worth as a human achievement and its significance for science (what we might call 'scientific criteria'), and on the grounds of conceptual complexity, inherent interest for children and relevance to everyday life (what we might call 'learner-oriented criteria'). Teachers are less accustomed to considering the role and status of that knowledge, and are relatively unskilled in designing learning materials to present their ideas on these matters to children. But this is precisely what is required as a corollary of a commitment to discuss the purpose of science as the generation of knowledge.

It would be counterproductive to allow too much to be made of the crude distinction between *descriptive* knowledge and *explanatory* knowledge (theories) that will have identified the key role of theories in making the world logical, comprehensible and predictable. Unfortunately, many science textbooks present a simplistic view of the origin and development of scientific knowledge. Often, theory generation is seen as no more than a process of looking for regularity in nature, and theory testing is regarded as simple confirmation or refutation, usually based on a single observation or critical experiment. Hodson (1988a) summarizes the problems of textbook distortion in the following terms:

> Theories are subordinated to experimentally gathered 'facts' and are assumed to be easily validated, or refuted, by direct observations and by

simple yes/no tests. As a consequence, children get an inflated sense of the importance of their 'experimental results' and a grossly misleading view of the relationship between observation, experiment and theory.

(Hodson, 1988a, p. 26)

A more appropriate and sound view is that theories are complex structures that stand or fall on their ability to describe, explain and predict observable phenomena, without being dependent on any single observation. In practice, no theory can accommodate all observations within its domain; there will nearly always be some observations that cannot satisfactorily be explained. History shows us that scientific theories grow and develop in order to accommodate observational evidence more fully. Hence, if we are to be faithful in our teaching to actual scientific practice, theories will undergo a process of refinement, development and replacement throughout a student's science education, and the degree of theoretical sophistication at any particular stage will be determined by the capacity of the theory to explain the phenomena the learners will encounter and the kind of enquiries they will undertake. It need not go further.

Once it is accepted that theories grow and develop, it is necessary to consider their status. As far as school science is concerned, there have traditionally been two extreme positions: naive realism and instrumentalism. In *naive realism*, scientific theory is believed to provide a true description of the world, whereas in *instrumentalism* the real world is considered to be described by means of imaginary scientific models. A major problem in science curriculum design is deciding which of these two positions to adopt. Sole use of either extreme position has serious limitations when compared with the actual practice and history of science, and so a *critical realist* position, able to accommodate both perspectives, may be more appropriate (Jacoby and Spargo, 1992).

Critical realists assert that scientists sometimes aim at a true description of the world and a true explanation of observable events. However, because they cannot know for certain that their findings and explanations *are* true, they regard them as conjectures about reality that are subject to critical scrutiny and test and, possibly, rejection. On other occasions, a 'true' description of the world may not be sought. Rather, a convenient predictive instrument is all that is required. Thus, critical realists can be realist about some theories (those that they believe to be true, or to be the 'current best shot at truth') and instrumentalist about others (those that they find useful, but do not accept as true). These latter are more appropriately termed *theoretical models*. From a critical realist position it is not illogical to retain a falsified or superseded theory in an instrumental capacity, provided that its status is recognized and acknowledged. It may be that within a restricted domain of application, and this applies particularly to school science, a theory that was once accepted but has now been falsified (and hence reduced to the status of a model) may be more useful than a 'true' (currently accepted) theory because it is simpler to use. Nor is it illogical to use alternative (even seemingly incompatible or contradictory) instrumental models for different aspects of the same phenomenon – for example, wave and particle models of light.

Table I Theory development in science and science education

(a) Tentative introduction of a model as one of several models
(b) A search for evidence through observation and experiment
(c) Selection of the best corroborated model by a process of criticism and discussion with others
(d) Further elaboration of the chosen model into sophisticated theory; during this stage concepts are refined and conceptual relationships are more clearly established
(e) Acceptance of the theory into the body of scientific knowledge – consensus within the class
(f) Use of the theory to explain phenomena; application of the theory in new situations
(g) Tests of the theory's capacity for prediction; during these later stages the theory may be made quantitative, as precise mathematical relationships are established

---

What students find confusing is that the role and status of theories and models are not made explicit. We leave students to form their own views from the classroom experiences we provide, many of which have not been planned with epistemological considerations in mind. At the very least, we need to be more careful in our use of terms *theory* and *model*, and we need to make it clear that conceptual structures are designed with particular purposes in mind (see also Gilbert, 1991). Role and status are inextricably linked. Moreover, the variety of specific purposes that motivate theory building and model building within the sciences ensures that the precise meaning attached to a concept will depend on the specific role that it has within a particular knowledge structure. Hence, attempts to integrate the sciences via 'large' concepts such as energy and force are fruitless (Hodson, 1992c).

As children become increasingly confident, and apply their conceptual understanding more widely, the theories they employ must be developed, becoming more detailed, more precise, and even, on occasions, mathematical. Theory development can be illustrated by steps (a) to (g) in Table 1.

The view that the conceptual structures of science are subject to growth, development and modification has striking parallels with contemporary views in constructivist psychology, holding out the prospect of a degree of harmony between the philosophical and psychological principles underpinning the curriculum (Duschl, 1990; Duschl et al., 1990; Nersessian, 1989; Villani, 1992). It is interesting that concept development in children seems to follow certain well-characterized 'learning histories', largely because of the common influences of everyday experience (Head, 1986; Solomon, 1987), and that these often reflect the concept's historical development (Clough et al., 1987; Driver et al., 1985). Hence, encouraging students to reflect on their own developing ideas is a way of illuminating the way in which scientific knowledge itself develops (Baird et al., 1991).

SCIENTIFIC METHOD

Perhaps the most significant feature of science curriculum change during the past twenty-five years has been the shift away from the teaching of science as a body of established knowledge towards the experience of science as a method of generating and validating such knowledge. Science teachers have been encouraged to provide courses which exemplify scientific method and put the learner in the position of 'being a scientist', and scientific method has come to be regarded as the major integrating feature of the sciences. Underlying these changes is the assumption that there is such a thing as a distinctive scientific method, and that it can be characterized and taught.

Consideration of the extensive literature in the philosophy of science fails to identify a single, universally accepted description of scientific method. Far from being dismayed by such lack of agreement, White (1983) regards it as an inevitable consequence of the complexity of the scientific enterprise, the myriad of possible starting points, and the differences in knowledge, experience and personality among individual scientists. Interestingly, children also regard it as inevitable. It is *teachers* who create the expectation of a single method through their continual reference to *the* scientific method (Hodson, 1990).

However, our failure to identify a single, simple method does not mean that scientists have no methods. Feyerabend's (1975) famous assertion that 'anything goes' implies the absence of a *prescribed* method, the absence of an algorithm, rather than the absence of methods. It should not be taken too literally. As Newton-Smith observes, 'Lazing in the sun reading astrology is highly unlikely to lead to the invention of a predictively powerful theory about the constituents of the quark!' (Newton-Smith, 1981, p. 269). Implying that the world of the scientist is totally anarchic does children (and science) as gross a disservice as implying that science has a single, all-powerful method. Science does have methods, but the precise nature of those methods depends on the particular circumstances: on the matter under consideration, on the theoretical knowledge the scientist possesses and chooses to employ, and on the investigative techniques and instrumentation devices available. By making a selection of processes and procedures from the range of those available and approved by the community of practitioners, scientists choose a 'method' they consider to be contextually appropriate. There are no universal decision criteria for what to do and how to do it. All decisions are 'local' – determined by the particular circumstances of individual investigations – and, therefore, *idiosyncratic*. In Percy Bridgham's words, 'the scientific method, as far as it is a method, is nothing more than doing one's damnedest with one's mind, no holds barred' (Bridgham, 1950, p. 278).

In making their selections and in implementing their chosen strategies, scientists utilize an additional kind of knowledge and understanding, often not well articulated or even consciously applied, which can be acquired only through the experience of *doing science* and which constitutes the central core of the art and craft of the creative scientist. This knowledge combines conceptual understanding with elements of creativity, experimental flair, the scientific equivalent of the gardener's 'green fingers' and a complex of affective attributes that provide the necessary impetus of determination and commitment. With experience, it develops into what Polanyi (1958) calls *connoisseurship*. In

Table 2 Key points towards a model of science

- Observation is theory dependent and, therefore, fallible (Hanson, 1958)
- Theories are complex structures produced by the creative activities of the human mind, rather than by inductive generalization from observational data; once produced, they have an objective existence, independent of individual minds (Popper, 1972)
- Theories may be retained and elaborated in spite of apparently falsifying observations; they need time to develop before they are subjected to rigorous testing (Kuhn, 1970)
- When observation and theory are in conflict, the fundamental assumptions of the theory may be protected by deflecting the apparent falsification to some of the subsidiary theoretical structure, perhaps to a theory of observation or instrumentation underpinning the collection of data (Lakatos, 1978)
- A new theory may have to be introduced to provide the evidence for the rejection of an existing theory; so long as old theory is retained, there may be no counter evidence; new theories enable scientists to view the world in new ways (Feyerabend, 1975)
- Scientific method, like the knowledge it produces, changes and develops; thus, there is no one method of science applicable at all times and in all situations; current scientific method suits the current situation, the stock of theoretical knowledge and of the techniques available; when the situation changes, the methods change

practice, scientists proceed partly by rationalization (based on their theoretical understanding) and partly by intuition rooted in their tacit knowledge of how to do science (their connoisseurship).

Because the ways in which scientists work are not fixed and not predictable, and because they involve a component that is experience dependent in a very personal sense, they are not directly teachable. That is, one cannot learn to do science by learning a prescription or set of processes to be applied in all situations. The only effective way to learn to do science is by *doing science*, alongside a skilled and experienced practitioner who can provide on-the-job support, criticism and advice. The implications of this for science education will be addressed later (see also Hodson *et al.*, 1992).

The key points listed in Table 2 constitute a model of science that is more suitable for the school curriculum than the inductivist view of scientific method that is usually presented to students. Some points can be made directly, during historical case studies and discussion topics, others can be teased out through reflection on laboratory experiences.

ASSESSMENT AND EVALUATION

By tradition, reproducibility of experimental results and consistency with 'observable facts' are held to be the criteria by which scientific theories are appraised. As a consequence, school science curricula invariably invest enormous faith in the capacity of observation and experiment to provide reliable data for making unequivocal decisions concerning the validity of theories. Even at a level of sophistication appropriate to the school curriculum it can be pointed out to students that there are some major problems associated with this position. First, 'consistency with the facts' does not confer any increased truth status on a theory. Such consistency simply means that the theory *may* be true (Duhem, 1962). But so may lots of other theories that might also correspond with the observations. Second, observation statements are fallible and theory dependent, so any conclusions based on them are also fallible and theory dependent. Third, experiments are messy and uncertain things that have to be interpreted using theoretical insights. They do not provide reliable and unambiguous data, because evidence can often be interpreted in a variety of ways, depending on the theory employed. Indeed, as Feyerabend (1975) asserts, a well-designed theory creates its own supporting evidence, thereby insulating it from attempts to falsify it. In practice, it is rarely possible to devise an experiment that represents a decisive test of a theory, and we seriously mislead students when we pretend to do so in class (Koertge, 1969; Millar, 1987).

The view advanced in many school textbooks is that theories are accepted or rejected when there is sufficient evidence. Of course, the ambiguity of 'sufficient' is never addressed: texts are non-committal about the *amount* of evidence required and are silent about the nature of that evidence. Textbook accounts that acknowledge the ways in which evidence may be interpreted differently, according to different theories, are rare. So, too, are those that acknowledge that a new theory may be required in order to provide the evidence necessary for the rejection of the existing one. Any discussion of a 'three-cornered fight' (between two rival theories and the variously interpreted 'observed facts') would, of course, undermine the assertion that theory rejection, on the basis of experimental evidence, is decisive – one of the cornerstones of the textbook image of science.

Problems arise because we delude children into thinking that the experiments they conduct in class are concerned with theory acceptance and rejection. In general, children are working within an accepted paradigm (at least, one that is accepted by the teacher!). The 'experiments' they conduct are concerned with the articulation and refinement of a previously accepted theory and, of course, with the development of their own learning, rather than with the critical testing of theories (Hodson, 1988b; Kirschner, 1992). The ways in which teachers prejudice learners in favour of a particular theory, by a selective presentation of 'facts', is well illustrated by Lambert *et al.* (1986) with respect to the teaching of natural selection, and might profitably be discussed with students as a way of showing them that in science lessons they are practising something more akin to Kuhn's *normal* science than to *revolutionary* science (Kuhn, 1970). If we consider it reasonable to require students to master the conceptual complexity of theories of genetics and chemical bonding, for example, it is reasonable to expect them to cope with a more sophisticated view of the procedures for accepting, developing and rejecting theories. The simple-minded descriptions presented in many textbook accounts of theory change are insulting, and often deviate quite markedly from real historical events.

If it isn't possible to perform critical experiments capable of furnishing theory-independent data, it follows that there are no purely logical criteria (in the familiar usage of the term) for establishing the superiority of one theory over another. In other words, theories are empirically underdetermined. Empirical adequacy is not enough in itself to establish validity. In practice, empirical inadequacy is frequently ignored by individual scientists fighting passionately for a well-loved theory (Mitroff and Mason, 1974), and is often considered subordinate to the 'context of discovery' by the community-appointed validators (Knorr-Cetina, 1983). Additional factors that may play a part in decision-making include:

- elegance and simplicity (the aesthetics of science);
- similarity and consistency with other theories;
- 'intellectual fashion', in the sense of compatibility with trends in other disciplines;
- social and economic considerations;
- cultural considerations;
- the status of the researchers;
- the views of 'significant others' (influential and powerful scientists, journal editors, publishers);
- priorities of research funding agencies.

In other words, knowledge is *negotiated* within the community of scientists by a complex interplay of theoretical argument, experiment and personal opinion.

Criteria of judgement include social, economic, political, religious, moral and ethical factors as they impact (sometimes unconsciously) on the decision-makers (Latour and Woolgar, 1979). Thus, science is not propelled exclusively by its own internal logic. Rather, it is shaped by the personal beliefs and political attitudes of its practitioners and reflects, in part, 'the history, power structures and political climate of the supportive community' (Dixon, 1973, p. 6).

By emphasizing that current ideas are no more than the latest in a series of views shaped and influenced by personal and social conditions and attitudes, historical case studies can reinforce understanding of the mechanisms of scientific practice and imbue children with a healthy scepticism regarding scientific claims. As Robert Young says,

Science is not something in the sky, not a set of eternal truths waiting for discovery. Science is practice. There is no other science than the science that gets done. The science that exists is the record of the questions that it has occurred to scientists to ask, the proposals that get funded, the paths that get pursued. . . . Nature 'answers' only the questions that get asked and pursued long enough to lead to results that enter the public domain. Whether or not they get asked, how far they get pursued, are matters for a given society, its educational system, its patronage system and its funding bodies.

(Young, 1987, pp. 18–19)

SCIENCE AS A CULTURAL PHENOMENON

Acknowledging that science is a human activity, driven by the aspirations and values of the society that sustains it, includes the possibility that different societies might define and organize science differently. Different societies will have different priorities for science and identify different technological problems, for which different 'criteria of success' are applicable. As a consequence, different knowledge bases will be generated, by different investigative strategies and methods. Hence, different theories and different technological solutions will emerge. In other words, scientific and technological knowledge are, to a significant extent, culturally determined and reflect the social, religious, political, economic and environmental circumstances in which science and technology are practised.

The admission that scientific practice and scientific knowledge are culturally dependent calls into question traditional assumptions about the rationality and objectivity of science. My view is that objectivity in science is both more dynamic and more diffuse than school science usually admits (Hodson, 1992c). Our so-called scientific observation of phenomena and events is always, and necessarily, influenced by our existing knowledge and experience of the world. From this position, it is but a short step to an admission that scientific objectivity includes our feelings and aspirations, and the consequent recognition that the objectivity and rationality of science are, themselves, cultural artefacts. Taking account of other cultural perspectives regarding the nature of scientific rationality is, of course, a key element in anti-racist education. Students can be confronted with the notion of a distinctive Islamic science (Sardar, 1989) or African science (Jegede, 1990), each with its characteristic ideological values and criteria of validity. Such matters, which are beyond the scope of this article, are addressed elsewhere (Hodson, 1992d).

This is not to say that science is simply a consequence of ethnocentric prejudice. According to Giere (1988), there may be certain predispositions to think in terms of spatial and geometrical relationships – as evidence of which he cites the rapid growth of molecular biology following the establishment of an acceptable spatial model for DNA and Einstein's insistence that visual models were of greater significance to him than mathematical ones. In one sense, this mirrors Holton's (1986) idea of long-standing *themata* in science that give structure and coherence to scientific development over time. According to Holton, it is the commitment to these themata, many of which occur as diadic or triadic choices (synthesis/analysis; constancy/evolution/catastrophic change) that guide research (rather in the style of Lakatos's 'positive heuristic'), permit bold and inventive leaps of imagination, and enable scientists to 'suspend their disbelief' when things are not going well. He identifies Milliken's selective reporting of the experimental results of his oil-drop experiments as a clear example of a powerful framework of beliefs and assumptions providing grounds for good judgements about discrepant events: 'The chief gain was the avoidance of costly interruptions and delays that would have been required to pin down the exact causes of discrepant observations.' (Holton, 1986, p. 12).

TOWARDS A MODEL OF SCIENCE FOR SCHOOL USE

The cathedral-building analogy employed by Ravetz (1971) may provide a suitable and readily accessible model of scientific practice for school science education. Ravetz sees science as a process with three phases: creation, validation and incorporation into the body of scientific knowledge. Scientific knowledge is the product of a complex social activity which precedes and follows the individual act of discovery or creation. An individual's confidence in new experimental results or in a new theoretical system is insufficient to establish it as part of scientific knowledge. It must stand up to criticism or testing by other practitioners. The criteria of truth and acceptability are determined by the community, and scientific knowledge is recorded for the community in a style approved by the community. This allows for the possibility of the community changing its mind about suitable criteria of judgement: using sociological criteria when beliefs cannot be justified rationally, or when 'the unexpected happens' (Laudan, 1977), or invoking Shapere's (1984) dictum that scientific rationality consists in finding beliefs that are free from *reasons* to doubt.

Although it will become increasingly important for students to see the interactive and reflexive nature of scientific inquiry (see later), there is some advantage early on in regarding science as comprising three major elements:

- an individual creative phase, starting from knowledge currently accepted by the community;
- an experimental phase, using procedures accepted and validated by the community;
- a recording and reporting phase, adopting language and forms approved by the community.

The creative phase

Creativity lies at the heart of scientific practice, yet an unfortunate consequence of teachers' praiseworthy concern to teach 'correct knowledge', and to eliminate misconceptions in children's understanding of science, is that they may tend (unconsciously) to discourage creative, divergent thought in children and thus foster the mistaken views that science is intolerant of individual opinion or ideas and science education offers little scope for creative, innovative thought.

A complete understanding of scientific practice requires that children be provided with opportunities to think creatively. Medawar (1969) identifies four kinds of scientific creativity: deductive intuition, inductive intuition, instant apprehension of analogy, and experimental flair. Whether or not he is correct in the detail of his analysis, it is clear that children need to be given ample opportunities to develop and practise a variety of creative skills. Technological problem-solving, computer-based activities and project work constitute some of the best vehicles for fostering such skills.

The experimental phase

Medawar (1969) identifies four types of experiments in science:

  (a) inductive (or Baconian) experiments, in which observational data pro-
      vide a base for making generalizations;
  (b) deductive (or Kantian) experiments, designed to examine the con-
      sequences of varying the axioms or presuppositions of a scheme of
      deductive reasoning;
  (c) critical (or Galilean) experiments, comprising actions carried out to test
      a hypothesis by examining the logical consequences of it;
  (d) demonstrative (or Aristotelian) experiments, designed to illustrate a pre-
      conceived belief and convince others of its validity.

Medawar asserts that most original research begins with Baconian experiments. As notions begin to form, it becomes necessary to distinguish between
them by critical experiments (which he sees as the principal demarcation between science and non-science). A Kuhnian analysis might recognize inductive
experiments as characteristic of a pre-paradigmic phase, deductive and demonstrative experiments as typical or normal science, and critical experiments as
part of the activity immediately preceding a scientific revolution.

  It is centrally important to good curriculum design that experimental work
in class has a clearly defined function. Children should be clear in their minds
whether they are simply collecting data (with a view to making an inductive
generalization), testing a hypothesis, or illustrating relationships within a conceptual structure. The relationship between experiment and theory is more
complex than many teachers and, indeed, many philosophers assume. Some
experimental work is generated entirely by theoretical speculation; so many
theories owe their origins to pre-theoretical experimentation; sometimes experimental findings have to wait 'in limbo' while theoreticians attempt to
account for them; occasionally, quite complex theories have no immediate
experimental or observational support.

  On occasions, theory and experiment develop together: experiments testing
the empirical adequacy of the theory and guiding theory construction and modification by 'filling in the gaps' and pointing out potentially fruitful avenues of
investigation. The complexity of these relationships is rarely made apparent in
school science, which tends to assume either a simple inductive or a critical role
for experiment and to confuse the teaching of an awareness of the role of
experiments with other pedagogic goals (Hodson, 1988b; Kirschner, 1992).

  The tendency of school curricula to cast experiments in either a simple
inductivist role or a Popperian critical role fails to acknowledge and develop
the idea that experimentation is part of theory construction and, therefore,
that the kinds of experiments employed at any one stage depend on the level of
theoretical sophistication already reached. The more developed the field, the
more likely it is that experiments are theory driven, in the sense that theoretical
speculation represents the starting point for experimentation. However, it is

absurd to suggest that such speculation always precedes experiment. In less well-developed fields, the more likely it is that practitioners engage in pre-theoretical observation – that is, observations to stimulate conceptualization. Thus, Liebig's assertion that an experiment not preceded by theory bears the same relation to scientific research as a child's rattle does to music, can be interpreted in either a 'strong' or a 'weak' sense (Hacking, 1983). Clearly, one must have thought about the experiment and the apparatus to an extent – a completely mindless investigation is no investigation at all! However, one need not always have a clear hypothesis to test. It is just as legitimate to carry out an experiment 'just to see what happens'. Experimental work cannot exist independently of all theory; at the very least it depends on theories of observation and instrumentation. But it does go on without there always being a specific hypothesis under test. Nor need hypotheses always be precisely formulated. It is perfectly legitimate simply to look for confirmation (or not) of a hypothesis as vague as 'x may have an effect'. The history of science furnishes many examples of experiments that are only theory guided in this 'weak' sense, experiments that are pre-theoretical in the sense that they are attempts to establish concepts and to stimulate theoretical development. In addition, there are examples of previously quite separate lines of experimentation and theoretical development suddenly providing mutual support, and cases of experiments designed to provide evidence for one theory actually furnishing evidence for another. Indeed, Einstein cited experiments conducted fifty years earlier as critical evidence for his theory of relativity.

In view of these considerations, it may be more sensible for science teachers to encourage students to regard theory and experiment as having an interdependent and interactive relationship: experiments assist theory building; theory, in turn, determines the kinds of experiments that can and should be carried out. In theory construction, experimentation has a twofold significance: first, in testing the empirical adequacy of the developing theory and providing retrospective evidence of theoretical propositions; second, in guiding the continued development of theory towards coherence and completeness. For example, experiments assist the refinement of concepts and the quantification of conceptual relationships, and establish the limits of applicability of the theory. Thus, experiment is seen to be an integral part of the decision-making of theory construction. In turn, theory has a twofold role in experimentation: first, in the generation of questions to be investigated and problems that require theoretical elucidation and explanation; second, as a guiding factor in the precise design of experiments to answer those questions and solve those problems (there may be other theories involved, too). This holistic, interactive view of the experiment–theory relationship provides a fruitful model for concept development in individuals.

The recording and reporting phase

Medawar (1967) and Ziman (1980) have observed that there is a marked difference between the way science is carried out and the way science is written

in research papers and textbooks. Science curricula fail to make students sufficiently aware of the difference, and of the reasons for it. An individual thinks
and works in a free and creative 'private language', but is constrained by the
community to present work for appraisal and publication in the formal 'public
language' of science. Science textbooks derive their style and content from
academic papers, and so tend to ignore the existence of 'private science' (Smolicz, 1970; Strube and Lynch, 1984). They also present science solely from the
perspective and within the assumptions of the prevailing paradigm, thereby
disguising the revolutionary nature of major scientific advances (Kuhn, 1970;
Siegel, 1978, 1979).

The actual chronology of experiment and theory is often rewritten in textbooks. This helps to sustain the myth that the path of science is certain and
assigns a simple and clear-cut role to experiment, thereby assisting the per-
petuation of further myths concerning experiments. Part of learning about
science should involve reading actual accounts of experiments, rather than the
more usual *post hoc* description and justification of actions, that reinterpret
the experimenter's motives and idealize the decision-making events in terms of
currently held theories. Children could be brought to an understanding that
research papers are written to persuade readers to accept conclusions, rather
than to describe what actually happened day by day during a research project,
by reading academic papers (appropriately edited to reduce conceptual, methodological and linguistic complexity) in conjunction with personal accounts by
writers such as James Watson, Richard Leakey and David Suzuki. Reinforce-
ment of this distinction could be achieved through children's own writing:
sometimes accounts of laboratory experiences could be expressed in 'private
language', or, alternatively, descriptions of procedures and results could be
expressed in community-approved 'public language'. Simulations involving
role playing (researcher, member of research committee, journal editor, etc.)
also have much to offer in this respect in encouraging an understanding of the
relationship between form and function, such that students are able to adopt a
style of writing that is appropriate to the particular content, purpose and
audience (see also Reid and Hodson, 1987).

TOWARDS HOLISTIC SCIENCE AND INTEGRATED SCIENCE
EDUCATION

Useful as the foregoing analysis can be, it is potentially misleading. Science is
not a set of discrete activities leading by inevitable linear progress from initial
speculation to final appraisal. Rather, it is a context-dependent and idiosyncratic activity. In approaching a particular situation, scientists refine their approach to a problem, develop greater understanding of it and devise more
appropriate and productive ways of proceeding *all at the same time*. As soon as
an idea is developed, it is subjected to evaluation (by observation, experiment,
comparison with other theories, etc.). Sometimes that evaluation leads to new
ideas, to further and different experiments, or even to a complete recasting of

the original idea or reformulation of the problem. Thus, almost every move that a scientist makes during an inquiry *changes* the situation in some way, so that the next decisions and moves are made in an altered context (see Stewart and Hafner (1991) for an extended discussion). Consequently, science is a holistic and fluid activity, not a matter of following a set of rules that requires particular behaviours at particular stages. It is an organic, dynamic, interactive activity, a constant interplay of thought and action.

Moreover, in engaging in scientific inquiry one also increases both one's understanding of what constitutes *doing science* and one's capacity to do it successfully. In other words, doing science is a reflexive activity: current knowledge and expertise inform and determine the conduct of the inquiry and, simultaneously, involvement in inquiry (and, crucially, reflection on it) refines knowledge and sharpens procedural expertise.

In order for students to gain an understanding of how the various phases and activities of scientific practice interact, they need to conduct scientific investigations for themselves. The educational value of such personal investigations can be more fully appreciated by regarding science education as having three major related elements:

- *learning science* – acquiring and developing conceptual and theoretical knowledge;
- *learning about science* – developing an understanding of the nature and methods of science, and an awareness of the complex interactions between science and society;
- *doing science* – engaging in and developing expertise in scientific inquiry and problem-solving.

In attempting to meet the *learning science* goal, we need to take cognizance of what recent research into children's understandings in science has revealed about concept acquisition and concept development, principally that learning is an active process in which learners construct and reconstruct their own understanding in the light of their experiences (Driver and Bell, 1986). This entails (a) creating opportunities for students to explore their current understandings and evaluate the robustness of their models and theories in meeting the purposes of science, and (b) providing suitable stimuli for development and change. Unfortunately, many of the so-called process-oriented science curricula seriously misjudge the nature of this enterprise, first by attempting to draw clear distinctions between the various processes of science, and, second, by insisting that the processes are independent of context and content and, therefore, are generalizable and transferable to other situations. In practice, employing the processes of science involves using concepts and theories, and involves using other processes. Because all processes are theory impregnated, and are inextricably linked with other processes, it is not possible to engage in theory-free investigations or to develop skills of observation, data collection, classification, inference, and so on, in isolation. Since one's capacity to use the processes of science effectively is dependent on one's theoretical understanding, it follows that teaching for process skill development is inseparable from teaching for concept development (Hodson, 1992b).

Given the interdependence of processes and concepts, it is reasonable to suppose that engaging in the processes of science *changes* one's conceptual understanding and that process skills play a crucial role in the development of understanding. In other words, encouraging students to deploy the processes of science (in conducting investigations and solving problems) is a way of developing their conceptual understanding. In its emphasis on (a) the inter-relatedness of conceptual and procedural knowledge and (b) the exploration and development of personal understanding, this argument is markedly different from those used by advocates of discovery learning and process-oriented teaching (Swatton, 1990).

A theory-driven approach to investigation, in which students *use* the processes and methods of science to investigate phenomena and confront problems as a means of enhancing and developing their understanding, provides a powerful integrative element for the curriculum. *At the same time*, students acquire a deeper understanding of scientific activity, and investigation (or 'exploration' as Qualter *et al.* (1990) call it) becomes a method both for *learning science* and *learning about science*. Further progress in *learning about science* can be made by encouraging students to reflect on the personal learning progress that has been made. For example, when students reconsider and reinterpret laboratory activities conducted earlier in the course, they are able to draw meaningful parallels between the development of their personal understanding and the growth of scientific knowledge. However, if it is to be effective, learning about science has to be afforded a much more explicit role in curriculum planning than has been common in the past (Hodson, 1990; Kirschner, 1992). In criticizing much of our contemporary approach to laboratory work, Woolnough and Allsop (1985) make a case for regarding practical work as having three major aspects:

- *exercises* – to develop skills and techniques;
- *experiences* – to 'get a feel for phenomena';
- *investigations* – to gain experience of doing science.

Clearly, this last one is a major contributor to children's understanding of the nature of science. However, a case can be made for a fourth category of practical work: what we might call 'getting a feel for scientific practice' (see Kirschner (1992) for a thorough and incisive discussion of this notion). Practical work in this context is not restricted to bench work. Rather, it includes all manner of other active learning experiences designed to bring about a clearer understanding of the nature of scientific activity – among them, the use of historical case studies, simulations and dramatic reconstructions (Brush, 1989; Burdett, 1989; Bybee *et al.*, 1991; Solomon, 1989; Solomon *et al.*, 1992; Wandersee, 1990), role playing and debating (Loving, 1991; van der Valk, 1989), purpose-built 'nature of science' units (Carey *et al.*, 1989), activities focused on topics where theoretical explanation is still controversial (Benson,

1989; Millar, 1989), utilization of socio-economic issues (Aikenhead, 1991, 1992), use of computer-based activities (Freidler *et al.*, 1990; Hodson, 1992f), 'paper and pencil' problem-solving (Gil-Perez *et al.*, 1990), and the elegant 'epistemological disturbance' strategy described by Larochelle and Désautels (1991).

Of course, investigation/exploration is also the means by which students *do science* – use the methods and processes of science to investigate phenomena, solve problems and follow interests that they have chosen for themselves. As I argued earlier, *doing science* is a context-dependent and idiosyncratic activity, for which practitioners develop expertise by hands-on experience. If scientists enhance their professional expertise through practice, it seems reasonable to suppose that students will learn to do science (and learn to do it *better*) by doing science – simple investigations at first, probably chosen from a well-tried list of 'successful' investigations designed and developed by the teacher, but whole investigations none the less. Then, as confidence, skill and knowledge grow, progress can be made to more complex, more challenging and more open-ended investigations. There is some evidence (Schauble *et al.*, 1991) that it may be more productive to begin with 'engineering-type problems' (where the goal is to optimize desired or interesting outcomes) and then to make a transition to 'science-type problems' (in which the goal is to identify and understand causal relationships among variables) because, as the authors argue, the former more closely match children's intuitive problem-solving strategies and their everyday ways of thinking. Eventually, students can proceed independently: choosing their own topics, and approaching them in their own way. In this way, they experience the whole process, from initial problem identification to final evaluation. Also, as Brusic reminds us, they experience 'the excitement of successes and the agony that arises from inadequate planning or bad decisions' (Brusic, 1992, p. 49). However, the teacher's role is still a crucial one: role model, learning resource, facilitator, consultant and critic (Hodson *et al.*, 1992). As Ravetz (1971) has commented, learning to do science occurs 'almost entirely within the interpersonal channel, requiring personal contact and a measure of personal sympathy between the parties. What is transmitted will be partly explicit, but partly tacit; principle, precept, and example are all mixed together' (Ravetz, 1971, p. 177).

When students are engaged in conducting their own investigations, under their own direction, they refine their conceptual knowledge and develop their procedural skills concurrently. Most importantly of all, they use their developing knowledge and expertise in real contexts. In such circumstances, there is much to be said for the use of an investigator's logbook, in which students reflect on the progress of their investigation: 'Where am I going?' 'Where do I go next?' 'Do I need to rethink, replan?' It is reflections like these, and the requirement to discuss them with the teacher, that gives students insight into the idiosyncratic and reflexive nature of scientific investigation and constitutes a major advance towards scientific literacy.

CONCLUSION

My view is that science education becomes more integrated when an investigative approach to learning science is adopted, because there is integration through the dynamic interaction of the processes of science and the conceptual understanding of each individual learner. Moreover, when students have adequate experience of doing science, there is integration through the interaction of observation, experiment and theory. In addition, because of the reflexive nature of scientific inquiry, there is integration between doing science, learning science and learning about science: students develop their conceptual understanding and learn more about scientific inquiry by engaging in scientific inquiry, provided that there is sufficient opportunity for, and support of, reflection.

Within this overall constructivist epistemology and psychology of learning, there are two major and closely related difficulties that have to be overcome if a satisfactory degree of integration is to be established:

(a) avoiding the trap of relativism, where any conclusion that students arrive at, for reasons that satisfy them, is deemed acceptable;
(b) ensuring that practical activities incline students towards currently accepted knowledge (in curriculum terms) without implying that knowledge is absolute or 'out there, waiting to be discovered'.

In both cases, the solution to the difficulty lies in a more explicit consideration of the ways in which scientific knowledge is constructed and social acceptance is negotiated, and in ensuring that such considerations are prominent in the design of laboratory activities. In many classrooms, serious mismatches occur between the professed 'philosophical stance' of the teacher and the curriculum experiences provided (Hodson, 1992a; Linder, 1992). It is not uncommon for teachers who explicitly promote the view that scientific knowledge is socially constructed (in historical case studies, for example) to design laboratory activities that implicitly promote a different view. In laboratory classes, 'experiments' are often designed to lead students to a particular view; they are regarded by teachers as a way of convincingly revealing meaning, rather than constituting an element in the negotiation or construction of meaning. As a consequence, the implicit curriculum message is that scientific theory is a body of authoritative knowledge revealed and authenticated by observation and systematic experimentation. In other words, students come to believe that there is a certainty about scientific knowledge. Ways need to be found for addressing these matters and the resulting confusions that students encounter. I hope that this article represents a small step in that direction. Further discussion of the issues, and of the possibilities for integrating science education through confrontation of a mix of socio-economic, environmental and moral–ethical issues, can be found in Hodson (1992c).

REFERENCES

Aikenhead, G. S. (1991) 'Transposing STS science curriculum policy into a higher school textbook'. Paper presented at the Annual Meeting of the Canadian Society for the Study of Education, Queen's University, Kingston, Canada.

Aikenhead, G. (1992) 'The integration of STS into science education', *Theory into Practice*, 31, pp. 27–35.

Baird, J., Fensham, P., Gunstone, R. and White, R. (1991) 'The importance of reflection in improving science teaching and learning', *Journal of Research in Science Teaching*, 28, pp. 163–82.

Benson, A. (1986) 'Children's understanding of science in four comprehensive schools'. Unpublished Ph.D. thesis, University of Manchester.

Benson, G. D. (1989) 'Epistemology and science curriculum', *Journal of Curriculum Studies*, 21, pp. 329–44.

Bridgham, P. W. (1950) *The Reflections of a Physicist*, New York, Philosophical Library.

Brush, S. G. (1989) 'History of science and science education', *Interchange*, 20, pp. 60–70.

Brusic, S. A. (1992) 'Achieving STS goals through experiential learning', *Theory into Practice*, 31, pp. 44–51.

Burdett, P. (1989) 'Adventures with N-rays: an approach to teaching about scientific theory and theory evaluation', in R. Millar (ed.) *Doing Science: Images of Science in Science Education*, Lewes, Falmer Press.

Bybee, R. W., Powell, J. C. and Ellis, J. D. (1991) 'Integrating the history and nature of science and technology into science and society studies curriculum', *Science Education*, 75, pp. 143–55.

Carey, S., Evans, R., Honda, M., Jay, E. and Unger, C. (1989) 'An experiment is when you try it and see if it works: a case study of grade 7 students' understanding of the construction of scientific knowledge', *International Journal of Science Education*, 11, pp. 514–29.

Clough, E. E., Driver, R. and Wood-Robinson, C. (1987) 'How do children's scientific ideas change over time?' *School Science Review*, 69, pp. 255–67.

Dibbs, D. R. (1982) 'An investigation into the nature and consequences of teachers' implicit philosophies of science'. Unpublished Ph.D. thesis, University of Aston.

Dixon, B. (1973) *What is Science For?* London, Collins.

Driver, R. and Bell, B. (1986) 'Students' thinking and the learning of science: a constructivist view', *School Science Review*, 67, pp. 443–56.

Driver, R., Guesne, E. and Tiberghien, A. (1985) *Children's Ideas in Science*, Milton Keynes, Open University Press.

Duhem, P. (1962) *The Aim and Structure of Physical Theory* (translated by Weiner, P. P.), New York, Atheneum Press.

Duschl, R. A. (1983) 'Science teachers' beliefs about the nature of science and the selection, implementation and development of instructional tasks: a case study', *Dissertation Abstracts International*, 45, p. 422-A.

Duschl, R. A. (1990) *Restructuring Science Education*, New York, Teachers College Press.

Duschl, R. A., Hamilton, R. and Grandy, R. E. (1990) 'Psychology and epistemology: match or mismatch when applied to science education?' *International Journal of Science Education*, 12, pp. 230–43.

Feyerabend, P. K. (1962) 'Explanation, reduction and empiricism', *Minnesota Studies in the Philosophy of Science*, III, pp. 28–97.

Feyerabend, P. K. (1975) *Against Method*, London, New Left Books.

Freidler, Y., Nachmias, R. and Linn, M. C. (1990) 'Learning scientific reasoning skills in microcomputer-based laboratories', *Journal of Research in Science Teaching*, 27, pp. 173–91.

Gardner, P. L. (1972) 'Structure-of-knowledge theory and science education', *Educational Philosophy and Theory*, 4, pp. 25–46.

Gardner, P. L. (1975) 'Science and structure of knowledge', in P. L. Gardner (ed.) *The Structure of Science Education*, Hawthorn, Longman.

Giere, R. N. (1988) *Explaining Science: A Cognitive Approach*, Chicago, University of Chicago Press.

Gilbert, S. W. (1991) 'Model building and a definition of science', *Journal of Research in Science Teaching*, 28, pp. 73–9.

Gil-Perez, D., Dumas-Carre, A., Caillot, M. and Martinez-Torregrosa, J. (1990) 'Paper and pencil problem-solving in the physical sciences as a research activity', *Studies in Science Education*, 18, pp. 137–51.

Hacking, I. (1983) *Representing and Intervening*, Cambridge, Cambridge University Press.

Hanson, N. R. (1958) *Patterns of Discovery*. Cambridge, Cambridge University Press.

Head, J. J. (1986) 'Research into alternative frameworks: promise and problems', *Research in Science and Technological Education*, 4, pp. 203–11.

Hodson, D. (1988a) 'Toward a philosophically more valid science curriculum', *Science Education*, 72; no. 1, pp. 1,940.

Hodson, D. (1988b) 'Experiments in science and science teaching', *Educational Philosophy and Theory*, 20, pp. 53–66.

Hodson, D. (1990) 'Making the implicit explicit: a curriculum planning model for enhancing children's understanding of science', in D. E. Herget (ed.) *More History and Philosophy of Science in Science Teaching*, Tallahassee, Florida State University.

Hodson, D. (1992a) 'Philosophic stance, curriculum experiences and children's understanding of science: some preliminary findings'. Paper presented at the Second International Conference on the History and Philosophy of Science and Science Teaching, Queen's University, Kingston, Canada.

Hodson, D. (1992b) 'Assessment of practical work: some considerations in philosophy of science', *Science and Education*, 1, pp. 115–44.

Hodson, D. (1992c) 'In search of a meaningful relationship: an exploration of some issues relating to integration in science and science education', *International Journal of Science Education*, 14, (5), pp. 541–62.

Hodson, D. (1992d) 'Towards a framework for multicultural science education', *Curriculum*, 13, pp. 15–28.

Hodson, D. (1992e) 'Anti-racist education: a special role for the history of science and technology'. Paper presented at the International Conference of the Physical-Mathematical Sciences and the Teaching of Science, Universidad Complutense, Madrid.

Hodson, D. (1992f) 'Redefining and reorienting practical work in school science', *School Science Review*, 73, pp. 65–78.

Hodson, D., Farmer, B. and Hanifin, E. (1992) 'Interactive teaching: from principles to practice'. Unpublished paper, The Ontario Institute for Studies in Education, Toronto.

Holton, G. (1986) *The Advancement of Science and its Burdens*, Cambridge, Cambridge University Press.

Jacoby, B. and Spargo, P. (1992) 'An appropriate science education for Africa: Deweyan instrumentalism or critical realism?' in S. Hills (ed.) *History and Philosophy of Science in Science Education*, 1, Kingston, Canada, Queen's University.

Jegede, O. (1990) 'Toward a philosophical basis for science education of the 1990s: an African viewpoint', in D. E. Herget (ed.) *More History and Philosophy of Science in Science Teaching*, Tallahassee, Florida State University.

Kirschner, P. A. (1992) 'Epistemology, practical work and academic skills in science education', *Science in Education*, 1, pp. 273–99.

Knorr-Cetina, K. D. (1983) 'The ethnographic study of scientific work: towards a constructivist interpretation of science', in K. D. Knorr-Cetina, and M. Mulkay (eds.) *Science Observed*, London, Sage.

Koertge, N. (1969) 'Toward an integration of content and method in science education', *Curriculum Theory Network*, 4, pp. 26–44.

Kuhn, T. S. (1970) *The Structure of Scientific Revolutions*, Chicago, University of Chicago Press.

Lakatos, I. (1978) *The Methodology of Scientific Research Programmes*, Cambridge, Cambridge University Press.

Lambert, D. M., Millar, C. D. and Hughes, A. (1986) 'Teaching the classic case of natural selection', *Rivista di Biologia-Biology Forum*, 79, pp. 117–23.

Lantz, O. and Kass, H. (1987) 'Chemistry teachers' functional paradigms', *Science Education*, 71, pp. 117–34.

Larochelle, M. and Désautels, J. (1991) 'The epistemological turn in science education: the return of the actor'. Paper presented at the International Workshop 'Research in Physics Learning. Theoretical Issues and Empirical Studies', Institute of Physics Education, University of Bremen.

Latour, B. and Woolgar, S. (1979) *Laboratory Life: The Social Construction of Scientific Facts*, London, Sage.

Laudan, L. (1977) *Progress and its Problems*, Berkeley, University of California Press.

Lederman, N. G. (1986) 'Relating teacher behavior and classroom climate to changes in students' conceptions of the nature of science', *Science Education*, 70, pp. 3–19.

Linder, C. J. (1992) 'Is teacher-reflected epistemology a source of conceptual difficulty in physics?' *International Journal of Science Education*, 14, pp. 111–21.

Loving, C. C. (1991) 'The scientific theory profile: a philosophy of science model for science teachers', *Journal of Research in Science Teaching*, 28, pp. 823–38.

Maxwell, N. (1984) *From Knowledge to Widsom*, Oxford, Basil Blackwell.

Medawar, P. B. (1967) 'Is the scientific paper a fraud?' *The Listener*, September 12, pp. 377–8.

Medawar, P. B. (1969) *Induction and Intuition in Scientific Thought*, London, Methuen.

Millar, R. (1987) 'Towards a role for experiment in the science teaching laboratory', *Studies in Science Education*, 4, pp. 109–18.

Millar, R. (1989) 'Bending the evidence: the relationship between theory and experiment in science education', in R. Millar (ed.) *Doing Science: Images of Science in Science Education*, Lewes, Falmer Press.

Mitroff, I. I. and Mason, R. O. (1974) 'On evaluating the scientific contribution of the Apollo Moon missions via information theory: a study of the scientist–scientist relationship', *Management Science: Applications*, 20, pp. 1,501–13.

Nadeau, R. and Désautels, J. (1984) *Epistemology and the Teaching of Science* Ottawa, Science Council of Canada.

Nersessian, N. J. (1989) 'Conceptual change in science and in science education', *Synthese*, 80, pp. 163–83.

Newton-Smith, W. H. (1981) *The Rationality of Science*, London, Routledge & Kegan Paul.

Polanyi, M. (1958) *Personal Knowledge*, London, Routledge & Kegan Paul, London.

Popper, K. R. (1972) *Objective Knowledge*, Oxford, Oxford University Press.

Qualter, A., Strang, J., Swatton, P. and Taylor, R. (1990) *Exploration: A Way of Learning Science*, Oxford, Basil Blackwell.

Ravetz, J. R. (1971) *Scientific Knowledge and its Social Problems*, Harmondsworth, Penguin.

Reid, D. J. and Hodson, D. (1987) *Science For All: Teaching Science in the Secondary School*, London, Cassell.

Sardar, Z. (1989) *Explorations in Islamic Science*, London, Mansell.

Schauble, L., Klopfer, L. E. and Raghavan, K. (1991) 'Students' transition from an engineering model to a scientific model of experimentation', *Journal of Research in Science Teaching*, 28, pp. 859–82.

Schibeci, R. A. (1981) 'Do teachers rate science attitude objectives as highly as cognitive objectives?' *Journal of Research in Science Teaching*, 18, pp. 69–72.

Shapere, D. (1984) *Reason and the Search for Knowledge: Investigations in the Philosophy of Science*, Dordrecht, Reidel.

Siegel, H. (1978) 'Kuhn and Schwab and science texts and the goals of science education', *Educational Theory*, 28, pp. 302–9.

Siegel, H. (1979) 'On the distortion of the history of science in science education', *Science Education*, 63, pp. 111–18.

Smolicz, J. J. (1970) 'Paradigms and models', *Australian and New Zealand Journal of Sociology*, 6, pp. 100–19.

Smolicz, J. J. and Nunan, E. E. (1975) 'The philosophical and sociological foundations of science education: the demythologizing of school science', *Studies in Science Education*, 2, pp. 101–43.

Solomon, J. (1987) 'Social influences on the construction of pupils' understanding of science', *Studies in Science Education*, 14, pp. 63–82.

Solomon, J. (1989) 'The retrial of Galileo', in D. E. Herget (ed.) *The History and Philosophy of Science in Science Teaching*, Tallahassee, Florida State University.

Solomon, J., Duveen, J., Scot, L. and McCarthy, S. (1992) 'Teaching about the nature of science through history: action research in the classroom', *Journal of Research in Science Teaching*, 29, pp. 409–21.

Stewart, J. and Hafner, R. (1991) 'Extending the conception of "problem" in problem-solving research', *Science Education*, 75, pp. 105–20.

Strube, P. and Lynch, P. P. (1984) 'Some influences on the modern science text: alternative science writing', *European Journal of Science Education*, 6, pp. 321–38.

Swatton, P. (1990) 'Process and content in the National Science Curriculum', *School Science Review*, 72, pp. 19–28.

Tyler, R. W. (1949) *Basic Principles of Curriculum and Instruction*, Chicago University of Chicago Press.

Van der Valk, T. (1989) 'Waves or particles? The cathode ray debate in the classroom', in R. Millar (ed.) *Doing Science: Images of Science in Science Education*, Lewes, Falmer Press.

Villani, A. (1992) 'Conceptual change in science and science education', *Science Education*, 76, pp. 223–37.

Wandersee, J. H. (1990) 'On the value and use of the history of science in teaching today's science: constructing historical vignettes', in D. E. Herget (ed.) *More History and Philosophy of Science in Science Teaching*, Tallahassee, Florida State University.

White, F. C. (1983) 'Knowledge and relativism III: the sciences', *Educational Philosophy and Theory*, 15, pp. 1–29.

Wolfe, L. F. (1989) 'Analyzing science lessons: a case study with gifted children', *Science Education*, 73, pp. 87–100.

Woolnough, B. and Allsop, T. (1985) *Practical Work in Science*, Cambridge, Cambridge University Press.

Young, R. M. (1987) 'Racist society, racist science', in D. Gill and L. Levidow (eds.) *Anti-racist Science Teaching*, London, Free Association Books.

Zeidler, D. L. and Lederman, N. G. (1987) 'The effect of teachers' language on students' conceptions of the nature of science'. Paper presented at the

National Association for Research in Science Teaching Annual Meeting, Washington, DC.

Ziman, J. M. (1980) *Teaching and Learning about Science and Society*, Cambridge, Cambridge University Press.

1.2

Three decades of science education reform in the USA

Senta A. Raizen

INTRODUCTION

History shows that science education reflects a sometimes uneasy marriage between science and education. In this article I argue that the tensions result from science being essentially élitist, whereas education has become increasingly populist. As industrialization and post-industrial developments have advanced, so have these two great adornments of Western culture: *science* as a way of knowing and understanding the natural world, and *education* for all citizens as a way of bringing about individual and collective improvement.

Both Alfred North Whitehead and Bertrand Russell recognized the need to make scientific knowledge and ways of thinking part of everyone's education. A report on science education by the National Science Foundation (NSF, 1965) starts with this quotation from Whitehead:

> In the conditions of modern life the rule is absolute: the race which does not value trained intelligence is doomed. . . . Today we maintain ourselves. Tomorrow, science will have moved forward yet one more step – and there will be no appeal from the judgment which will then be pronounced on the uneducated.
>
> (Whitehead (1916) cited in NSF, 1965, p. 1)

Nearly two generations later, Bertrand Russell (1962) observed that the increasing power over matter that science has made possible is the chief cause of change in the modern world. He saw the understanding of natural processes and the orderliness of the universe as an empowerment of the human species. He went on to argue, however, that this power must 'be brought into the service not of this or that group . . . but of the whole human race' (Russell, 1962, p. 25).

Both Whitehead and Russell anticipated the need for everyone to have adequate command of the ever-growing body of scientific knowledge and technical capability, so that all could share in the power conferred by science and its

Adapted by the author from 'The reform of science education in the USA: *déjà vu* or *de novo?*' *Studies in Science Education*, (1991) Vol. 19, pp. 1–41.

applications. This article explores the efforts, over the last three decades, to realize this vision in the schools of the USA.

GROWING SCIENCE, GROWING EDUCATION

In order to understand how the two enterprises involved in science education reform came to relate and influence each other in particular ways, I trace, briefly, the historical roots behind the expansion of both, science and education.

Science and government

The growth of the US scientific establishment has been closely associated with war. In each of the country's major military conflicts – the Civil War and the First and Second World Wars – the contribution scientists made to the war effort provided evidence of the utility of science. Consequently, the federal government developed policies for engaging the scientific community in special ways.

The National Academy of Sciences

The founding of the National Academy of Sciences, the most prestigious of US scientific institutions, was a direct consequence of the Civil War. Its charter was established by the US Congress and President Lincoln in 1863. One of the Academy's stated purposes was to serve as an official adviser upon request and without fee to the federal government on questions involving science or technology.

The operating arm of the Academy, the National Research Council, was established in 1916. An important reason for its creation was that the advice requested by the federal government accelerated during the war. Volunteer committees proved inadequate and had to be supported with paid staff to ensure timely delivery of advice. The Presidential charter, together with the mandate to provide advice to the government, was renewed in 1918 at the request of President Wilson.

At present, the National Academy of Sciences continues its unique relationship to the federal government. Even though it is a private, self-perpetuating body which selects its own membership on the basis of outstanding scientific contribution, it serves as key adviser to the government on a wide variety of scientific, technical, and policy matters.

The National Science Foundation

The second major US scientific institution to grow out of a recognition of wartime contributions made by scientists is the National Science Foundation (NSF), a government agency that supports basic research. Even before the USA entered the Second World War, an Office of Scientific Research and Development was established to sponsor research and development in advanced weaponry. Headed by Vannevar Bush, this office provided the model for NSF and for the support of academic science based on peer review. Based on his experience with civilian control of wartime research, Bush (1945) wrote the landmark report *Science – The Endless Frontier*, in which he recommended the establishment of a new federal agency devoted to supporting the work of university scientists.

NSF did not come into existence until five years after Bush's report was delivered to the President. The debates surrounding NSF's creation turned largely around who was to exercise control over the proposed agency – the scientific community through a board of scientists and a scientist-director or representatives of various sectors of the public. In the end, a compromise solution provided for a governing board of scientists and a director recommended by the scientific community but appointed by the President and approved by the Congress.

Initially, the budget of the fledgling agency was quite modest: $3.5 million in the first year, growing to only $16 million by the sixth year. Early programmes concentrated on grants to individual scientists and fellowships to promising graduate students. Both NSF's programmes and budget levels expanded considerably as a result of the launching of the Russian Sputnik in 1957 which, in the atmosphere of the cold war, was considered as something akin to a military challenge. A decade later, NSF's budget had grown to nearly $500 million, and the education programmes had expanded to encompass initiatives at all levels, including secondary and elementary schools. Yet, supporting basic research, the principal focus of Bush's report, remains the Foundation's central mission, together with the cultivation of the best minds to advance the frontiers of science. The involvement of government with science was expected to yield high benefits – advancement of scientific knowledge and its application to a variety of problems. The ninety years that separate the creation of the Academy and NSF illustrate both the growing interest in the contributions of science and the changing conceptions of appropriate means for collaboration between the scientific establishment and the polity. The Academy is an exclusive, private body which has as one of its main purposes the recognition, through bestowal of Academy membership, of scientific work of highest calibre. Because of its position at the heart of the scientific establishment, the Academy is able to call on outstanding individuals to serve on committees to advise on issues at the intersection of scientific knowledge, technical expertise, and governmental policy. Committee members still serve without compensation, but the costs of the staff and other expenditures incurred in providing this advice come largely from the budgets of federal agencies and ultimately from the taxpayer.

NSF is a government agency expressly created to disburse public funds to support scientific research. While it does so on the basis of authorization and appropriations recommended by the President and legislated by the Congress, decisions on grant actions are based on peer review by fellow scientists, generally drawn from outside the government. Despite periodic challenges from

Congress about the extent to which the scientific community should be the sole arbiter of NSF investments in research, this mode of operation continues.

The expansion of schooling

The antecedents of schooling in the USA and the roots of national education policy present a complex interaction of élitism and populism. Both upper and lower educational institutions in the colonies originated with the need to prepare individuals for the learned professions – doctor, minister, lawyer. These institutions were highly selective and presented traditional curricula anchored in the study of classical languages and culture. For example, Harvard was founded in 1636 by an English clergyman, and Boston's Public Latin School ('Public' in the British rather than the US sense) in 1635. These institutions continue to select their students on the basis of excellence. Schools were not open to all who desired an education; even access to elementary education depended on one's location and means. Even Jefferson, deeply committed to education and founder of the University of Virginia, thought that children should, after three years of common schooling, be divided into two classes – labour, and leisure and learning, the former to become apprentices and the latter to go on to further education.

The next two centuries saw a profound change, brought about by rapid industrialization and by the perceived need to acculturate the streams of immigrants flowing into the burgeoning cities. Again, Massachusetts led the way by establishing a pattern of six years of schooling for all children. The great school leaders of the era, who pushed for universal education before the Civil War, saw education and national progress as inevitably related, with a close connection between freedom, self-government, and an educated citizenry.

Vocationalism had its first success with the Morrill Act of 1862, which created agricultural and mechanical arts colleges intended to advance research and education in scientific farming. The creation of these institutions illustrates populism in US education and faith in the power of knowledge to bring about the betterment of communities.

In the 1870s several experimental schools were created to provide an appropriate balance between mental and manual labour. Instruction in academic subjects was combined with instruction in such manual arts as woodworking and ironworking. This approach to secondary education was opposed by the traditionalists who saw schools as the institutions connecting students to the great cultural wealth and information stored in books (Cremin, 1964). Nevertheless, the movement to require manual arts training of all students gained momentum. Slowly, this turned into vocational education in the schools, taking the place of apprenticeships in factories. The landmark Smith–Hughes Act of 1917 marked the beginning of the involvement of the federal government in lower education. The purpose was to increase the supply of skilled workers, socialize the children of immigrants, and reduce the problem behaviours exhibited by delinquent adolescents. 'The vocational education movement . . .

had the appearance of a new religion . . . the panacea of the moment' (Grubb, 1979, p. 196).

Less than two decades later, vocational education became the target of heavy criticism for creating a dual educational system, for its narrowness of training, for its lack of economic pay-off, for its failure to address unemployment of unskilled and underskilled young people, and for not offering a viable alternative to traditional academic schooling for the college-bound. The vocational education programmes have continued to the present day, and so have the debates.

Progressive education

In parallel with vocational education came pedagogic developments concerning effective ways of learning, as exemplified by progressive education, usually associated with John Dewey. Two critical principles of the 'practice schools' that Dewey, his forerunners and his disciples created in the fifty years between 1880 and 1930 were to move the child to the centre of the educative process and to interrelate the several subjects of the curriculum so as to enhance their meaning for the child.

In these schools much of the pupils' work in the early years was to be conducted around major projects simulating activities in the home and the community. Children created their own stories in order to read and write. Science was begun in the form of nature studies conducted during field trips. The children took their observations and descriptions back to the classroom, thus integrating their work in science with their studies in language and art. Mathematics was frequently introduced in connection with this laboratory work, as were manual training activities. Geography was started with explorations of the surrounding countryside or city streets. As the children moved through the grades, the work was designed to expand the students' horizon and knowledge, so that by age twelve or thirteen they would engage in projects in the academic disciplines.

The job of the teacher was to start where the children were and lead them through their explorations and project work into the disciplinary knowledge. Dewey recognized, as some of his disciples did not, that this kind of teaching required considerable subject-matter knowledge on the part of the teacher and explicit goal setting to govern the instructional process (Cremin, 1964). The Dewey's Laboratory School, established at the University of Chicago in 1896, drew on distinguished Chicago science faculty to work directly with the children and the teachers.

Adaptations of progressive education eventually came under criticism for lack of integrity in their curricular offerings, meagre and formalistic instruction, and willingness to accept low-level performance from the students. The children were perceived to be doing sloppy work, and their immersion in concrete activities did not necessarily lead to improved learning. The key problem appeared to be finding teachers both willing *and* able to teach effectively in the new manner.

To students of reform efforts in science education, the attempt to introduce activity-based education intended to allow the child to make meaning of his education, the difficulties encountered, and the consequent criticisms have a familiar ring. It is sobering to observe that the roots of the current reform efforts in science education as well as those of the 1960s – together with the criticisms – go back nearly a century in the USA.

Testing and grouping students

The two world wars spurred the growth of science in the USA. They also spawned the extensive testing of students which has come to dominate US education. When the USA entered the First World War, the US Army, encouraged by the American Psychological Association, developed a number of tests to help place recruits within the Army. This experience led to the introduction of intelligence testing into US education. Eventually intelligence tests were widely used to track children according to their mental ability in order to make instruction more efficient.

Concurrently, progressive schools of all kinds grew in number. To some degree they maintained the twin progressive notions of child-centred education and focus on community life. In one variation, teachers were responsible for developing the curriculum geared to students' individual needs. This plan worked under the strong leadership of the superintendent who had instituted it. In other settings, however, it deteriorated to endless meetings of teacher committees, the principal purpose of which became discussions of the *process* of curriculum development rather than curriculum development itself (Cremin, 1964).

Calls for reform

In the decades between the two world wars, education had become nearly universal. A great diversity of students was flocking to the schools, causing educators to question whether all students were being prepared adequately, not only academically, but for work and citizenship. Progressive education provided an attractive response to these concerns, and it became the orthodoxy of US public schools. The progressivism of Dewey had been transmuted, however, through infusion of a strong element of social efficiency, into school as a mechanism to adjust the individual to society (Ravitch, 1983).

By the 1950s and 1960s criticisms were mounting. The industrial development of the war and post-war years increased the need for well-trained workers; the cold war required more professional manpower. In the face of these needs, academics found the school curriculum greatly diluted by the wholesale adoption of the rhetoric of progressive education and the life-adjustment movement. The nature of the criticisms is reflected in the titles of some of the most influential books: *Educational Wastelands* (Bestor, 1953), *Quackery in the Public Schools* (Lynd, 1953) and *Let's Talk Sense About Our Schools* (Woodring, 1953). Critics urged a return to what they saw as the main function of the school: intellectual training based in the academic disciplines – history, English, science, mathematics and foreign languages. They blamed the deterioration of the schools at least in part on the separation between university scholars and secondary education that had occurred since the 1920s (Wooton, 1965). When the then USSR launched the first space satellite in October 1957, criticisms of the schools and their watered-down curricula in science and mathematics multiplied.

In 1958 the National Defense Education Act was passed in response to the apparent technological superiority of the USSR, marking the entry of the federal government into pre-college science education. NSF was to deal exclusively with science (including mathematics) and operate mainly through scientific societies and universities, whereas the Office of Education was to strengthen all areas of education by dealing primarily through state and local school systems.

The hitherto modest forays by NSF into pre-college education became a rapidly growing and highly visible effort. In 1959 over 50 per cent of NSF obligations were devoted to education programmes – a high-water mark never achieved before or since. The rise and decline of two mainstays of the 1960s reforms in science education – teacher institutes and curriculum improvement projects – are chronicled below.

SCIENCE EDUCATION REFORMS IN THE 1960s AND 1970s

'In the tug of war between élitists and levellers the National Science Foundation is nearly always pulled toward the quality side' (England, 1982, p. 227). The first education programme started by NSF in 1952 was support for graduate fellows chosen by the National Academy of Sciences on the basis of their outstanding undergraduate record. The fellows had (and have) the right to choose their graduate schools, taking their stipends with them, with the result that they tended to cluster at a very small number of the most prestigious research universities. However, outside pressures began to break down NSF's exclusive focus on graduate education. A 1976 report summarized the agency's ambivalence on getting involved in pre-college education (Library of Congress, 1976, pp. 42–3):

> In retrospect, it could hardly be said that the Foundation entered the pre-college education field on its own initiative. The problem was thrust upon it by circumstances, and responsibility to take action was resisted [. . .] the senior administration of the Foundation and the National Science Board would have been pleased on a number of occasions to have surrendered this responsibility to any other auspices.

Teacher institutes

The original Bush report, *Science – The Endless Frontier* (Bush, 1945), noted that high school was a critical transition for prospective students of science and that the teaching of science in the high schools was inadequate. One cause was seen to be the separation of teacher education from the faculties of arts and sciences. After alarms were raised about college enrolments in science dropping and the country falling behind the USSR in producing technical manpower (DeWitt, 1955), NSF began efforts to re-educate teachers in order to attract more high-school students to science and prepare them better (Library of Congress, 1976).

The success of institutes for high-school teachers sponsored by industry, universities, and private foundations encouraged NSF to initiate its first such institute in 1954. Early budget requests were modest, but pressure from the very highest levels of government and the science community caused NSF to increase the programme. By 1956 there were twenty-seven institutes, although the Foundation still regarded the programme as experimental.

Fiscal year 1957 marked a watershed: programme funds grew in a single year from 7 per cent of the NSF budget to 25 per cent; the number of institutes nearly quadrupled. Some 300 teachers received instruction in the summer of 1955; the number rose by about 1,000 in 1956 and then grew to over 6,500 the next year. By 1957 there were summer institutes in all but five states and in three territories. The institutes programme continued to grow, though more slowly; in 1965 there were nearly 450 institutes with 21,000 high-school teachers as participants (Krieghbaum and Rawson, 1969). NSF could boast that there was an institute in every Congressional district – its steady defence against charges of élitism in its fellowship and research support programmes. Congress made sure the agency would continue to favour programmes for high-school teachers through an annual earmarking of NSF appropriations. In 1959 this was the tidy sum of $30 million, over 20 per cent of all NSF funds for that year, amounting to 38 per cent of all education funds.

The teacher institutes started out presenting advanced knowledge in a specific discipline, taught, if possible, by eminent scientists imported from leading universities. As the institutes increased in number, they began to include general science and sometimes even elementary subject matter related to the teacher's classroom teaching. By the mid-1960s, institutes served to update and upgrade teachers who were inadequately prepared, as well as providing advanced training (Krieghbaum and Rawson, 1969). An additional function was to help teachers use the new curricula produced with NSF support.

The popularization of the institutes not only increased the numbers of teachers able to participate, but also broadened course offerings. By the late 1960s NSF had supported 50 per cent of all secondary science and mathematics teachers in some form of institute. Nevertheless, the programme did not reach the teachers who probably needed it the most as at least half of them never applied to go to an institute. The formidable challenge posed by the country's 1,100,000 elementary school teachers was not even attempted.

The institutes reached their highest level in the mid-1960s (nearly $40 million and over 35,000 participants per year) and maintained close to that level through 1971 (Committee on Science and Technology, 1975). For reasons detailed below, 1973 marked the beginning of decreases in NSF funding of teacher training. By 1975 funding levels were below those of 1959, and by 1976 the programme received almost no funding.

Improvement of science curricula

The launching of Sputnik resulted in a big boost in NSF's budget and the chance to try out and expand a variety of educational programmes which tried to follow the wishes of both the scientific community and the Congress. Most prominent was the course content improvement programme, initiated in 1956 and modelled on the school mathematics development initiated by Max Beberman at the University of Illinois in 1951. The first major NSF grant under the new programme, actually made before Sputnik, went to the Massachusetts Institute of Technology (MIT) for the Physical Sciences Study Committee (PSSC, 1960).

A fundamental axiom of the programme was that the improvement of curricula needed to enlist outstanding research scientists. One of the key leaders of PSSC, Jerrold Zacharias, was recognized for his contribution to the war effort; he had worked on the Manhattan project to develop the atomic bomb. His mind-set and that of many of his colleagues was shaped by this experience of 'big science'. It was assumed that by assembling teams of highly capable scientists and science teachers, one could successfully address the intellectual problems of the science curriculum, just as the teams of the Manhattan project had addressed the engineering challenges of developing an atomic bomb. Similarly conceived projects soon followed in the next four years in biology and chemistry. Concurrently with the developments in science, a major effort was being made to reform school mathematics, starting with the reform of mathematics courses at the secondary level and eventually reformulating mathematics for elementary schools.

The high-school science and mathematics curriculum materials being developed were intended for students enrolled in the pertinent courses. PSSC, in particular, was aimed then as now at the small minority of students enrolling in Grade 12 physics (the last year of high school). The course was designed to bring modern physics to high-school students through a variety of challenging curricular materials; it was also intended to be a demonstration of the power of an intellectually rigorous system constructed by science. A later attempt to humanize physics through the inclusion of historical material and astronomy (Rutherford *et al.*, 1970) succeeded no better in its purpose of attracting additional students to physics.

The curriculum development programmes encouraged eminent research scientists to become involved in pre-college education. The guiding principles were:

- leadership and work by scientists of stature;
- fundamental rethinking of content and approach;

- science presented as systems of inquiry rather than as bodies of knowledge;
- laboratory experiences designed to have students learn for themselves by using the modes of attack of scientists confronting problems;
- curriculum content reflecting the structure of the discipline, with no watering down for the less science oriented;
- scrutinizing of all assumptions on when and how to introduce or develop a topic;
- no single effort or curriculum study in any one discipline or level of education; and
- careful classroom trial of any new materials.

(NSF, 1965, pp. 25–6)

The costs of the writing teams, trials in schools, the development of laboratory manuals, apparatus, films, and other teaching aids made the NSF projects expensive. The approach was quite different from the traditional method of preparing pre-college textbooks in which one or two authors, not usually scientists themselves, would write the first edition, with subsequent editions often only minimally revised.

Expansion into elementary school

In 1960 the Foundation commissioned a study of science education in elementary and junior high schools, which concluded that a curriculum effort was needed in this area. The rationale was not concern for the development of the scientific workforce, but rather science for all students as a basic part of their general education in the lower grades. The approach to curriculum development was to be similar: no single common national curriculum in science, stress on teaching science in the spirit of discovery characteristic of science itself, preparation of curriculum materials by the combined efforts of scientists and teachers. The need for new instructional materials for in-service and pre-service programmes for science teachers was recognized as well.

From 1961 to 1964 the NSF funded several feasibility projects at the elementary school level, four of which became major curriculum development efforts: the Science Curriculum Improvement Study (SCIS) at the University of California, Berkeley; the Elementary Science Study (ESS) at Education Development Corporation; the Minnemast Project at the University of Minnesota; and Science: A Process Approach at the American Association for the Advancement of Science.

Implementation issues

NSF had begun its programmes in pre-college education with the assumption that improving the subject-matter knowledge of secondary school teachers would improve science education for students. Next it turned to the reform of the text materials and laboratory exercises the teachers were using in their classrooms but, even better-trained teachers did not spontaneously turn to the new curricula, some of which were a radical departure from their classroom practices and from the science teaching they had experienced in their college courses. It appeared that special training and technical assistance were necessary to ensure that the investment in improved curricula would pay off in the form of better science instruction in the classroom. So in 1959 the NSF began supporting institutes to train teachers in the use of the curricula it had sponsored. By 1975, 80 per cent of the teacher-training support was for the dissemination and utilization of the new curricula (Welch, 1979).

Another significant aspect of these curriculum development initiatives was the relationship of the NSF projects to the publishing industry. Scientists controlled the curriculum development process within the NSF projects and publishers were involved only in the late stages, when the materials were close to being finished. Projects had different strategies for interacting with the commercial sector. For example, the biology group (BSCS) closely controlled the production of its three different versions of high-school biology. It licensed each version to a different publisher and controlled each revision. On the other hand, one of the chemistry groups (Chem Study) sold off its interest in the materials once the pilot stage was completed. Several different publishers acquired the rights to produce their own versions and subsequently were in charge of all revisions. Other groups distributed materials as non-copyrighted, experimental editions in soft covers in order to encourage commercial publishers' textbooks to make their own adaptations.

At the outset a number of the publishers were uneasy with what they considered an unwarranted incursion by the federal government into the development of instructional materials. They held that materials should be in the public domain and that they might have helped make them more marketable, had they been involved earlier. Nevertheless, the prestige of the NSF-supported projects was such that, as a rule, they had little problem in attracting commercial publishers (Committee on Science and Technology, 1975).

Congressional criticism

Of all NSF's pre-college programmes, the institutes were the Congressional favourites. The curriculum development efforts enjoyed a less favourable reception. Curriculum development projects seemed never-ending and expensive and, unlike institutes, they were concentrated in a few sites. The new approaches took extensive testing; films and laboratory apparatus were difficult to distribute.

Business arrangements for the publication and distribution of NSF-sponsored materials were questioned, particularly of hands-on kits and other unconventional course materials that did not find ready distributors. It was, in fact, Congressional investigation of the dissemination mechanisms for one such course, 'Man: A Course of Study', which led to the abandonment of the whole 1960s' curriculum improvement effort, aided and abetted by a variety of factors operating in the decade between 1965 and 1975. Because 'Man: A Course of Study' involved a multi-media approach and dealt with a controversial subject (human adaptation to the natural environment as illustrated by various animal adaptative behaviours), it proved especially unattractive to the private sector. To disseminate the materials, NSF invested not only in teacher training, as it had done with other curricula, but also in the publication of the materials themselves. The content of the materials, no matter the eminence of the scholars who had created them, was easy prey for individuals and groups who saw it as a perversion of traditional values. In their view, the federal government, through supporting the dissemination and implementation of the course, was imposing these values upon the schools. The controversy escalated and led to several governmental investigations that soon broadened their inquiries to take in all of NSF's pre-college programmes, their effectiveness, and their management (Committee on Science and Technology, 1975).

Changing circumstances

The turmoil over 'Man: A Course of Study' took place in the broader context of a shift in educational priorities in the mid-1960s. The civil rights movement of the early 1960s changed concerns from building the nation's scientific manpower to spotlighting the populations traditionally underserved by the schools. New federal programmes dealt with desegregating the schools and making funds available for special programmes for minority children, poor children, children with a variety of disabling conditions, and children not proficient in English. NSF saw little reason to engage with these new priorities, even though the elementary curricula had proved quite successful with some of the populations of concern.

Two other circumstances affected NSF's pre-college programmes in the mid-1970s. First, in some sense the investment in research and science education seemed to have been almost too successful. As the science education programmes entered their second decade, concerns arose about a surplus of scientists and engineers, some of whom were experiencing difficulties in finding employment commensurate with their training. The costs of the war in Vietnam and the accompanying inflation and recessions resulted in decreased federal spending on research and new space initiatives, which had previously commanded the talents of scientists and engineers. The President's budget office urged decreases in spending on science education, starting with support of graduate students, as a way of containing the expansion of a community ever hungry for more grant funds.

An even more significant change was the shift in school enrolment downward, a decrease of 15 per cent between 1971 and 1973 and projected to go down even further to give an overall decrease of 20 per cent by 1990 (National Center for Education Statistics, 1987). A decrease in funding for education accompanied the decrease in enrolment, again exacerbated by the Vietnam war and the recessions of 1973–4 and 1981–2. The willingness to try innovations, which characterized the educational expansion after the Second World War, gave way to the need for retrenchment. Instead of experimenting with new curricula, schools focused on the basics. Instead of using expensive, hard-to-maintain kits and laboratory materials, teachers returned to a heavy reliance on textbooks.

Impact of the 1960s' reforms

What was the impact of the 1960s' science education reforms? Answers depend in part on when the appraisals were made. Early studies conducted by the projects themselves concentrated on the results of the pilot trials of the materials, but as project materials became widely available, commercial sales figures began to be used as an indicator cf success. The results might have been predicted from the large amount of literature on educational innovation: the more radical a curriculum was, the more difficulties it experienced in the marketplace. For example, the Chemical Bond Approach curriculum found little usage compared to the Chem Study materials, which represented a more traditional approach to the teaching of high-school chemistry. Similarly, the BSCS blue version based on a biochemical or molecular approach to biology far outsold the BSCS green version which represented a then radically new environmental or ecological approach.

Educational sociologists became interested in how well the project objectives and materials fared in the schools where they had been adopted. Sarason (1973) ascribed failure to accomplish the intended fundamental changes to lack of attention to the school culture by the outsiders who had designed and were pushing the reforms. Similarly, Marsh (1964) noted the PSSC committee members had great experience in the administration of scientific research but little in the institutional organization and behaviour of schools. In his view, it was the classroom physics teachers who made the programme viable (Marsh, 1964, pp. 266–7).

In the late 1970s NSF commissioned several studies to evaluate the lasting effects of the curriculum reforms. One of these, a national survey of science, mathematics, and social studies programmes, suggested that about 19 million children, or 43 per cent of the school population, were using the reform materials (Weiss, 1978). Just what use meant, however, might be disputed. A parallel investigation, consisting of intensive case studies (Stake and Easley, 1978), proved disappointing about actual classroom practices. There seemed to be little evidence that the hands-on orientation and the investigative approaches that characterized the NSF curricula were being implemented by teachers.

Yet, when the curricula were used appropriately, they appeared to meet some important objectives. A meta-analysis of 20 years' worth of studies on the effects of the new science curricula showed that they were effective in teaching some of their key objectives, such as problem-solving and logical thinking, while doing no worse in such traditional objectives as memorizing science knowledge (Shymansky et al., 1983). Resnick and Resnick (1982) concluded that students exposed to the new curricula in mathematics and science experienced demanding standards and up-to-date learning.

SCIENCE EDUCATION REFORM IN THE 1980s

In 1983 the first federal budget prepared under President Reagan gave very little money to the NSF pre-college science education programmes;

only $160,000 was expended for materials development, research, and informal science education and a little over a million dollars for teacher preparation.

This coincided with renewed concern among scientists and educators for the inadequacies of US science education. A plethora of education reports were published in 1982 and 1983. Some of these reports dealt specifically with science and mathematics (National Academy of Sciences, 1982; National Science Board, 1983); others documented the poor state of education in the nation's schools (Boyer, 1983; Goodlad 1984; National Commission on Excellence in Education, 1983; Sizer, 1984); several linked the nation's economic future to the technical competencies of its workforce, found to be wanting as a result of deficient schooling (Task Force on Education for Economic Growth, 1983; Twentieth Century Fund Task Force, 1983). Evidence on the poor science and mathematics performance of US students, whether compared to their counterparts a decade or two earlier or to students in other countries, was cited frequently and publicized in the media (National Assessment of Educational Progress, 1983a, b; Wolf, 1977).

The report of the National Commission on Excellence in Education, *A Nation At Risk* (1983), proved particularly influential, thanks, in part, to its startling language: 'If an unfriendly foreign power had attempted to impose on America the mediocre educational performance that exists today, we might well have viewed it as an act of war' (National Commission on Excellence in Education, 1983, p. 5). The reports mentioned above helped educational reform gain new currency in the 1980s. The momentum is being maintained. In the autumn of 1989, the President and State Governors jointly proclaimed six national education goals for the 1990s, several involving mathematics and science education. In particular, goal 4 states: 'By the year 2000, US students will be first in the world in mathematics and science achievement' (National Governors' Association, 1990, p. 5).

The locus and nature of initial reforms

It is a mistake to think that the National Science Foundation can solve the problems of science education in this country. . . . It does not reach the bulk of the educational activities going on, particularly in the schools which serve the poorer students, the poorer States.

(Committee on Education and Labor, 1983, p. 284)

This statement from Representative Brown of California during congressional hearings for NSF's 1984 budget reflected the reform mood in the country quite well. In the 1960s no one in the schools or even among the public was much concerned about the quality of education; the harsh judgements came from the scientific and university communities. In the 1980s it was different. Concern may have been triggered by the highly visible national reports and the baleful test scores, but it was shared by influential policy-makers, particularly at the state level, and abetted by some vocal sectors of the business community.

Educational reform was everybody's business, spurred on by the perception that the USA was losing its competitive edge in the global economy.

The heightened activity at the state level, totally absent in the 1960s, was no accident. States have acquired much greater responsibility for education, largely through assuming a larger share of the support for public education. The rationale for this was usually economic, that is that a state's economic growth depended on the technical capabilities of its workforce. This led several states to create special high schools offering advanced science and mathematics training for the most able students. It was also argued that technical capability needed to be widely distributed throughout the workforce, implying the necessity of a sound scientific and mathematical education for everyone, not just the élite.

Increasing high-school graduation requirements

One of the first widespread reforms of the 1980s was to implement some of the recommendations of the *A Nation At Risk* report (National Commission on Excellence in Education, 1983).

Five years after publication of the report, thirty states had increased their high-school graduation requirements in science (Firestone *et al.*, 1989), although as of 1990, only four states had achieved the three years of science recommended by the report (Coley and Goertz, 1990). In some states the increases were quite dramatic. California, for example, previously had no science requirement; neither had Florida, which decided on the full three-year recommendation of Clune (Clune, 1989). Perhaps more influential for the college-bound students were the actions of state universities and colleges, which increased their requirements for admission at about the same time as states increased their graduation requirements (Goertz and Johnson, 1985).

Despite some initial concerns, the higher graduation requirements have not increased the number of students dropping out of school; however, the additional courses provided to lower-ability students may not be very rigorous. Firestone *et al.* (1989) found that the students taking additional academic classes because of state requirements were mostly middle- and low-achievers, and the schools offering the extra courses reported that they were at the basic, remedial or general level. Tacking on additional courses does not necessarily produce a high-level academic curriculum for all students.

Testing and accountability

A second reform initiative generated largely by the states was a drive towards accountability through increased student testing. Over forty new state testing provisions went into effect in the 1980s. Generally these cover basic proficiencies in reading, mathematics and the language arts, but about half the states have also instituted tests that students must take to become eligible for promotion to the next grade or for high-school graduation. The number of students, the grade levels included, the subjects being tested, and the types of tests being used have all greatly expanded in the last decade.

Unfortunately, most states and districts still rely heavily on commercial, norm-referenced tests. These tests have been criticized on a number of grounds (Archibald and Newmann, 1988; Hein, 1990; Raizen *et al.*, 1989, 1990; Schwartz and Viator, 1990; Wiggins, 1989): tests are not linked to state frameworks or school curricula; they misrepresent the nature of the subject; they distort and narrow instruction; and they provide poor assessment models for teachers (Dorr-Bremme and Herman, 1986). Testing seems to have its biggest impact on the elementary curriculum. About two-thirds of the elementary teachers interviewed by Firestone *et al.* (1989) in their study of the progress of reform said testing influenced what they taught. With the tests in use in most states, having teachers teach to the test is unlikely to improve the curriculum.

Teachers

The quantity and quality of the teaching workforce has also received attention. Even in the face of disagreements on the extent of the teacher shortage in science and mathematics (Darling-Hammond and Hudson, 1990; Feistritzer, 1986), the states took action. Teacher licensure, more easily changed than teacher preparation, was addressed early. A number of states instituted teacher certification tests (Firestone *et al.*, 1989). Another popular reform involved alternative routes toward certification for individuals with science backgrounds, relieving them of the need to go through traditional teacher education programmes.

A reform that cost real money and is an indication of state and local commitment is the increase in teacher salaries. Between 1980 and 1985 average teacher salaries increased nationally by 45 per cent (unadjusted for inflation), outstripping inflation as well as increases received by all other workers. This brought teachers back to the relative position compared to other workers they had held in 1971 and 1972 (Firestone *et al.*, 1989). One reason for the salary increases was the projection of an impending teacher shortage, due to an ageing teacher population likely to retire in great numbers (Haggstrom *et al.*, 1988) just as student enrolments were climbing again. There was concern about the quality of individuals going into teaching. Studies had found that students who majored in education had lower verbal test scores than those who did not, and that the teaching profession had special problems in recruiting and retaining the academically able (Vance and Schlechty, 1982). The increases in teacher salaries were deemed necessary to build a high-quality teaching workforce.

Curriculum frameworks

As part of the reform movement, a number of states began efforts to exercise leadership in curriculum and instruction. All but three states now have some general curriculum guidelines in science, but these vary greatly in specificity and in accompanying implementation measures. California, probably the outstanding example of using this reform strategy, involved hundreds of teachers and university faculties in the development of a state framework in science (as well as in other subjects), intended to guide course content for each year of schooling (all twelve grades) (California Department of Education, 1990). The development of the framework was accompanied by in-service training for teachers, using as tutors many of the teachers who had helped create the framework. The reform of the state testing programme in science is also based on the philosophy and content of the new framework.

Armstrong *et al.* (1989) found that state curriculum frameworks can produce greater local emphasis on science, particularly at the elementary level, and improve the quality of local curricula, materials, and teacher in-service training. This is not the case, however, unless there is an integrated approach, such as California's, with broad involvement from many sectors and considerable emphasis on dissemination and implementation. Even then, classroom practice remains difficult to change (Cohen, 1990).

Professional societies have also been active in developing curriculum guidelines. The American Association for the Advancement of Science (AAAS) (1989) has laid out a set of recommendations on the science understandings and habits of mind essential for all citizens in a scientifically literate society. A number of states have adopted the AAAS vision and framework; six school districts are currently engaged in developing curricula that will make the recommendations a reality in the classroom. The National Science Teachers Association (Aldridge, 1989) has recommended a co-ordinated scope and sequence for science courses in secondary schools. Their recommendations are undergoing further development in several states and local districts.

A new chemistry course developed by the American Chemical Society (1988) gives a flavour of current directions. The text, rather than being organized along traditional disciplinary lines, concentrates on eight chemistry-related technological issues, for example water needs, chemistry and health, understanding food. The units stress problem-solving and decision-making, in addition to major chemical concepts and laboratory skills.

The NSF programmes of the 1980s

As a result of the new concerns about mathematics and science education, the NSF education programmes enjoyed a meteoric rise from the low point of 1983. By 1990 the materials development programme had escalated to $48 million, teacher preparation and enhancement programmes to $81 million. The word 'pre-college' had been banned from NSF's lexicon of division titles and programme names, telegraphing the new interest in scientific accomplishments for all students, not just the college bound. NSF investments were not confined to the school years (kindergarten to Grade 12). For example, graduate fellowships have increased to nearly $37 million and a new programme of undergraduate science, engineering, and mathematics education, started in 1985, received $34 million.

There were some clear differences in operating principles compared to the 1960s. In contrast with the 1960s a much larger range of organizations were to be eligible for NSF awards, including lower education systems, and the programmes called for participation by many sectors of the community, not just scientists and teachers, but also school administrators, private businesses, and governmental entities outside education. The elementary grades were declared to be a high priority, particularly in curriculum reform.

The new materials development projects

As curriculum development efforts slowly re-emerged in NSF's revitalized science education programme, some of the apparent lessons of the 1960s were being applied to the new projects. The NSF staff in the science education division now included representatives of the education community whereas, in the 1960s, it drew entirely from the scientific community. This affected the design of the new programmes, most notably in the case of the 'Triad' projects for developing elementary and middle school science and mathematics curriculum materials. NSF required that there be three equal partners involved in any proposed project: the developers themselves (to include scientists and science educators), the prospective publishers or distributors of the materials, and school districts. No university or research and development centre could apply for a grant under this programme unless it had pre-signed a publisher who would pledge a large amount of money to help develop and distribute the materials, underwrite some of the pilot testing, and engage in subsequent teacher training.

In 1987 NSF funded three full-scale Triad projects at the elementary level (NSF, 1989):

- the Life Lab Science Programme, intended as a kindergarten to Grade 6 life-science programme, with financial support ($2.4 million) from Addison-Wesley Publishing Company;
- a BSCS project to develop a science/health programme consisting of twenty-eight activity-based modules for kindergarten to Grade 6, with Kendall/Hunt Publishing Company to invest $2.9 million;
- a project focused on students in urban systems (largely minority and largely poor), intended to integrate the life, physical, and earth sciences, to receive $2 million from Sunburst Communications, Inc.

Another four Triad elementary projects were not as ambitious; they were intended as adjuncts rather than replacements for the existing curriculum.

The trials were funded for four years of development and pilot trials. They were to be ready for commercial dissemination in 1991. NSF is now engaged in a review to determine whether the Triad concept is effective in getting the project materials into schools.

Partnerships

The successors to the old institutes programmes for teacher preparation and enhancement also stress co-operation with others. The names alone of several of the programmes underline their rationale: 'Private Sector Partnerships', intended to encourage business and industry to work with schools; 'Science and Mathematics Education Networks', intended to promote dialogue and consensus about educational improvement among scientists and educators. NSF programme announcements encourage 'collaboration among such partners as the Federal government, colleges and universities, state and local education agencies, business and industry, cultural institutions and media, scientists and science educators, and teachers, school administrators, and parents' (NSF, 1989, p. xvi).

State-wide systemic initiatives

Perhaps the most radical departure from NSF's pre-college education programmes of the 1960s was a programme inaugurated in 1991 to support a select group of states in systemic reform of the science (and/or mathematics) education in their schools. The awards were made through co-operative agreements rather than grants, a mechanism that made NSF an active partner in each project. The proposal solicitation (NSF, 1990) stressed the need to involve state leaders, school system leaders, leaders in science-rich institutions (universities and colleges, museums, science laboratories), the private sector, parent groups and other community organizations, and teacher-preparing institutions. Proposing states had to address a variety of components in concert, including:

- organizational structure;
- provision and allocation of resources (including non-NSF contributions);
- recruitment, preparation, and retention of teachers;
- curriculum content and learning goals;
- delivery of instruction, including facilities and equipment;
- assessment of student achievement and external evaluations; and
- articulation within the system.

The first round of awards went to ten states (thirty submitted proposals), the second to eleven states. There was to be one more competitive round. The programme has high visibility in Congress and, of course, among the state governments.

SPECULATIONS ABOUT THE FUTURE

The US science education reforms of the 1980s have set themselves a tall order: that *all* students become scientifically literate by the end of twelve years of school. The reforms started from a low point of support for science education in the early 1980s; they have shown surprising staying power. They started with 'quick fixes', legislation and mandates to increase the amount of time spent on science and the academic rigour of the curriculum. They continued with measures that required financial commitments at the local, state and national levels. They now confront the difficult task of changing science instruction in nearly every classroom in the nation. That not much progress has been made to date is confirmed by the continuing discouraging test results (International Association for the Evaluation of Educational Achievement, 1988; LaPointe *et al.*, 1989, 1992; Mullis and Jenkins, 1988) and by surveys of current practice and teaching conditions (Weiss, 1987; Weiss and Boyd, 1990).

Much has been learned about the need to involve the many interested constituencies in working toward science education improvement. Will the current efforts, therefore, be more successful than those of the 1960s in bringing the power of science into the service of all? It is too early to tell, but formidable obstacles remain.

First, there is no unanimity on what represents scientific literacy or consensus that it is an appropriate goal (Shamos, 1988). Teachers, school administrators, academic scientists, industrialists and college students hold different conceptions about the meaning of the phrase (Champagne *et al.*, 1989).

At its simplest, scientific literacy means familiarity with scientific terms. More commonly, it means sufficient knowledge to comprehend and apply scientific information in the news media and encountered at work, in caring for oneself and family, and in making decisions affecting one's community. Such a conception of scientific literacy often leads to an emphasis on understanding technology as well as science, since most problems involve both (Bybee *et al.*, 1989; Hickman *et al.*, 1987). Technology, however, presents a new field of knowledge and practice to most teachers, even those with a strong science background. The dangers of diluting both the science and the technology components of the curriculum are very real.

A third view of scientific literacy is that taken by the AAAS in *Project 2061: Science for All Americans* (AAAS, 1989). This report urges that individuals acquire considerable depth of conceptual understanding of major scientific theories and of the methods of science, as well as acquiring scientific attitudes and the disposition to use science knowledge for self and society. This is an ambitious goal and far from the science taught and tested in today's classrooms.

Second, the need for improvement is greatest in the classrooms that serve ethnic minority students, students from poor communities, and students with physical disabilities or language deficiencies. Yet, these are the very classrooms that tend to have the fewest science resources, whether competent teachers, rich curricula and choice of appropriate courses, high aspirations for students, or material resources devoted to science. These disparities are becoming more acute as the student population is becoming more diversified (Hodgkinson, 1985). In California, for example, already the majority of elementary school children come from minority groups and this will become the case for other states. It has already happened for the school populations in most large cities.

There is much understanding of science learning by children not profiting or excluded altogether from current science instruction (Beane, 1985; College Board, 1990; Malcom *et al.*, 1984). Yet schools continue to stream children early according to standardized reading and arithmetic tests. Students assigned to lower tracks receive an education that becomes poorer and poorer in science as they move through the grades, with the consequence that they are not able to participate in higher-level courses in upper secondary school (Oakes, 1990). Streaming in this way tends to exclude, from higher-level science instruction, the very groups currently underrepresented in science. This practice with its deep roots in American education makes scientific literacy for all a difficult goal to achieve.

Third, the current wave of education reform started and has been sustained during a period of relative prosperity in which increased spending on education was politically feasible. This prosperity has waned in the last three years, and school systems are retrenching. Perhaps history will not be a guide, and the investment in science education will continue its upward trajectory. Having learned that educational change does not come easily nor quickly, that it takes persistence and time, one can only hope that the political will continues to carry through the reform agenda in science education.

REFERENCES

AAAS (American Association for the Advancement of Science) (1989) *Project 2061: Science for all Americans*, Washington, DC, American Association for the Advancement of Science.

Aldridge, W. G. (1989) *Essential Changes in Secondary School Science: Scope, Sequence, and Coordination*, Washington, DC, National Science Teachers Association.

American Chemical Society (1988) *ChemCom: Chemistry in the Community*, Dubuque, Ia., Kendall/Hunt Publishing Company.

Archibald, D. A. and Newmann, F. M. (1988) *Beyond Standardized Testing: Authentic Academic Achievement in the Secondary School*, Reston, Va., National Association of Secondary School Principals (NASSP) Publications.

Armstrong, J., Davis, A., Odden, A. and Gallagher, J. (1989) *Designing State Curriculum Frameworks and Assessment Programmes to Improve Instruction*, Denver, Colo., Education Commission of the States.

Beane, D. (1985) *Mathematics and Science: Critical Filters for the Future of Minority Students*, Washington, DC, The Mid-Atlantic Center for Race Equity, The American University.

Bestor, A. (1953) *Educational Wastelands: The Retreat from Learning in our Public Schools*, Urbana, University of Illinois Press.

Boyer, E. L. (1983) *High School: A Report on Secondary Education in America*, New York, Harper & Row.

Bush, V. (1945) *Science – The Endless Frontier*, Washington, DC, republished by the National Science Foundation in 1980.

Bybee, R. W., Buchwald, C. E., Crissman, S., Heil, D. R., Kuerbis, P. J., Matsumoto, C. and McInerney, J. D. (1989) *Science and Technology Education for the Elementary Years: Frameworks for Curriculum and Instruction*. A report of the National Center for Improving Science Education, Andover, Mass., The NETWORK, Inc.

California Department of Education (1990) *Science Framework for California Public Schools Kindergarten through Grade Twelve*, California, California Department of Education.

Champagne, A. B., Lovitts, B. E. and Calinger, B. J. (eds.) (1989) *Scientific Literacy: This Year in School Science 1989*, Washington, DC, American Association for the Advancement of Science.

Clune, W. H. (1989) *The Implementation and Effects of High School Graduation Requirements: First Steps toward Curricular Reform*, New Brunswick, NJ, Rutgers University, Centre for Policy Research in Education.

Cohen, D. K. (1990) 'Revolution in one classroom: the case of Mrs Oublier', in D. K. Cohen and P. L. Peterson (eds.) *Effects of State-Level Reform of Elementary School Mathematics Curriculum on Classroom Practice*, East Lansing, Mich., The Center for the Learning and Teaching of Elementary Subjects, Michigan State University.

Coley, R. J. and Goertz, M. E. (1990) *Educational Standards in the 50 States: 1990*, Princeton, NJ, Educational Testing Service.

College Board (1990) 2nd edition *Academic Preparation in Science: Teaching for Transition from High School to College*, New York, College Entrance Examination Board.

Committee on Education and Labor, US House of Representatives (1983) *Hearings on Mathematics and Science Education*, Washington, DC, US Government Printing Office.

Committee on Science and Technology (1975) *National Science Foundation Curriculum Development and Implementation for Pre-college Science Education*, Washington, DC, US Government Printing Office.

Cremin, L. A. (1964) *The Transformation of the School: Progressivism in American Education 1876–1957*, New York, Vintage Books, Random House.

Darling-Hammond, L. and Hudson, L. (1990) 'Pre-college science and mathematics teachers: supply, demand and quality', in C. B. Cazden (ed.) *Review of Research in Education*, Washington, DC, American Educational Research Association.

DeWitt, N. (1955) *Soviet Professional Manpower – Its Education, Training, and Supply*, Washington, DC, US Government Printing Office.

Dorr-Bremme, D. W. and Herman, J. L. (1986) *Assessing Student Achievement: A Profile of Classroom Practices*, Los Angeles, Center for the Study of Evaluation, University of California.

England, J. M. (1982) *A Patron for Pure Science: The National Science Foundation's Formative Years, 1945–57*, Washington, DC, National Science Foundation.

Feistritzer, E. (1986) *Teacher Crisis: Myth or Reality?*, Washington, DC, National Center for Educational Information.

Firestone, W. A., Fuhrman, S. H. and Kirst, M. W. (1989) *The Progress of Reform: An Appraisal of State Education Initiatives*, New Brunswick, NJ, Center for Policy Research In Education.

Goertz, M. E. and Johnson, L. M. (1985) *State Policies for Admission to Higher Education*, New York, The College Entrance Examination Board.

Goodlad, J. I. (1984) *A Place called School*, New York, McGraw-Hill.

Grubb, W. N. (1979) 'The effects of national policy on vocational education evaluation', in D. Henry (ed.) *The Planning Papers for the Vocational Education Study*. Prepared by the National Institute for Education, Washington, DC. US Government Printing Office.

Haggstrom, G. W., Darling-Hammond, L. and Grissmer, D. W. (1988) *Assessing Teacher Supply and Demand*, Santa Monica, Calif., The Rand Corporation.

Hein, G. (ed.) (1990) *The Assessment of Hands-on Elementary Science Programs*, North Dakota Study Group on Evaluation, Center for Teaching and Learning, University of North Dakota.

Hickman, F. M., Patrick, J. J. and Bybee, R. W. (1987) *Science/Technology/Society*, A framework for curriculum reform in secondary school science and social studies, Boulder, Colo., Social Science Education Consortium, Inc.

Hodgkinson, H. L. (ed.) (1985) *All One System: Demographics of Education, Kindergarten through Graduate School*, Washington, DC, The Institute for Educational Leadership, Inc.

International Association for the Evaluation of Educational Achievement (IEA) (1988) *Science Achievement in Seventeen Countries: A Preliminary Report*, Elmsford, NY, Pergamon Press.

Krieghbaum, H. and Rawson, H. (1969) *An Investment in Knowledge*, New York, New York University Press.

LaPointe, A. E., Meade, N. A. and Phillips, G. W. (1989) *A World of Differences*, Princeton, NJ, Educational Testing Service (ETS).

LaPointe, A. E., Askew, J. M. and Mead, N. A. (1992) *Learning Science*, Princeton, NJ, Educational Testing Service (ETS).

Library of Congress (1976) *The National Science Foundation and Pre-College Science Education: 1950–1975*, Report prepared for the Committee on Science and Technology, US Congress, Washington, DC, US Government Printing Office.

Lynd, A. (1953) *Quackery in the Public Schools*, Boston, Little, Brown.

Malcom, S. M., Aldrich, M., Hall, P., Quick, B. and Stern, V. (1984) *Education in the Sciences – Equity and Excellence: Compatible Goals*, Washington, DC, Office of Opportunities in Science, American Association for the Advancement of Science.

Marsh, P. E. (1964) Wellsprings of strategy: considerations affecting innovations by the PSSC, in B. Miles (ed.) *Innovation in Education*, New York, Teachers College, Columbia University.

Mullis, V. S. and Jenkins, L. B. (1988) *The Science Report Card. Elements of Risk and Recovery*, National Assessment for Educational Progress, Report No. 17–S–01, Princeton, NJ, Educational Testing Service.

National Academy of Sciences (1982) *Science and Mathematics in the Schools: Report of a Convocation*, Washington, DC, National Academy Press.

National Assessment of Educational Progress (1983a) *Reading, Science, and*

Mathematics Trends: A Closer Look, Denver, Colo., Education Commission of the States.

National Assessment of Educational Progress (1983b) *The Third National Mathematics Assessment: Results, Trends, and Issues*, Denver, Colo., Education Commission of the States.

National Center for Education Statistics (1987) *The Condition of Education: A Statistical Report*. A report of the US Department of Education, Office of Educational Research and Improvement, Washington, DC, Superintendent of Documents, US Government Printing Office.

National Commission on Excellence in Education (1983) *A Nation at Risk: The Imperative for Educational Reform*, Washington, DC, US Department of Education.

National Governors' Association (1990) *National Education Goals*. Adopted by the membership on 25 February, 1990, Washington, DC, National Governors' Association.

National Science Board Commission on Pre-College Education in Mathematics, Science and Technology (1983) *Educating Americans for the 21st Century*, Washington, DC, National Science Foundation.

NSF (National Science Foundation) (1965) *Science Education in the Schools of the United States*. Report to the Committee on Science and Astronautics, US Congress, Washington, DC, US Government Printing Office.

NSF (National Science Foundation) (1989) *Directory of Awards: Fiscal Years 1987 and 1988*, Washington, DC, Directorate for Science and Engineering Education.

NSF (National Science Foundation) (1990) *Statewide Systemic Initiatives in Science, Mathematics, and Engineering Education 1989*, Washington, DC, Directorate for Science and Engineering Education.

Oakes, J. (1990) *Multiplying Inequalities: The Effects of Race, Social Class, and Ability Grouping on Students' Opportunities to Learn Mathematics and Science*, Santa Monica, Calif. The RAND Corporation.

PSSC (Physical Sciences Study Committee) (1960) *Physics*, Boston, D.C. Heath.

Raizen, S. A., Baron, B., Champagne, A. B., Haertel, E., Mullis, V. S. and Oakes, J. (1989) *Assessment in Elementary School Science*. A report of the National Center for Improving Science Education, Andover, Mass., The NETWORK, Inc.

Raizen, S. A., Baron, B., Champagne, A. B., Haertel, E., Mullis, V. S. and Oakes, J. (1990) *Assessment in Science Education: The Middle Years*. A report of the National Center for Improving Science Education, Andover, Mass., The NETWORK, Inc.

Ravitch, D. (1983) *The Troubled Crusade: American Education, 1945–1980*, New York, Basic Books.

Resnick, D. P. and Resnick, L. B. (1982) 'Standards, curriculum, and perspective', *Educational Researcher*, 14(4), pp. 5–20.

Russell, B. (1962) *Power*, New York, Barnes & Noble.

Rutherford, F. J., Holton, G. and Watson, F. G. (1970) *Project Physics*. Republished in 1981 by Holt, Rinehart & Winston, New York.

Sarason, S. B. (1973) *The Culture of the School and the Problem of Change*, Boston, Allyn & Bacon.

Schwartz, J. L. and Viator, K. A. (eds.) (1990) *The Prices of Secrecy: The Social, Intellectual, and Psychological Costs of Current Assessment Practice*, Cambridge, Mass., Harvard Graduate School of Education, Educational Technology Center.

Shamos, M. H. (1988) 'The lesson every child need not learn', *The Sciences*, 28, (4), pp. 14–20.

Shymansky, J. A., Kyle, W. C. and Alport, J. M. (1983) 'The effects of new science curricula on student performance', *Journal of Research in Science Teaching*, 20, (5), pp. 387–404.

Sizer, T. (1984) *Horace's Compromise: The Dilemma of the American High School*, New York, Houghton Mifflin.

Stake, R. E. and Easley, J. A. (1978) *Case Studies in Science Education*. NSF SE-78-74. Available from the US Government Printing Office, National Science Foundation, Washington, DC.

Task Force on Education for Economic Growth (1983) *Action for Excellence: A Comprehensive Plan to Improve our Nation's Schools*, Denver, Colo., Education Commission of the States.

Twentieth Century Fund Task Force (1983) *Report of the Twentieth Century Fund Task Force on Federal Elementary and Secondary Education Policy*, New York, Twentieth Century Fund.

Vance, V. and Schlechty, P. (1982) 'The distribution of academic ability in the teaching force: policy implications', *Phi Delta Kappan*, 63, p. 23.

Weiss, I. R. (1978) *Report of the 1977 National Survey of Science, Mathematics, and Social Studies Education*. Prepared for the National Science Foundation. Available from the US Government Printing Office, Supt. of Doc. no. 083–000–00364–0, Washington, DC, National Science Foundation.

Weiss, I. R. (1987) *Report of the 1985–86 National Survey of Science and Mathematics Education*, Research Triangle Park, NC, Horizon Research, Inc.

Weiss, I. R. and Boyd, S. E. (1990) *Where Are They Now? A Follow-Up Study of the 1985–86 Science and Mathematics Teaching Force*, Chapel Hill, NC. Horizon Research, Inc.

Welch, W. W. (1979) 'Twenty years of science curriculum development: a look back', in D. C. Berliner, (ed.) *Review of Research in Education 7*, Washington, DC, American Educational Research Association.

Wiggins, G. (1989) 'A true test: toward more authentic and equitable assessment', *Phi Delta Kappan*, 70, (9), pp. 703–13.

Wolf, R. M. (1977) *Achievement in America*, New York, Teachers College Press.

Woodring, P. (1953) *Let's Talk Sense About our Schools*, New York, McGraw-Hill.

Wooton, W. (1965) *SMSG: The Making of a Curriculum*, New Haven, Yale University Press.

1.3

Science education in Japan and the United States: are the Japanese beating us at our own game?

Anton E. Lawson

A COMPARISON OF REASONING ABILITIES

During September of 1986 the National Science Foundation and the Japanese Ministry of Education supported a conference of American and Japanese science educators held at the East-West Center on the campus of the University of Hawaii in Honolulu to discuss the status of science education in the two countries. Discussions were far reaching but focused primarily on data comparing scientific reasoning abilities of seventh, eighth, and ninth grade students from the two countries (Takemura *et al.*, 1985; Mattheis, Spooner and Coble, 1986). The Japanese sample consisted of 4,397 students randomly selected from throughout Japan. The American sample, regrettably not a random sample of the United States, consisted of 3,291 randomly selected students from throughout the state of North Carolina.

Using a slightly modified version of the Classroom Test of Formal Reasoning (Lawson, 1978), both samples of students were tested on their ability to conserve displaced volume, control variables, and use proportional, probabilistic, and combinatorial reasoning. The data then, in effect, allowed a comparison of Japanese and North Carolina students' reasoning abilities at three grade levels. How did the Japanese and North Carolina samples compare? In short, the Japanese students outperformed the North Carolina students on virtually all reasoning tasks at all grade levels. The comparative data for the combined grades, reported by Takemura *et al.* (1985) are reproduced in Figure 1.

Although the North Carolina sample cannot be considered as representative of the entire United States it should be pointed out that many of the same reasoning tasks have been administered to a wide range of students in many parts of the United States. The North Carolina sample's performance on the test is not atypical. Lawson and Bealer (1984), for example, compared performance of a San Francisco Bay Area sample of students with a suburban and a rural sample of students in Arizona on their ability to use proportional,

From: *Science Education* (1990) Vol. 74, no. 4, pp. 495–501.

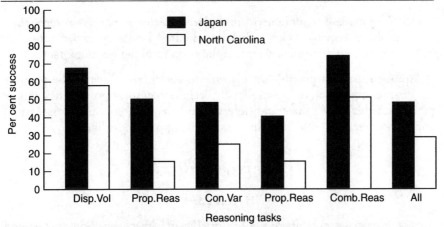

Figure 1 Comparison of reasoning abilities of a representative sample of 4,397 Japanese students with a representative sample of 3,291 North Carolina students (grades seven, eight and nine). Disp. vol. = displaced volume; Prop. reas. = proportional reasoning; Con. var. = control of variables; Prob. reas. = probalistic reasoning; Comb. reas. = combinatorial reasoning; All = all tasks combined (from Takemura et al., 1985)

probabilistic, and correlational reasoning. They found performance to vary but the average to be generally at the levels of the North Carolina sample.

At first blush the Japanese superiority in reasoning seems surprising in light of the fact that a primary objective of American education has long been to develop rational thinking abilities (cf. *The Central Purpose of American Education*, Educational Policies Commission, 1961) while the Japanese are well known for the Confucian tradition of group ordering by clearly defined roles. The Japanese emphasis on group harmony might to some appear not to provoke the development of rational thought processes whose primary aim is to test diverse ideas via logical argumentation and evidence. To what can the Japanese superiority be attributed?

POSSIBLE CAUSES OF THE DIFFERENCE

During the September 1986 conference the participants engaged in a discussion to explore possible causes of the observed difference in reasoning performance. The following hypotheses were suggested:

(1) Japanese students are innately more intelligent.
(2) Parental involvement and educational expectations are greater in Japan.
(3) Japanese students spend more time on learning tasks.
(4) Japanese students come in contact with a greater diversity of potentially conflicting, hence thought provoking, cultural perspectives.
(5) Religious and philosophical doctrines in Japan (e.g., Shinto and Buddhism) do not oppose scientific thought as Christianity often does in the United States.
(6) Test items, when translated into Japanese, were altered and made easier.

(7) The Japanese school curriculum places greater emphasis on reasoning, problem solving, open-ended questioning, hands-on experimentation and argumentation, and less emphasis on recalling textbook facts.

Although it is not possible at this time to determine which of the possible causes or combination of causes play the largest role, some possibilities appear more plausible than others and deserve our attention, continued discussion, and future research. Which of the possibilities appear most likely?

MOST LIKELY CAUSE(S)

Hypothesis 1

Japanese students are innately more intelligent. Stevenson, Stigler, Lee and Lucker (1985) reported the results of a carefully conducted and thorough cross-cultural comparison of Japanese, Chinese, and American first and fifth grade students on a variety of tests of basic cognitive performance (intelligence) and academic achievement. After carefully controlling for differences in socioeconomic level and eliminating minority and/or non-native speaking children from their sample, they found similarity in level, variability, and structure of intellectual abilities among the three cultures. However, Chinese children surpassed Japanese and American children in reading scores while both Chinese and Japanese children obtained higher scores in mathematics than did the American children. Their results suggest that higher achievement of the Chinese and Japanese children is not due to higher intellectual abilities but must be related to their experiences at home and at school.

Hypothesis 1 is, therefore, weakened. Nevertheless, it is likely that the samples tested by Stevenson *et al.* (1985) were much less heterogeneous than the North Carolina sample tested by Mattheis *et al.* (1986). Therefore, the average level of intelligence of the North Carolina sample may, in fact, be less than that of the Japanese sample.

Hypothesis 2

Parental involvement and educational expectations are greater in Japan. There seems little doubt that the overall level of parental involvement and educational expectations are greater in Japan than in the United States. This is reflected by the extensive role played by mothers who teach small groups of children in after-school lessons called *juku* and by mothers working individually with their children. The typical Japanese mother places great emphasis and considerable effort into her children's education and their success on all important entrance examinations. In fact the effort mothers put into their children's examinations has even been given a special term – the Kyoiku mama syndrome. In contrast to the Western notion of independent effort and personal achievement, the Japanese consider academic achievement to be the result of considerable cooperative effort and planning so much so that the mother is sometimes portrayed as one who is totally identified with her children's success or failure and has, therefore, no identity of her own. To the Kyoiku mama, educating the children is a full time job (Ranbon, 1985).

While this emphasis on education may have its positive effects on the child, it may also be a matter of too much too soon. Further, it is not clear what things are taught by the mothers. Clearly the possibility exists for an emphasis on learning that would have no positive impact on reasoning (e.g., the memorization of capital cities of the Prefectures), therefore, it is not possible, and perhaps not even reasonable, to conclude that this emphasis will translate into improved reasoning performance in the junior high school years.

Hypothesis 3

Japanese students spend more time on learning tasks. Schools in Japan operate at least 220 to 240 days each year as opposed to the normal 180–185 in the United States. Generally the Japanese student attends school five and one half days per week for over 40 weeks. The school day typically begins at 8:30 a.m. and lasts until 5:00 p.m. Academic work typically concludes at 2:30 p.m. with sports and other extracurricular activities filling the remaining time. The school year begins in April and ends in March of the next year. Summer vacation lasts about one and one half months and students are given assignments to be completed during that time. The assignments are collected and graded by the same teachers who gave them as teacher changes do not occur until March. Thus the possible benefits of work over the summer, as well as time spent in class, greatly favours the Japanese.

Hypothesis 4

Japanese students come in contact with a greater diversity of potentially conflicting, hence thought provoking, cultural perspectives. Formal reasoning patterns are generally viewed as cognitive tools one uses to assess the validity of alternative causal hypotheses. As one reaches adolescence one may come into contact with various alternative explanations and points of view which may be in contradiction (e.g., God created all living things during six days versus living things evolved to their present forms gradually over millions of years). Thus it seems likely that the intellectual diversity of the culture would increase the likelihood of contact with alternative conceptions and in turn would provoke the acquisition of formal reasoning patterns.

Which culture, the Japanese or the American, is more diverse intellectually? At first glance one would think that the Japanese culture is less intellectually diverse than the American culture; therefore, it would be less conducive to the intellectual development of its youth. Gakusesika (1984) reports that 98.6% of the Japanese have pure Japanese origin (i.e., nonracially mixed) and 90% of the people think of themselves as middle class. According to Nakayama (1987) social norms such as uniformity, conformity, and group consciousness have been formed under these demographic conditions. Yet this homogeneity of background may actually mask a heterogeneity of thinking as Japan has a long history of looking to other countries for ideas. Takemura (1983) for example, stated, 'Japanese people have always adopted, adapted, co-opted – or even borrowed the best of the West and East, yet sometimes discarded the borrowing to think and act according to their own unique characteristics' (p. 153). In the same vein, Nakayama (1987) claims that technological development in Japan has been based upon copies and clever combinations of technical ideas imported from overseas.

According to some observers, Japan has a long history of competing goals and values and nowhere is this societal questioning more clearly evidenced than in the schools. From the West come ideas of freedom, individualism, and equal opportunity. From the Confucian tradition come ideas of group ordering by clearly defined roles, stressing family ties, and shared moral tenets (Ranbon, 1985). Thus it would appear that in Japan racial and socioeconomic homogeneity has not at all provoked cultural and intellectual isolation. The situation in North Carolina could well be viewed as much the opposite where racial and social heterogeneity may foster intellectual separation and isolation and hence serve to retard, not enhance intellectual development.

Hypothesis 5

Religious and philosophical doctrines in Japan (e.g., Shinto and Buddhism) do not oppose scientific thought as Christianity often does in the United States. This hypothesis must be viewed as speculative as I know of no studies which bear directly on its validity. Clearly, however, one can see a long history of conflict of Christianity with science in the history of science. This conflict is highlighted by the Copernican theory, which put the sun, rather than the earth, at the centre of the universe, and by the theory of evolution which claims humans evolved from non-human ancestors rather than being created by an act of God and in God's image. Clearly untested faith in any position is not acceptable in science yet this is precisely what Christianity often requires. To the extent that Western religion fosters a lack of willingness to consider alternatives and the untested acceptance of any position, this would presumably restrain the development of reasoning skills. Although I am by no means an authority on Eastern religion, the Japanese science educators claimed that no such conflict arises between science and their Eastern religious views.

Hypothesis 6

Test items, when translated into Japanese, were altered and made easier. Although this hypothesis cannot be totally ruled out it appears to be unlikely. The reasoning test administered to the Japanese students was of course written in the Japanese language. It was translated from the English version by Japanese science educators who were not only very knowledgeable about issues related to assessing reasoning abilities but very competent in English. Therefore, it seems unlikely that the Japanese translation would be less difficult than the original English version. It should also be pointed out that the Japanese superiority was consistent from one test item to the next which also argues against this hypothesis. If item difficulty varied between the two versions due to differences in wording of questions in different languages, one would expect Japanese superiority to appear on some, but not all of the items.

Hypothesis 7

The Japanese school curriculum places greater emphasis on reasoning, problem solving, open-ended questioning, hands-on experimentation, and argumentation, and less emphasis on recalling textbook facts. When the Japanese participants were asked which of the seven hypotheses they favoured, this was the clear winner. Further, when asked what aspect of the curriculum they felt best encouraged the development of reasoning abilities, they were almost unanimous in the view that it is the way science is taught that makes the most difference. Of course their view is based on very little 'hard' evidence yet it is clear that the Japanese know what science is being taught in grades 1–9, they know how much science is being taught and further they know how it is being taught.

Japan has a very centralized system of education in which the Ministry of Education sets the national curriculum as well as the number of class hours which must be devoted to each subject. In the elementary school the total number of class hours devoted to science is 68 for the first grade, 70 for second grade, 105 for third through seventh grades, and 140 hours for eighth and ninth grade. Among these hours approximately 70 per cent are recommended for practical activities and laboratory work.

According to Nakayama (1987), 'the development of cognitive skills in science is one of the most important goals of science education in Japan' (p. 25). Further, this is done by letting students '. . . have first hand experience with real objects and understand the ideas from real things and phenomena through problem solving processes' (p. 25). In other words, science is taught in grades 1–9 and not only that, it is taught largely via inquiry procedures and 'hands-on' activities. This stands in stark contrast with grades K–6 science education in the United States where the normal pattern is to teach little or no science and what little that is taught is generally through textbook readings which most science educators would not view as teaching science at all.

INTERIM SUMMARY

Of course it is not possible at this time to determine how much each of the alternative hypotheses contributes to the observed difference in reasoning between the Japanese and North Carolina sample. But would it not be ironic if the science curriculum proved to be a major cause as it could forcefully be argued that Japanese science educators came to their view that the study of science in the early years should be 'hands-on' and group inquiry-oriented through their study of curriculum development efforts of the 1960s and 1970s in the United States? These efforts included the development of inquiry-oriented programmes such as the Elementary Science Study, Science: A Process Approach and the Science Curriculum Improvement Study. It seems safe to say that science educators in the United States and Japan generally agree that these types of programmes and what they stand for are what an early education in science should be. In Japan they have been able to put this philosophy and methodology into the schools. In the United States, due I think, to our lack of a central educational authority, and due to a lack of effective teacher training, we have not been able to put these programmes into the majority of schools. In other words, the Japanese seem to be beating us at our own game. This, to at least one science educator in the United States, represents an extremely frustrating state of affairs.

An excellent beginning bibliography of English language publications concerning science education in Japan, as well as a list of resources for research on science education in Japan, can be found in Klopfer (1986). The interested reader is urged to consult these and other references for additional information.

REFERENCES

Educational Policies Commission (1961) *The Central Purpose of American Education*, Washington, DC, National Education Association of the United States.

Gakuseisha, R. (1984) *Nippon: The Land and its People*, Nippon, Nippon Steel Corporation.

Klopfer, L. E. (1986) 'Resources for research on science education in Japan', *Science Education*, 70, (3), pp. 347–54.

Lawson, A. E. (1978) 'The development and validation of a classroom test of formal reasoning', *Journal of Research in Science Teaching*, 51, (1), pp. 11–24.

Lawson, A. E. and Bealer, J. M. (1984) 'Cultural diversity and differences in formal reasoning ability', *Journal of Research in Science Teaching*, 21, (7), pp. 735–43.

Mattheis, F., Spooner, W. E. and Coble, C. R. (1986) 'A study of logical thinking skills, integrated process skills, and science attitudes of North Carolina middle grade students: a summary report'. Paper presented at the US – Japan Seminar on Science Education, Honolulu, Hawaii.

Nakayama, G. (1987) 'Perspectives on educational settings and school science curricula in Japan compared with the United States'. Unpublished joint research report, East Carolina University and Hiroshima University.

Ranbon, S. (1985) 'Schooling in Japan: the paradox in the pattern', *Education Week*, February 20.

Stevenson, H. W., Stiger, J. W., Lee, Shin-Ying and Lucker, G. W. (1985) 'Cognitive performance and academic achievement of Japanese, Chinese, American children', *Child Development*, 56, pp. 718–34.

Takemura, S. (1983) People, society and science education in Japan, in D. E. Hadary and Vicentini (eds.) *Proceedings of US – Italy Joint Seminars in Science Education for Elementary School Children*, Washington, DC, The American University.

Takemura, S., Matsumoto, K., Yoshida, A., Matsumoto, S., Hioki, M., Saruta, Y., Kadaya, S., Nakayama, H., Matsubara, V. U., Tadokoro, Y. and Makayama, G. (1985) Unpublished research report. The Japan–US Cooperative Science Program, Hiroshima University.

1.4

International comparisons in science education

Elaine Brown

INTRODUCTION

In 1992 a report was published entitled *Science Achievement in Twenty-Three Countries* (Postlethwaite and Wiley, 1992) to complement *Science Education and Curricula in Twenty-Three Countries* (Rosier and Keeves, 1991) and *Changes in Science Education and Achievement, 1970–1984* (Keeves, 1991), both published in 1991. A further volume on the international assessment of science practical skills is being prepared. The series presents the results of the Second International Science Study (SISS).

This article considers some of the information covered by this study.

THE SECOND INTERNATIONAL SCIENCE STUDY

The Chair(man) of IEA (International Association for the Evaluation of Educational Achievement), in his foreword to one of the reports, claims 'that in the early 1980s, science education had lost direction in most countries of the English speaking world' (Rosier and Keeves, 1991, p. vii). This is given as the reason why this second science study was proposed and why some thirty countries initially expressed interest in participating, the first science study having been done in 1970–1 (Comber and Keeves, 1973). Whatever the reason(s), twenty-six countries were prepared to fund their own participation in the study. Each designated a research institute to be responsible for the international co-operation needed for the design and conduct of the study, data collection, and preparation and publication of national reports.

Most of the data were collected in 1983–4 and the national reports were seen as the primary outcome of the study. Each country tailored the study to suit local conditions while attempting to provide data that would contribute to the aims of the international study which were:

- to measure, by means of large-scale survey procedures, the current state of school science education across the world;
- to examine the ways in which science education has changed since the early 1970s;

- to identify the factors which explain differences in the output of science education programmes across countries, and between students within countries, with particular attention to the role of the science curriculum as an explanatory factor;
- to investigate changes in the patterns of relationships between the explanatory factors and the outputs between the early 1970s and the early 1980s;
- to assist all participating countries, especially less-developed countries, to carry out associated national studies of science education in order to investigate issues of particular interest in their own countries.

(Keeves and Rosier, 1981, as quoted in Keys, 1987, p. 3)

THE POPULATIONS AND THE DATA COLLECTED

The study sought to measure the science achievement of students in three age groups and to provide information to allow links to be made between science achievement, the intended curriculum, the sex of students, their attitude to science, their perception of science lessons and various other factors influencing home or school life.

The working language of the study was English and translations were made into sixteen other languages.

The final samples ('achieved' populations) totalled in excess of 200,000 students, their teachers and school/college principals. Data were collected by five-option multiple-choice tests and through questionnaires or 'opinionnaires' (Jacobson and Doran, 1988) which utilized rating scales. The achieved population comprised students who had attempted at least three items on the core test of science achievement; teachers who had answered at least one question on the questionnaire; and schools attended by at least three students with qualifying results (whether or not data on their school were available).

Table I Sample sizes and response rates P1 and P2

	Population 1			Population 2		
	Target population (millions)	Achieved sample (thousands)	Per cent response from designed sample	Target population (thousands)	Achieved sample (thousands)	Per cent response from designed sample
Philippines (largest sample)	1.1	16.9	92	573	10.8	88
Nigeria (smallest sample)	2.2	0.9	36	441	0.8	15
England	0.6	3.7	62	708	3.1	53
Japan	2.0	7.9	99	1,819	7.6	95
Korea	0.9	3.4	99	861	4.5	100

Based on information given in Postlethwaite and Wiley, 1992, pp. 187 and 188.

Table 2   Sample sizes and response rates P3 and P3 subgroups

	Largest achieved sample			Smallest achieved sample		
	Country	Per cent students in school	Achieved sample	Country	Per cent students in school	Achieved sample
All students	Canada (Eng. system)	68	9,452	Ghana	1.2	494
Physics	Hong Kong	20	6,025	Ghana	0.6	291
Chemistry	Hong Kong	20	5,952	Hungary	1	143
Biology	Korea	38	3,319	Italy	4	147
Non-scientists	Italy	34	2,455	Singapore	8	297

Based on information given in Postlethwaite and Wiley, 1992, pp. 6 and 189–93.

Variables were only included in the final databank if more than 80 per cent of the achieved population had provided information. Various statistical procedures were used to test for sampling errors and to minimize either differences in sample size and/or the percentage of each 'designed' sample qualifying for inclusion in the analysis. Tables 1 and 2 give some indication of the statistical manipulation required. The target populations were as follows:

- Population 1 (P1): students aged 10:0 to 10:11 or all students in the grade where most were 10 years old. (These would probably have had class teaching.)
- Population 2 (P2): students aged 14:0 to 14:11 or all students in the grade where most were 14 years old. (These would probably have been taught by subject specialists.)
- Population 3 (P3): subgroups of students in their final year of full-time school. (The students themselves would have specialized.)

The survey found almost all ten-year-olds to be in school, between 97 and 99 per cent for the countries taking part. Attendance was not so uniform for fourteen-year-olds where a sharp distinction was evident between seventeen of the countries, all reporting over 90 per cent and the rest where the range was shown to be from as low as 11 per cent. The variation in P3 was vast and further confused by variations in vocational training programmes.

THE INTERNATIONAL TESTS

The intended uses of the data from the survey included: comparisons with the findings of the 1970–1 survey (Comber and Keeves, 1973); cross-national comparisons of science achievement; quantification of 'growth' (IEA, 1988), that is the change in achievement from P1 to P2 and from P2 to P3; and identification of characteristics influencing the science achievement within 'élite' and 'mass' education systems. (At the time of the study senior educational policy-makers in various countries were particularly interested in such measures (IEA, 1988).)

Table 3 Listing used for classification of test items and for the analysis of the curricula taught

Earth science	P1*	P2*	P3*	Chemistry	P1	P2	P3
Solar system	3	3	1	Introductory chemistry	2	7	6
Stellar system	1	0	1	Electro-chemistry	0	0	5
Meteorology	3	4	1	Chemical laws	0	2	5
Constitution of Earth	0	0	0	Chemical processes	0	1	4
Physical geography	1	2	1	Periodic system	0	0	2
Soil science	0	0	0	Energy relationships in chemical systems	0	0	1
				Rate of reactions	0	0	3
Physics	**P1**	**P2**	**P3**	Chemical equilibrium	0	0	2
Measurement	2	3	3	Chemistry in industry	1	1	1
Time and movement	1	0	3	Chemical structure	0	2	3
Forces	4	4	3	Descriptive inorganic chemistry	1	1	2
Dynamics	1	0	4	Organic chemistry	0	1	2
Energy	0	0	3	Environmental chemistry	0	0	0
Machines	2	2	0	Chemistry of life processes	1	0	1
Mechanics of fluids	1	1	0	Nuclear chemistry	0	0	2
Introductory heat	2	3	2				
Change of state	1	2	1	**Biology**	**P1**	**P2**	**P3**
Kinetic theory	0	1	2	Cell structure and function	0	0	0
Light	1	1	1	Transport and cellular material	0	0	2
Vibration and sound	2	2	1	Cell metabolism	0	0	0
Wave phenomena	0	0	3	Cell responses	0	1	1
Spectra	0	0	1	Concept of the gene	0	0	6
Static electricity	1	0	1	Diversity of life	4	2	1
Current electricity	1	3	4	Metabolism of the organism	3	7	7
Electromagnets/alternating currents	2	1	2	Co-ordination and behaviour of the organism	0	1	3
Electronics	0	0	1	Regulation of the organism	0	1	4
Molecular/nuclear physics	0	0	3	Reproduction and development of plants	6	3	1
Theoretical physics	0	0	0	Reproduction and development of animals	5	2	4
				Human biology	4	3	2
				Natural environment	0	2	1
				Cycles in nature	0	1	1
				Natural groups and their segregation	0	0	0
				Population genetics	0	0	0
				Evolution	0	0	6

* Columns P1, P2 and P3 show the number of test items for each of these populations. Adapted from Table 2 in IEA, 1988, p. 19.

An international test of science had been constructed prior to the 1970–1 survey based on content areas judged by the IEA Science Committee to represent the common science curriculum across the world. With a few changes this was still considered suitable in 1980. Each topic was specified in terms appropriate to the populations, for example 'Physical geography' became 'Weathering by wind and water/Fossils' for P1; 'Surface features/Igneous sedimentary and metamorphic rocks/Folding and faulting/Fossils and fossilization' for P2; and 'Geomorphology, stratigraphy, oceanography and palaeontology' for P3. A grid was developed to guide the selection of test items and establish curriculum indices (see below), on which these topics were charted against three types of science achievement:

- simple information;
- the understanding of a principle;
- the application of information and understanding to solve a practical problem.

In the earlier study some items had been criticized as 'wordy', making them more a test of reading than science, and there had been concern that pencil and paper tests could not be valid measures of practical work in science. It was decided, therefore, to make greater use of diagrammatic material in framing questions and that all test items should relate to scientific content.

Table 3 shows the number of test items related to each topic. Any new items were tried out in at least five countries; 'old' items from the 1970–1 study were included; and, a substantial number of identical items were used in either the P1 and P2 tests or the P2 and P3 tests.

The resultant tests were regarded as equally 'fair' or 'unfair' with respect to the education systems of all the participating countries.

A 'core' test for each population was done by all samples. The 'core' tests for P1 and P2 contained twenty-four and thirty test items, respectively. In addition to the core test the achievement of each sample was also assessed on any two of a number of additional tests available for use in rotation.

The initial international comparisons (IEA, 1988) were made using the results on the core tests only. Comparisons using data from all three tests (core plus two of the rotated tests) were included in the more recent report (Postlethwaite and Wiley, 1992). The additional information reinforces the original comparisons (see Table 4).

These comparisons may have achieved the international aims of the study, including the identification of areas warranting explanation or further investigation by participating nations, but they were also prone to simplistic interpretation. The preliminary report (IEA, 1988) reported rank orders of countries by achievement according to core test scores. It claimed that the large samples used allowed accurate estimates to be made of the mean scores for each national system of education: valuable statistics for policy-makers and politicians. The fact that almost all countries clustered within one standard deviation of each other is unlikely to be pointed out or explained.

Table 4 Some comparative mean scores

	P1			P2		
	Core test (24 items) means score as %	Rank*	All test data mean score as %	Core test (30 items) mean score as %	Rank*	All test data mean score as %
England	49	14	54	56	12	56
USA	55	9	Not given	55	14	Not given
Japan	64 (highest)	1	66	67	2	69
Nigeria	32 (lowest)	18	35	41	17	42
Hungary	60	6	62	72 (highest)	1	71
Philippines	40	17	42	38 (lowest)	18	40
All countries	53			57		

* Rank is given for the same eighteen countries according to core test scores.

Based on information in Postlethwaite and Wiley, 1992, pp. 19 and 26–7, and IEA, 1988, pp. 26 and 32.

Other league tables can be constructed, for example to show the range of achievement within a country's schools or the number of schools in a country achieving lower scores than the lowest scoring school in the highest scoring nation. It appears from the data that in Japan and Sweden all schools achieve much the same results whereas in Hungary there are considerable between-school differences. In England 61 per cent of primary schools achieve scores lower than the lowest in Japan – a statistic difficult to ignore.

DATA FROM TEST ITEMS

The scores achieved on particular test items reflect the school curricula of the candidates. The patterns of scoring for students in different countries is of interest to curriculum developers as it may provide reasons for re-examination of syllabuses and educational objectives. The test item (example 1) was answered by P2 students and by the biology, physics and chemistry students in P3 (IEA, 1988). Table 5

Table 5 Scores for five countries on test item, example 1

	A		B		C*		D		E		No response		Increase from P2 to P3 (%)
	P2	P3	P2	P3	P2	P3	P2	P3	P2	P3	P2	P3	
England	12	10	41	10	26	76	9	2	8	1	4	1	50
Finland	11	12	44	22	26	55	9	5	8	3	2	3	29
Japan	21	12	22	9	51	73	3	3	2	2	1	1	22
Hungary	13	6	26	9	52	80	3	2	4	1	2	1	28
Korea	14	0	36	0	28	0	12	0	10	0	1	0	0

* C is correct answer.

Based on information given in IEA, 1988, pp. 116 and 119.)

shows the scores for P2 and P3 students for this particular test item. The pattern of results suggests that the curriculum for P2 students varies from country to country.

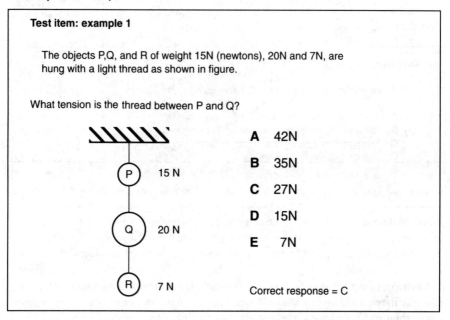

Test item: example 1

The objects P,Q, and R of weight 15N (newtons), 20N and 7N, are hung with a light thread as shown in figure.

What tension is the thread between P and Q?

P   15 N

Q   20 N

R   7 N

A   42N

B   35N

C   27N

D   15N

E   7N

Correct response = C

Source: IEA, 1988, p. 115.

Other test items show different anomalies. The data for test item (example 2) answered by P2 students show atypically low scores for Japan (20 per cent) and Korea (16 per cent). The country with the highest score on this item was Hungary (76 per cent) (Postlethwaite and Wiley, 1992, p. 52). It suggests the need for further investigation. Are different facts being taught? Did something get changed in the translation?

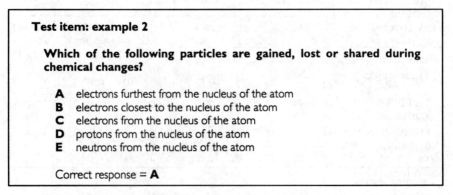

Test item: example 2

Which of the following particles are gained, lost or shared during chemical changes?

A   electrons furthest from the nucleus of the atom
B   electrons closest to the nucleus of the atom
C   electrons from the nucleus of the atom
D   protons from the nucleus of the atom
E   neutrons from the nucleus of the atom

Correct response = **A**

Source: Postlethwaite and Wiley, 1992, p. 52.

Influence on science achievement is not confined to the planned curriculum and this is reflected in the data for some test items. Surprise was expressed (IEA, 1988, p. 103) at the relatively low scores on the test item (example 3) for P1 students from Asian countries where it is hot and humid all the time. Could it be that their experience of raw milk was negligible?

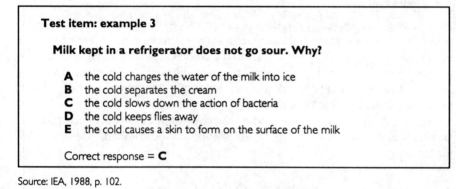

Test item: example 3

Milk kept in a refrigerator does not go sour. Why?

- **A** the cold changes the water of the milk into ice
- **B** the cold separates the cream
- **C** the cold slows down the action of bacteria
- **D** the cold keeps flies away
- **E** the cold causes a skin to form on the surface of the milk

Correct response = **C**

Source: IEA, 1988, p. 102.

CURRICULUM INDICES

A major concern in any study is comparing like with like, implying fair assessments. The test items used by the SISS were related to the 'common science curriculum across the world' and were not necessarily a 'fair' test of achievement with respect to the curriculum of any one country. Curriculum indices were needed to show the learning opportunities in each country. These were of three kinds: a curriculum coverage index, a test relevance index and a test coverage index.

The first is a measure of the match between the intended or planned curriculum in a particular country and the topics specified for each age group by the study; the second a measure of the degree to which students might encounter the content areas associated with test items; the third, and most important as far as test validity goes, the extent to which the test items covered the intended curriculum of a country.

Responsibility for obtaining curriculum indices rested with each country. They covered the content of the curriculum and what were termed the process objectives of science teaching. Eleven aspects of science teaching were given as a classification of teaching objectives (Rosier and Keeves, 1991, pp. 39 and 285).

These objectives are summarized as four general objectives:

- applications of science;
- manual skills;
- attitudes, interest and values;
- limitations of science and scientific methods;

and a hierarchy of seven process objectives:

- knowledge and understanding;

- observation;
- measurement;
- problem-solving;
- interpretation of data;
- formulation of generalizations;
- model building.

Establishing indices for the science content of the curriculum was easier in countries with a standardized curriculum even when the topics were organized in different ways, for example as part of life studies (Sweden) or environmental science (Finland). Considerable resistance was shown to the requirement to create indices for the process objectives, especially by countries who had not previously considered science teaching in this way.

The curriculum indices were used to calculate adjustments for each country and each sample to compensate for differences in the students' opportunities for learning.

LOCAL CONTEXTS

Data in the international analysis were treated as congruent and it is impossible to determine the range or magnitude of variation from one country to another. Variations in the implementation of the original sampling plan caused obvious incongruence in the data. Less obvious are variations caused by the superimposition of national objectives on the original plan. For example, the role of the study within a national curriculum development programme will have affected the allocation of resources to the study and the emphasis of the national report.

In some of the participating countries this study was just one of many contributing to knowledge of science education. Such studies range from individual teachers closely observing pupil performance and questioning the suitability of a particular curriculum for a particular learner, to the preparation of case studies which described national education systems and sought to identify indicators which limited or promoted achievement in science.

For example, at the time this study (SISS) was being planned (1980–1), extensive Department of Education and Science (DES)-initiated work was examining science education. The objectives were to monitor performance and raise standards. The work of the Assessment of Performance Unit (Science) (APU (S)), various in-service initiatives (aimed at improving classroom practice, especially in primary schools), and the Secondary Science Curriculum Review (which encouraged groups of teachers to develop science courses suitable for all students aged eleven to sixteen), contributed to an unprecedented scrutiny of the teaching of science.

England did not join the SISS until 1983 and the data collected were not primarily intended to provide a detailed description of students' science achievement; that was the job of the APU (S) (Eggleston, 1991). The national purpose of the SISS study in England was to provide baseline data against which the effects of curriculum development initiatives could be measured (Keys, 1987).

Late entry into the project gave little time for testing or modification of the international data-collecting instruments (tests and questionnaires) to suit the science education provided by English schools.

The impact of national objectives on the results submitted to the study is not made explicit in the international reports.

BASELINE DATA

The SISS study provided an enormous amount of data not just about student achievement in science and variations in the science curriculum from one country to another, but many other factors that might affect that achievement.

The questionnaires that were completed by students, teachers and school principals have provided valuable data against which future studies can be compared. These range from factual information, for example size of school, numbers of years teaching experience, sex of student, sex of teacher, number of siblings, etc.; through less rigorous measures, for example number of hours homework, socio-economic status of a student's home, adequacy of science equipment, etc.; to subjective judgements, for example views of and interest in science, enjoying school, classroom effort, etc.

The national and international reports used these data in attempts to identify predictor variables that determine the science achievement of students. For the analysis of the data for English students the predictor variables were grouped into the following five blocks (Keys, 1987, p. 126).

Block 1: Attitudes towards school and education

educational aspirations;
enjoyment of school.

Block 2: Teaching and learning

student-directed learning;
practical work;
calculator for own use;
science homework;
opportunity to learn;
use of calculators in class;
science in initial training;
time teaching science;
age of teacher.

Block 3: The home

home background;
computer at home;
family size.

Block 4: The school

relative size of science department;
science class size;
school type;
PTA social activities;
location;
region;
size of year group (P1);
computer at school.

Block 5: The student

numerical ability;
verbal ability;
sex of student;
age of student.

Analysis was also made of students' responses to individual items from the 'Description of science learning inventory' and the 'Attitude inventory'. These analyses describe aspects of science education at the time that the data were collected (1983), see Tables 6 and 7 (Keys, 1987).

Data collected for the Second International Science Study are presented in Postlethwaite and Wiley (1992) in ways which allow comparisons between countries. These comparisons are inconclusive.

Making comparisons between nations on the basis of the data collected is fraught with problems especially when many circumstances have changed since the data were collected nearly ten years ago. Consider just one major

Table 6   The responses of P2 students in England to items concerned with student-directed learning

	Often (%)	Some-times (%)	Never (%)
We use books other than textbooks for learning science	15	47	37
We are allowed to make our own choice of science topics to study	5	13	82
We do fieldwork outside the classroom as part of our science lessons	2	28	70
In our practical work we make up our own problems and then the teacher helps us to plan experiments to solve them	7	25	69
When we do experiments the teacher gives us problems to solve and then leaves us to work out our own methods and solutions	18	54	28
In our practical work we make up our own problems and work out our own methods to investigate problems	5	26	68

Source: Keys, 1987, Table 7.2, p. 112.

Table 7 The responses of P1 students in England to items concerned with teaching methods

	Often (%)	Some-times (%)	Never (%)
We use a textbook for our science lessons	29	33	28
We watch the teacher do experiments during our science lessons	31	45	24
During the science lessons we copy the teacher's notes from the blackboard into our own books	38	47	15
We have tests on what we have learned in science	16	48	36

Source: Keys, 1987, Table 7.5, p. 114.

change in England and Wales. The project reported that there was no national control on curriculum content. Since the introduction of the National Curriculum this has changed from 0 per cent to 100 per cent.

The SISS has provided data that cause the effectiveness of science teaching to be questioned from many different perspectives. They provide the basis for hypotheses to be set for future study. They do not provide a recipe for providing the ideal. Tables of comparison are powerful tools. Once set in print it is easy to accept the information without question and without consideration of the confidence that should be placed in any rank or percentage point.

(I have used the term 'national' in this article to describe the samples. In some cases this is inaccurate as samples were drawn from educational systems. Canada, for example, provided two sets of data – French and English.)

REFERENCES

Comber, J. C. and Keeves, J. P. (1973) *Science Education in Nineteen Countries*, Stockholm, The International Association for the Evaluation of Educational Achievement/Almqvist & Wiksell.

Eggleston, J. (1991) *The 1980–82 APU Science Survey – An Independent Appraisal of the Findings*, London, School Examinations and Assessment Council (SEAC).

IEA (International Association for the Evaluation of Educational Achievement) (1988) *Science Achievement in Seventeen Countries*, Oxford, The International Association for the Evaluation of Educational Achievement/Pergamon.

Jacobson, W. J. and Doran, R. L. (1988) *Science Achievement in the United States and Sixteen Countries: A Report to the Public*, New York, International Association for the Evaluation of Educational Achievement.

Keeves, J. P. (1991) *Changes in Science Education and Achievement, 1970–1984*, Oxford, The International Association for the Evaluation of Educational Achievement/Pergamon.

Keys, W. (1987) *Aspects of Science Education in English Schools*, Windsor/England, Nuffield Foundation for Educational Research (NFER)/Nelson.

Postlethwaite, T. N. and Wiley, D. E. (1992) *The IEA Study of Science II: Science Achievement in Twenty-Three Countries*, Oxford, The International Association for the Evaluation of Educational Achievement/Pergamon.

Rosier, M. J. and Keeves, J. P. (1991) *The IEA Study of Science I: Science Education and Curricula in Twenty-Three Countries*, Oxford, The International Association for the Evaluation of Educational Achievement/ Pergamon.

1.5

Laboratory practice in further and higher education: developments in the design of practical work

Mark Atlay and Dee Edwards

INTRODUCTION

One of the characteristic features of science courses is their laboratory-based component. This is particularly true in higher education where laboratory work is given a high priority, sometimes accounting for over half of the formal teaching time. In traditional courses, whether in schools, further or higher education, practical work involved students assembling apparatus, following procedures and writing reports according to set 'recipes'. The aim was to elucidate basic principles and to instil in the student, through repetition, a strict scientific practice. Thankfully these days have now long gone; today the emphasis is on the development of a much wider range of skills and the dividing line between what constitutes classroom studies and laboratory work is blurred.

In this article we look at some of the key factors underpinning practical work and at some of the developments that it has undergone during the last decade. We will examine, in particular, developments at the further/higher education interface but many of the issues raised are applicable to science teaching at any level both in the laboratory and in the classroom.

The broad aims of laboratory courses have been identified by Klopfer (1971):

- knowledge and comprehension;
- processes of scientific inquiry;
- observing and measuring;
- seeing a problem and seeking ways to solve it;
- interpreting data and formulating generalizations;
- building, testing and revising a theoretical model;
- application of scientific knowledge and methods;

This article is based around *Teaching in Laboratories* by Boud, D., Dunn, J. and Hegarty-Hazel, E. (1986) SRHE and NFER-Nelson, London, pp. 13–18, 19–22, 32–33 (extract 1); and *Science: Core and Option Unit Specifications and Sample Learning Activities*, BTEC Publications, London, pp. 15–19 (extract 2).

- manual skills;
- attitudes and interests;
- orientation;
- literature skills.

To this list Boud (1985) has added communication skills.

Unlike practice in schools, where practical work, activities and more formal teaching now form part of an integrated programme, the relationship between laboratory and lecture theatre is less easy to define. Not only are they physically different rooms but they often involve different lecturers (supervision is often undertaken partly by graduate students) and in a modular system units may be entirely laboratory based with no associated lecture component. With current pressures on scarce laboratory space and time, students may find themselves carrying out practical work alongside those studying other units.

The first part of this article consists of an extract from a chapter by Boud which examines some of the factors to be considered when designing practical courses and presents some of the research which has been carried out in this area. Boud advocates a behavioural approach to course design; for a fuller description of the setting of objectives and assessment see Boud, Dunn and Hegarty-Hazel (1986) from which this extract was taken.

The behavioural approach was one adopted by the Business and Technician Education Council, later renamed the Business and Technology Education Council (BTEC), in their design of both practical and classroom syllabuses in the early 1980s. They subsequently modified their approach to adopt a less prescriptive system. The second half of this article is based on extracts of materials produced by BTEC, and compares two similar laboratory-based units of a modular scheme written before and after the change from the setting of behavioural objectives and discusses some recent developments in this area.

EXTRACT 1 (BOUD ET AL., 1986): AIMS, OBJECTIVES AND COURSE PLANNING

There is much discussion today about the need to specify goals, aims and objectives for courses of all kinds in higher education, but more emphasis has been placed on it with respect to laboratory teaching than to any other area.

Rather than become involved in the details of the debate, we intend to examine some of the reasons why it is particularly important to think about general goals, aims and objectives in the context of laboratory work, to explore ways of generating and formulating them and to discuss the uses to which they can be put in planning laboratory courses. [. . .] We shall be focusing on [. . .] two components: values and general goals, and aims and objectives. We shall examine the implications these have for how courses should be planned and how they should be structured. One matter which complicates our task is that the literature on laboratory teaching rarely distinguishes clearly between general goals, aims and objectives. These terms can be regarded as falling along a spectrum from the general to the specific. Most authors would agree, however, on the need to consider each in turn when planning a course and they would stress the importance of ensuring that course aims are consistent with general goals and that more specific objectives are consistent with course aims.

Before exploring these issues, and before focusing on the aims of laboratory courses, we must clarify what we mean by the term 'lab work' and where it fits into the overall scheme of a science course. Is it a synonym for teaching experimental science? Or is it simply what commonly occurs in the slot marked 'laboratory' in students' timetables? The distinction is not a trivial one, as it is becoming increasingly common to find activities labelled laboratory which appear to be peripheral to experimental science as such. As the laboratory component of courses appears to be the most flexible, and often the most ill-defined, it is not surprising to find that it is the home for computing, demonstrating phenomena, and various hands-on experiences and tutorial activities which pursue goals other than those of the experimentalist.

General goals and aims

Any discussion of aims and objectives needs to be conducted in the overall context of the general goals to be pursued in a degree programme. There are two broad approaches to this which have been adopted in science courses in recent years. The first is what might be termed the traditional approach of the pure sciences and is based upon a view of the structure of the discipline. Its starting point is in questions such as 'What is required for an appreciation of this aspect of inorganic chemistry?' or 'What does a student need to know to understand experimentation?' These require an analysis of the demands of the subject and regard it as the central organizing feature around which the course is built.

In the discipline-centred approach, laboratory topics and problems are chosen for the light which they shed on important techniques, methods or concepts. The resulting teaching may bear little or no resemblance to the current activities of practitioners in the field, but should relate to key ideas in the discipline of either a practical or theoretical nature. A clue to whether this approach is being adopted is in such remarks as 'We couldn't allow someone to graduate with a *physics* degree if they hadn't covered . . . in the lab' or 'I know they haven't used this technique in industry for years, but it is such a good illustration of the concept of . . .'. This approach is particularly important in training future academic scientists who will have responsibility for advancing their subjects.

A second approach is based upon needs and takes a view of what is required of the student either for future employment or in subsequent courses. Its starting point is in questions such as 'What skills does a graduate physicist need?' or 'What are the requirements of a chemist working in an analytical laboratory?' Some of these needs will be related to the discipline but others may well relate to professional practice or to more general needs of graduates, such as in the area of communication skills.

The needs-based approach has been discussed extensively in recent years in the science-based professional subjects such as medicine (Barrows and Tamblyn, 1980; Neame, 1981) and agriculture (Bawden et al., 1984), using the term problem-based learning (Boud, 1985). Entire degree programmes have been established which are formed around events in professional practice rather than by the traditional method of building up from a foundation of the basic sciences. Laboratory activities focus directly on the problems with which practitioners are commonly involved. They do not necessarily link the scientific principles on which they are based to the framework of the subject.

Although motives may differ in these two approaches, and there may be different starting points, the construction of a laboratory course planned within a framework may follow similar lines and use very similar techniques to that developed in the other. No matter what approach is adopted it is necessary to consider the goals of laboratory teaching and to examine how these particular goals can be incorporated into a programme.

Hofstein and Lunetta (1982) pointed out that many goals for the laboratory are almost synonymous with those defined for science courses in general. They identified a need to define goals where laboratory work could make a special and significant contribution and to capitalize on the uniqueness of this form of teaching. Anderson (1976) focused particularly on laboratory teaching in his book *The Experience of Science* and he proposed four purposes for it:

(1) The laboratory is a place where a person or group of persons engage in a human enterprise of examining and explaining natural phenomena.
(2) The laboratory provides an opportunity to learn generalized systematic ways of thinking that should transfer to other problem situations.
(3) The laboratory experience should allow each student to appreciate and in part emulate the role of the scientist in inquiry.
(4) The result of laboratory instruction should be a more comprehensive view of science including not only the orderliness of its interpretations of nature, but also the tentative nature of its theories and models.

Scientific inquiry

One of the most important general goals in laboratory teaching concerns scientific inquiry. If one takes the view that laboratories are important places where knowledge is generated and validated in the experimental sciences, and if students are to gain an appreciation of these processes and to develop the abilities required to contribute to them, then scientific inquiry could be regarded as the *raison d'être* of laboratory-based learning. Although laboratory teaching may have other purposes, such as the inculcation of specific skills or the appreciation of particular aspects of a subject, the characteristic feature of laboratory work is active inquiry. It includes such things as observing and measuring, seeing problems and seeking ways to solve them, interpreting data and making generalizations, and building explanatory models to make sense of findings. Some of these activities could take place in other settings, but it is in the laboratory that they are all put together. In many instances it is difficult to see how goals concerned with the processes of scientific inquiry could be satisfactorily developed in any other context, a difficulty that is apparent if we refer to examples from Klopfer's (1971) categorization. One of his subsets of aims is 'Processes of scientific inquiry: 1 Observing and measuring':

- observation of objects and phenomena;
- description of observations using the appropriate language;
- measurements of objects and changes;
- selection of appropriate measuring instruments;
- estimation of measurements and recognition of limits in accuracy.

Although it is possible to pursue some of these aims in places other than laboratories, great care would need to be taken to ensure that the experience for students did not become an artificial one, possibly misleading them about the practice of scientific inquiry. Seeing and solving problems is a good example in this area. If in the laboratory students are only exposed to problems whose solution involves a straightforward application of given knowledge, they can easily fail to appreciate that one of the most important, and challenging, aspects of problem-solving in real scientific situations is being able to identify a problem and translate it into a form which is amenable to the application of particular known techniques.

Lucas (1971) provided a useful summary of the use of the term 'inquiry' as discussed in the science education literature. In his view it can be used to refer to:

(a) what scientists do in obtaining answers from nature (their techniques and procedures);
(b) the logical processes used in science;
(c) the teaching technique that
    (i) enables the (student) to solve problems by asking questions to gather information, or
    (ii) uses a semi-structured discussion intended to develop skill in probing or searching;
(d) a combination of the meanings: using the technique (c above) to teach about inquiry (a above).

We consider that 'science as inquiry' should be given first priority. It would be a nonsense for any course to portray science as a fixed body of knowledge; but it is not necessary for 'learning as inquiry' to be used to present this notion. However, unless at some stage students learn about the processes of scientific inquiry through being engaged in it, it is unlikely that they will be in a position to reach a full appreciation of the practice of science and be able to contribute to this enterprise themselves. Simple involvement in 'learning as inquiry' activities is not sufficient in itself for students to come to an appreciation of scientific inquiry. They may need also to be involved in an explicit examination of the processes through which scientists create knowledge.

From aims to objectives

Black and Ogborn (1979) proposed three clusters of aims which are implicit in much writing about laboratory work:

- training in techniques;
- learning the ideas of the subject;
- learning how to carry out experimental inquiries.

According to these authors, techniques include: manipulation, such as the use of particular equipment or experimental techniques; observation, such as counting and adequate recognition of biological materials; and mental techniques, for example the analysis of errors or aspects of report writing. Learning ideas requires an exposure to phenomena and the complexity of real situations. Learning the process of experimental inquiry may involve project work in which students are responsible for the conduct of inquiry in an apprenticeship fashion. Clearly these clusters of aims are different in kind as well as content. The pursuit of objectives in the first two could well take place quite independently of the third, although some elements of the first two are required for the third. Laboratory work can be designed to encompass any or all of these clusters depending on the overall intentions of the programme of which it forms a part.

Many authors have proposed sets of aims for laboratory work which focus on the purposes of laboratory activities and which expand the rather brief categorizations listed earlier. For example, in the context of developing methods for the evaluation of laboratory courses Boud (1973) derived the list in Table 1 from the literature at that time on laboratory teaching [. . .] and from interviews with university physics teachers. Similar lists have also been used by Lynch and Gerrans (1977) and Gabb and Mander (1984).

Lists of this type are based on what teachers claim laboratory courses are concerned with and are useful for checking in general terms the extent to which particular courses are pursuing desired aims and objectives, but they have severe limitations. Despite having used them in our earlier work we find them in retrospect rather naive and not focused on any clear concept of the role of laboratory work. The aims in the list in Table 1 are relatively content-free; that is, they do not refer to the subject matter which will be associated with each aim. They mix what teachers will do with what is expected of students: they are not explicitly related to student outcomes. For example, No. 20 would be less ambiguous if it were stated as 'to give practice in communicating technical concepts' and indicated the type of performance expected of a student. Some of the items have very little to do with laboratory work or are of such a general nature as to make them of very little use. For example, No.

Table I List of aims for undergraduate laboratory courses in science (from Boud, 1973, as expressed in Boud et al., 1980)

(1) To instil confidence in the subject
(2) To teach basic practical skills
(3) To familiarize students with important standard apparatus and measurement techniques
(4) To illustrate material taught in lectures
(5) To teach the principles and attitudes of doing experimental work in the subject
(6) To train students in observation
(7) To train students in making deductions from measurements and interpretation of experimental data
(8) To use experimental data to solve specific problems
(9) To train students in writing reports on experiments
(10) To train students in keeping a day-to-day laboratory diary
(11) To train students in simple aspects of experimental design
(12) To provide closer contacts between staff and students
(13) To stimulate and maintain interest in the subject
(14) To teach some 'theoretical' material not included in the lectures
(15) To foster 'critical awareness' (for example extraction of all information from data, avoiding systematic errors)
(16) To develop skill in problem-solving in the multi-solution situation
(17) To simulate the conditions in research and development laboratories
(18) To provide a stimulant to independent thinking
(19) To show the use of 'practicals' as a process of discovery
(20) To familiarize students with the need to communicate technical concepts and solutions
(21) To provide motivation to acquire specific knowledge
(22) To help bridge the gap between theory and practice

12, 'to provide closer contacts between students and staff, says nothing about why closer contacts should be sought, what the nature of such contacts should be nor how one would recognize close contacts. Lists of this kind would be more useful if attention were given to clarifying the items, splitting those aims which include more than one idea and removing the ambiguities in interpretation. Hellingman (1982) and his colleagues created such a list of aims and objectives for assessment purposes.

Lists of aims would not in themselves provide a sufficient basis for the planning of a laboratory programme. In any course it is essential that aims are linked to the subject matter through which they will be pursued, which should be done in such a way that the purposes of laboratory activities are not lost in the detail of scientific procedure and subject content. Many authors suggest that the pursuit of many aims is subject-specific (cf. Gardner, 1975), so that a student trained in making observations of physical phenomena would not necessarily be able to perform at the same level, or indeed at any level at all, when confronted with the need to make biological observations. [. . .]

Expressing aims and objectives

There are many ways in which aims and objectives can be formulated. What all formulations have in common is that they assist laboratory teachers to think clearly about their intentions. The simplest form of expression is in terms of what the teacher or demonstrator will do: for example 'train students in making deductions from measurements'. This is a statement of the intention of the teacher, which may or may not be embodied in the teaching materials provided. It does not say what *students* are expected to be able to do: will students know *about* making deductions, or will they simply be expected to make deductions from given measurements? Not only is the statement formulated in terms of what the teacher will do, but it is also vague: it does not make the intentions explicit.

A more useful way of formulating aims and objectives is in terms of what it is that students should be able to do following the learning experience. What is ultimately important is what students learn, not what teachers teach, and it is helpful if this attitude is adopted throughout discussions of teaching activities. Not all that students learn can be demonstrated, but it is desirable for teachers to be able to obtain evidence from student behaviour that learning has taken place. Therefore, objectives need to be formulated which are student-oriented, specific and precise. However, it should be emphasized that the overall goals and aims of the enterprise occupy the place of importance and guide the formulation of specific objectives.

Mager (1975) has identified three characteristics of a good objective of this kind: it should include a description of the behaviour a student is expected to demonstrate, the conditions under which the student should be able to demonstrate it, and the standards to be attained. Two examples of such behavioural objectives are:

- The student will be able to set up a given cathode ray oscilloscope so that a sinusoidal signal of a given magnitude is displayed centrally on the screen.
- At the end of this experiment the student will be able to:
  (a) read the volume of liquid in a burette to two decimal places;
  (b) deliver a quantity of the given liquid precisely from the burette;
  (c) read the final volume of liquid in the burette to two decimal places, and hence by subtraction determine the accurate volume delivered.

It is not always necessary or even desirable to specify all objectives in minute detail. While being a good discipline for clarifying the designer's intentions, such a process can nevertheless lead to a fragmentation of purposes if great care is not taken. Macdonald-Ross (1973) has discussed the limitations of behavioural objectives, and his summary of advantages of and objections to them is given in Table 2. Some benefits accrue from the specification of objectives because they are stated in terms of behaviour, others because they are specific, others because they are precise, still others because they are student-oriented. Most of the advantages listed in Table 2 follow because the objectives are specific or student-oriented not because they are behavioural.

It is quite easy to write behavioural objectives for fairly simple educational aims, such as being able to solder wires to a given level of competence or being able to make certain measurements. It is much more difficult, and in some

Table 2 Advantages of, and objections to behavioural objectives (from Macdonald-Ross, 1973)

The advantages claimed for behavioural objectives
They form the basis of the only well worked-out method of rational planning in education
They encourage educators to think and plan in detailed, specific terms
They encourage educators to make explicit previously concealed values
They provide a rational basis for evaluation
They prescribe the choice of instructional means
They form the basis of a self-improving system
The system eventually achieves internal consistency
And the system eventually realizes in practice the aims set in theory
Objectives serve as a medium of communication
Objectives can be made the basis for individualized instruction

The objections to behavioural objectives
No consistent view exists as to the origin of objectives
In the educational domain no well-defined prescriptions are available for deriving objectives
Defining objectives before the event conflicts with voyages of exploration
Advocates do not show how teachers can use objectives to guide unpredicted classroom events
There are an extremely large number of paths through any body of knowledge, thus reducing the effectiveness of objectives in design
In some disciplines criteria can only be applied after the event
Objectives do *not* prescribe the validity of test items
Objectives are inherently ambiguous
The level of specificity problem has never been solved
Objectives do not communicate intent unambiguously, especially to students
Trivial objectives *are* the easiest to operationalize, and this *is* a problem
The relevance of goal-referenced models of education can be questioned
Weak prescriptions lead to cycling; this can be costly
Lists of behaviours do not adequately reflect the structure of knowledge

cases impossible or undesirable, to do so for less tangible outcomes, particularly those of an attitudinal nature.

One of the practical limitations on the use of objectives in the design of laboratory work is that not all important objectives can be identified sufficiently clearly in advance to enable them to be drawn up at the outset. Aims and objectives can often be inferred from actual laboratory activities and from student assessment requirements, and it is usually easier to start to refine them then than at the initial stage of planning. The fact that some teachers in higher education resist the specification of aims and objectives might be related to this point. Some books on the topic might be taken to imply that it is simply a matter of sitting down and working out what you want to do before entering the teaching laboratory, which is unrealistic. It is a non-trivial matter to determine exactly what it is that students are expected to do in laboratories and whatever can be done to simplify the task should be done. Inevitably, no matter what attempts are made to clarify aims and objectives, it will not be until after students have engaged in the laboratory work that it will be

apparent how much can realistically be achieved. It is therefore necessary to
ensure that there are always opportunities to revise objectives. [. . .]

Using aims and objectives to guide student learning

One of the common complaints of students on science courses is that laboratory work is not connected to what happens in the rest of the course. The
criticism is often countered by staff who argue that it is not possible to organize laboratory work to synchronize with lectures when there are limitations
imposed by insufficient equipment or problems in timetabling. It is also ob-
jected that the laboratory course is not primarily designed to illustrate lectures.
The fact that this story is a familiar one in many science subjects suggests that
there is a problem underlying such symptoms: a problem probably arising
from a lack of clarity about the purposes of teaching laboratories, or, more
particularly, from a failure to communicate their purposes to students.

Once the aims and objectives have been decided there are many effective
ways of providing activities which address them. For example, if the illustration of lecture content is the aim, as is common in some first-year courses, then
demonstration experiments may be used that are either timetabled as part of
other laboratories' activities or available on a self-service basis (for example,
see Cryer and Rider, 1977; Price and Brandt, 1974). Such demonstration
experiments can be constructed so that the appropriate experiment is always
available at the right time. If the aim is to teach experimental skills, then there
may be no need for there to be any direct relationship between lectures and
laboratory. In this case the laboratory class would need to be completely self-
contained and provide opportunities for students to practise and develop their
skills in experimental work. The use of formal input sessions and tutorials may
need to be considered to supplement laboratory activities. Once students know
why they are engaging in a particular activity they can fit it into the framework
they are developing for the subject and feel more confident that what they are
doing is of wider importance than the isolated collection and analysis of
results.

There is conflicting evidence on the ways in which the detailed specification
of objectives can assist students to learn more effectively. Davies (1976), in his
extensive review of objectives in curriculum design, drew two conclusions
from the literature: supplying objectives facilitates learning in some situations
but not in others; and making objectives available benefits some students more
than others. Although he did not discuss laboratory teaching specifically, his
findings imply that it is more profitable to present students with objectives in
those situations where they are without explicit instructions in laboratory
manuals.

Obviously, unless there is a certain minimum level of specification of aims
and objectives students will not be aware of what it is they should do and
whether they have reached the desired end point. Many studies have indicated
that there is often a substantial difference in the ways in which staff and

students perceive the aims of laboratory courses (for example, Chambers, 1966; Boud, 1973; Lynch and Gerrans, 1977), and that this can lead to problems of communication. For example, if students believe that the main purpose of an activity is to make precise observations while staff believe that it is to analyse and account for the observations, then students could miss the point of the exercise and devote their energies to the wrong end.

When students have to select laboratory experiments for themselves, aims and objectives can be used to ensure that all the important goals of the course have been pursued while placing a minimum of restriction on student choice. [. . .]

Providing students with lists of objectives is in itself not a very satisfactory way of communicating intentions: it would be rare for students to have a sufficient appreciation of any given objective until they had started to engage in an exercise related to it, or for such lists easily to be fitted into their existing knowledge structure. Rothkopf (1976) suggests that objectives are more useful to students if they can be closely allied to teaching materials. Students can then see the objectives in the context of the tasks which they are expected to complete rather than as abstract lists. [. . .]

Afterword

Implicit in this chapter has been the assumption that the specification of aims and objectives is desirable. This may be challenged by some readers who feel that such an approach is reductionist, that important goals can be trivialized by being described in minute detail and that many important goals cannot be specified anyway. These criticisms may have some substance in certain areas, especially where research-type investigations are concerned: if we always knew what we would find in laboratory experiments then there would be little point in continuing to conduct them. However, this is to confuse educational ends with scientific ones. In any planned educational experience the teacher needs to know something of what it is that the student will achieve by it, otherwise the teacher cannot be said to be engaged in a teaching act. Even at the final-year level, when students are given a task to complete for which the specific outcome is not known, then there must still be some clear educational reasons for asking them to conduct the investigation in the first place. Without them, there is every reason to believe that the students might more profitably spend time on some other matter more closely related to the purposes of the course. Objectives do not always need to be described in completely operational terms. Much can be gained solely by providing rather more information on educational intentions than is commonly the case at present.

FROM BEHAVIOURAL TO NON-BEHAVIOURAL COURSE DESIGN

The Business and Technology Education Council (BTEC) is responsible for courses which span the curriculum between A-levels and degree-level work. Whilst, increasingly, BTEC National awards are finding their way into the school curriculum, BTEC Higher National awards have been the province of the further/higher education sector. These awards attempt to span the divide between academic and vocational areas by providing a college-based education with a large industrial/workplace component. Two types of award are possible: Certificates, where the student is working full time and receives day-release to study in college; or Diplomas, where the student is a full-time student but has to complete a significant work-placement or work-experience component in order to receive the award.

BTEC schemes are modular in nature. In 1984 each unit was framed in behavioural terms, such as defines, describes or compares, and lists, etc., were widely used. An examination of one laboratory-based unit, Laboratory Techniques III, illustrates the behavioural approach more clearly. This unit would be taken in the first year of a Higher National award. The aims of this unit were:

(1) to further familiarize students with, and develop their confidence in, the assembly and use of scientific apparatus;
(2) to make the students conversant with a reasonable variety of techniques;
(3) to enable students to work safely in the laboratory;
(4) to develop students' ability to draw honest and meaningful conclusions from results;
(5) to develop students' awareness of the limitations inherent in a measurement and of possible sources of error;
(6) to develop good techniques in the students' work.

There are nineteen different subject areas (A to T) which could go to form this unit depending on the individual emphasis an institution required. For example, a college wishing to use this unit as part of a biology course would select from those areas which contain a biological component. The weighting of each subject area was not equal and was defined by its expected contribution to the total assessment of the unit. Thus a biological-based unit might be made up from a selection of subject areas as shown in Table 3.

Table 3 Possible composition of a biological-based unit

Unit/subject area	Title	Topic area as % of assessment
N	Microscopy	25
Q	Animal physiology	30
R	Haematology	15
T	Plant physiology	30

In each case the assessment is further broken down into contributions from motor skills and intellectual skills (information, comprehension and application).

Examples from three different topic areas of this unit are given below; in each case only part of the complete topic area is given. All objectives should be prefixed by the words 'The expected learning outcome is that the student . . .'

From the topic area of Electrical Measurement:

1 Understands and uses commercial bridge and potentiometer circuits.
   1.1 Determines an unknown capacitance using an ac bridge and a standard capacitor.
   1.2 Determines the conductance of a solution using a suitable ac bridge.
   1.3 Describes the construction of a commercial potentiometer.
   1.4 Identifies simple faults in a commercial potentiometer system.
   1.5 Describes the special measurement requirements of a pH meter and indicates how these may be met in practice.
   1.6 Describes the construction of a potentiometric chart recorder.
   1.7 Identifies simple faults in a potentiometric chart recorder.

From the topic area of Further Chromatography:

12 Knows the basic principles of liquid column chromatography and uses the technique for the separation of mixtures.
   12.1 Explains the meanings of the terms stationary phase, mobile phase, solid support, eluent, eluate and elution.
   12.2 Describes how to pack a column for column chromatography.
   12.3 Draws a diagram to show a typical experimental arrangement for column chromatography.
   12.4 Sets up, packs and uses a chromatographic column (either adsorption or partition) for separating a given mixture and collects the separated components.

From the topic area of Biochemistry:

32 Describes the principles, techniques, applications and limitations of separation techniques commonly used in biochemistry.
   32.1 Compares the cell disintegration techniques of:
      (a) grinding tissue with a pestle and mortar
      (b) the Potter–Elvheim homogenizer
      (c) ultrasonication
   32.2 States the principles and applications of both preparative and analytical centrifugation.
   32.3 Describes the principles of, and performs a fractional precipitation of proteins from a suitable preparation.
   32.4 Describes the applications of chromatographic and electrophoretic processes to the separation of proteins.
   32.5 Performs a separation of proteins by a chromatographic and electrophoretic technique.

By 1988 BTEC philosophy on course design had changed markedly. The behavioural nature of the syllabus had disappeared to be replaced by one which was more process oriented. The replacement Laboratory Techniques III unit is known as Laboratory Techniques N and is reproduced below. In the new scheme the unit has a distinctly chemical bias, the other subject areas having moved to other units.

EXTRACT 2 (SCIENCE: CORE AND OPTION UNIT SPECIFICATIONS
AND SAMPLE LEARNING ACTIVITIES):
BTEC-DEVISED UNIT

Unit title	Laboratory Techniques
Value	1.0
Learning support time	Typically 60 hours in respect of part-time courses (where it is complemented by experiential learning) with up to 90 hours being more usual in full-time courses.
Level	N

Rationale	a	This unit is presented as a set of process objectives. The unit does not specify any content and only seeks to describe the skills that students should acquire, no matter what technique is used as the vehicle for learning. The course team should decide what specific techniques they will use for the content of the unit.
	b	This unit is designed for students joining National Award courses from a variety of backgrounds, for example, BTEC First Qualification, a diversity of 'O' level/GCSE courses and with a variety of future interests.
	c	The course team should consider: the nature of the employment of day-release students; the career ambitions of full-time students; the industry that the programme has been designed to serve; and the previous experience of the students.
	d	Centres may change, after consultation with the moderator, the specific content of the unit from year to year.
	e	Two forms of guidance are offered: • how a specific technique can be treated within this format: sample learning activities for core studies. • a list of techniques that could constitute a full unit.

Summary of aims		The Aims are:
	a	to encourage awareness of scientific practice in a number of areas;
	b	to develop industrially relevant competence in a number of specific laboratory techniques;
	c	to foster a responsible attitude to work in the laboratory;

	d	to develop effective communication within a laboratory;
	e	to acquaint students with the need to balance accuracy, speed and cost in laboratory work.
Teaching and learning strategies	1	Teaching methods should take into account: • the students' achievements in scientific studies • the laboratory facilities available to students at work • likely future employment opportunities.
	2	Learning will take place through the student's own activities, by carrying out experiments, observing and reporting, using reference material. The scientific process of enquiry and investigation should occur in all of these activities.
	3	Students should have the opportunity to discuss information they have obtained from the library and other sources.
Assessment	1	The provisions of the General Guideline *Assessment and Grading* apply.
	2	Assignment activities will provide the only vehicle for assessment of this unit.
	3	Grading criteria should give emphasis to skills development, speed, accuracy, communication of findings and safe working practise.
Special notes	1	We wish to emphasise that the content list is for guidance only.
	2	When preparing a submission for validation, centres should include a list of the specific content they propose to cover initially.
Content	1	The Principal Objectives and indicative content cannot be satisfactorily interpreted in isolation from the above statements on *Aims, teaching and learning strategies* and *assessment* and should be read in conjunction with them.
	2	The indicative content helps to interpret each Principal Objective or provide for possible developments. It is entirely possible for centres to design assignments which do not correspond precisely with the Principal Objectives; assignments should, however, emphasise activity-based learning and be in accordance with the Aims of the unit.

**Principal
Objectives**

1 Analyse a given problem
   - What has to be done
   - How accurately it has to be done
   - What safety factors need consideration
   - How quickly it needs to be done
   - What cost can be allowed for the job
   - What manpower is required and available
   - Who needs the results and what for
   - How the results are to be presented

2 Select an appropriate technique
   - List alternative methods with costs, speed, accuracy etc
   - Select most appropriate method for the job in hand
   - Justify the final choice of technique to a superior with reference to cost, time and accuracy

3 Prepare to undertake the task
   - Prepare a suitable environment
   - Ensure apparatus is clean to an appropriate level
   - Undertake preliminary calibrations
   - Check calibration against a known standard
   - Prepare means of recording results, particularly any computer systems

4 Carry out the procedure to the required degree of accuracy in the appropriate time scale
   - Work to the specified degree of accuracy
   - Work with proper attention to safety
   - Work with due regard to eliminating pollution
   - Work to a commercially accepted time scale
   - Check for internal consistency of results
   - Determine where repeat work is needed, and carry this out
   - Record results as they are derived

5 Present the results in the form most valuable to the user
   - Work through any necessary calculations
   - Draw up results in the form required by the end user
   - Record the circumstances under which the results were derived, the time taken and the accuracy

6 Clear away
   - Clean, reset or otherwise prepare for storage, any apparatus used
   - Safely dispose of unwanted by-products or reagents used and reclaim any expensive material

- Complete laboratory notebook including the difficulties encountered and how these were overcome
- Note and report any equipment defects
- Initiate the reordering of stock depleted below an agreed level
- Suggest for the future reductions in the time or cost of the operation and/or an increase in accuracy

Indicative Content	The indicative content may be achieved by a selection from the following items. The percentages given to each activity refer to the proportion of a 60-hour unit that might be devoted to it. Alternative laboratory investigations may be substituted. Centres should clearly state the chosen content at the time of application for approval
(20%)	• Quantitative determination of substances by titrimetry
(15%)	• Quantitative determination of substances by absorptiometry (colorimetry)
(25%)	• Preparation and investigation of pure samples of inorganic and organic substances, making use of isolation and purification techniques
(15%)	• Quantitative separation of mixtures using ion exchange
(20%)	• Investigation of enzyme kinetics by physical methods
(20%)	• Quantitative separation of mixtures by electrophoresis
(15%)	• Quantitative determination of substances, using ultraviolet/visible spectrophotometry
(15%)	• Estimation of elements using atomic absorption or flame photometry
(15%)	• Qualitative and quantitive separation of mixtures using gas chromatography
(20%)	• Investigation of high vacuum systems and their operation and uses
(15%)	• Investigation of unknown substances, using infrared spectrometry
(10%)	• Qualitative and quantitative separation of mixtures, using hplc
(20%)	• Investigation of crystal lattices by X-ray powder photography

EXAMINING THE CHANGE

The change away from behavioural objectives described above was not the only change in approach. One of the other key areas to undergo fundamental change, and which affected laboratory work, was the development of so-called 'common skills'. In the 1984 syllabus, units of 'General and Communication Studies' were designed to develop student skills. These were isolated units, remote from the main subject content of the course and often taught by non-scientists. In the new scheme 'common skills' units do exist but the emphasis is on the integration of skills development, subject knowledge and understanding. They also serve to alleviate one of the problems with modular courses; that of each unit being seen in isolation. Thus the emphasis is on student-based activities that integrate across unit boundaries and develop such skills as identifying problems, solving problems, working in groups, applying knowledge, evaluating information, writing reports, etc., in 'real-life' situations.

The setting of behavioural objectives may have a role to play in formulating both practical and lecture syllabuses. Their advantages and disadvantages are broadly those set out in Table 2 of Extract 1. As Boud points out, unless great care is taken they can 'lead to a fragmentation of purpose' (Boud *et al.*, 1986, p. 20) and the advantages follow 'because the objectives are specific or student-oriented not because they are behavioural' (Boud *et al.*, 1986, p. 21). An additional problem is that the prescriptive nature of the way in which they define the syllabus leaves little scope for experiential learning.

The need to provide more scope for college initiatives, responsive to local needs, and to allow for the integrated development of skills led BTEC to move away from setting behavioural objectives on a national basis. What problems the new course guidelines will produce remain to be seen. The emphasis on skills is now a key element in many courses including the National Curriculum and gNVQs (general National Vocational Qualifications).

REFERENCES

Anderson, O. R. (1976) *The Experience of Science: A New Perspective for Laboratory Teaching*, New York, Teachers College Press.

Barrows, H. S. and Tamblyn, R. M. (1980) *Problem-Based Learning: An Approach to Medical Education*, New York, Springer Publishing.

Bawden, R. J., Macadam, R. D., Packham, P. J. and Valentine, J. (1984) 'Systems thinking and practices in the education of agriculturalists', *Agricultural Systems*, 13, pp. 205–25.

Black, P. J. and Ogborn, J. (1979) 'Laboratory work in undergraduate teaching', in D. McNally (ed.) *Learning Strategies in University Science*, University College Cardiff Press, ICSU Committee on the Teaching of Science, pp. 161–201.

Boud, D. J. (1973) 'The laboratory aims questionnaire. A new method for course improvement?' *Higher Education*, 2, pp. 81–94.

Boud, D. J. (ed.) (1985) *Problem-Based Learning in Education for the Professions*, Sydney, HERDSA.

Boud, D. J., Dunn, J. and Hegarty-Hazel, E. (eds.) (1986) *Teaching in Laboratories*, Guildford, SHRE and NFER-Nelson.

Boud, D. J., Dunn, J., Kennedy, T. and Thorley, R. (1980) 'The aims of science laboratory courses: a survey of students, graduates and practising scientists', *European Journal of Science Education*, 2, pp. 415–28.

Chambers, R. G. (1966) 'The teaching of practical physics', in S. C. Brown and N. Clarke, (eds.) *The Education of a Physicist*, London, Oliver & Boyd, pp. 73–83.

Cryer, N. and Rider, J. G. (1977) 'A "do-it-yourself" demonstration laboratory', *Physics Education*, 12, pp. 389–93.

Davies, I. K. (1976) *Objectives in Curriculum Development*, London, McGraw Hill.

Gabb, R. G. and Mander, A. H. (1984) 'Laboratory work at school and university', *Research and Development in Higher Education*, 5, pp. 101–8.

Gardner, P. L. (1975) 'Science and the structure of knowledge', in P. L. Gardner (ed.) *The Structure of Science Education*, Hawthorne, Victoria, Longman pp. 1–40.

Hellingman, C. (1982) 'A trial list of objectives of experimental work in science education', *European Journal of Science Education*, 4, pp. 29–43.

Hofstein, A. and Lunetta, V. N. (1982) 'The role of laboratory in science teaching: neglected aspects of research'. *Review of Education Research*, 52, pp. 201–18.

Klopfer, L. E. (1971) 'Evaluation of learning in science', in B. S. Bloom, J. T. Hastings and G. F. Madaus (eds.) *Handbook of Formative and Summative Evaluation of Student Learning*, New York, McGraw Hill.

Lucas, A. M. (1971) 'Creativity, discovery and enquiry in science education', *Australian Journal of Education*, 15, pp. 185–96.

Lynch, P. P. and Gerrans, G. C. (1977) 'The aims of first year chemistry courses, the expectations of new students and subsequent course influences', *Research in Science Education*, 7, pp. 173–80.

Macdonald-Ross, M. (1973) 'Behavioural objectives – a critical review', *Instructional Science*, 2, pp. 1–52.

Mager, R. F. (1975) *Preparing Instructional Objectives* (2nd edition), Belmont Ca., Fearon.

Neame, R. L. B. (1981) 'How to . . . construct a problem-based course', *Medical Teacher*, 3, (3), pp. 94–9.

Price, R. M. and Brandt, D. (1974) 'Walk-in laboratory: a laboratory for introductory physics', *American Journal of Physics*, 42, pp. 126–30.

Rothkopf, E. Z. (1976) 'Writing to teach and reading to learn: a perspective on the psychology of written instruction', in N. L. Gage (ed.) *The Psychology of Teaching Methods*, Chicago, University of Chicago Press, pp. 91–129.

1.6

Exemplary practice in science classrooms

Kenneth Tobin and Patrick Garnett

High level cognitive learning has been an elusive goal of science programmes for many years. Despite the innovations incorporated in science curricula developed since the 1960s, there is evidence to suggest that traditional teaching methods are still utilized and student outcomes are associated with memorization of science facts and algorithms to solve problems without necessarily understanding how the algorithms work. Research has indicated that when the curriculum is implemented insufficient emphasis is placed on the development of student understanding and high level cognitive outcomes. Stake and Easley (1978) found that teachers emphasized learning facts about science and provided students with few opportunities to develop the high level thinking skills that most courses purported to develop. The courses were very textbook oriented and students tended to lack motivation to learn about applications of science to the world outside of the classroom. Tests and examinations were found to be powerful motivating forces in most of the observed classrooms. A similar trend was reported by Mitman, Mergendoller, Packer and Marchman (1984) in a study of 11 junior high science classes. Mitman *et al.* noted that few academic tasks required students to use high level cognitive skills. The authors reported that assessment tasks having most weight assigned to them (e.g. tests) had low cognitive demands.

Parallel findings were reported by Tobin and Gallagher (1987) in an Australian study of 15 high school science teachers. Tobin and Gallagher reported that science teachers emphasized completion of academic work to the possible detriment of students' understanding of the content. Teachers' emphasis on 'getting the work done' seemed to be associated with concerns that students cover the content to perform well on tests and to succeed at the next educational level. Teachers felt a responsibility to cover the work in the assigned time and planned and implemented lessons with a focus on covering course content. This emphasis on covering course content in the assigned time was

From: *Science Education* (1988) Vol. 72, no. 2, pp. 197–208.

often at the expense of developing students' understanding of the subject matter and their high level cognitive skills.

In some classes where teachers endeavoured to emphasize high level cognitive outcomes, barriers to high level learning were evident. Gallagher and Tobin (1987) described an interaction between classroom management and the cognitive demands of academic work in high school science activities. When the cognitive demands of the work were high, students demonstrated task avoidance behaviours that taxed the teacher's managerial affectiveness. In low ability classes teachers were able to retain control by changing activities so that students could engage without risk of failure. When the cognitive demands of the academic work were reduced the students were content to engage. In one high ability class, students asked to engage in a high level cognitive task underwent a period of restlessness in which most of the class was off-task. These examples suggest that students engage in task avoidance behaviours when the cognitive demands of the academic work are high for sustained periods of time.

Penick and Yager (1983) concluded that past case studies only highlighted the plight of science education and held little promise for stimulating improvements. They argued that case studies of excellence provided opportunities to identify aspects of science programmes that did work so that other 'school programs could begin building on what was known to work' (p. 621). Penick, Yager and others at the University of Iowa initiated a project in the US known as Search for Excellence. This project was seen as a 'new focus upon successes, exciting experiments, the positive facets of school science' instead of 'focusing upon failures, problems, and negative aspects' (Yager, 1984, p. 1). Because the focus of the Search for Excellence was on *programmes*, the initial output from the study included case studies of over 50 excellent science programmes published as several volumes by the National Science Teachers Association (e.g., Penick, 1983; Penick & Bonnstetter, 1983; Penick and Lunetta, 1984).

The philosophy underlying the Search for Excellence had considerable appeal to our group of researchers who decided to conduct a somewhat similar research effort in Western Australia. Our study, The Exemplary Practice in Science and Mathematics Education (EPSME) project, was based on the assumption that much could be learned from case studies from the best science and mathematics teachers. Also, we believed that such case studies of exemplary practice could lead to improvements in science and mathematics teaching by motivating and guiding teachers' attempts to improve their practice. In some respects our philosophy was similar to that espoused by Penick and Yager. However, there was one fundamental difference. Our group was committed to intensive classroom observations of teachers who were nominated and eventually invited to participate in the study.

OVERVIEW OF THE STUDY

The EPSME study involved a research team of 13 science and mathematics educators from Western Australia, and 26 teachers in schools in the metropolitan area of Perth, Western Australia. Thirteen science teachers and 13 mathematics teachers participated in the study. Eleven teams were formed to conduct case studies of the specific teachers involved in the study. Each team consisted of one or two researchers and focused on specific teachers in specific contexts. For example, different teams examined physics, chemistry, biology and general science at the high school level.

The teachers involved in the study were identified through a nomination process. Key educators in Western Australia, including teachers, State Education personnel and lecturers from tertiary institutions were asked to nominate outstanding teachers of science or mathematics. Nominators were selected because of their expertise in science education and were not provided with a list of criteria on which to base their nominations. Teachers who were nominated most frequently were invited to participate in the study.

Of course exemplary practice comes in many forms and is a subjective term that is interpreted in different ways by different educators. In this study, the term exemplary practice was not meant to imply that the nominated teachers were 'perfect' in the way that they taught. The teachers were considered effective in a broad sense of providing a learning environment in which students could develop concepts, inquiry skills and positive attitudes. Consequently, exemplary teachers were likely to employ a range of teaching strategies and organizational structures successfully in order to facilitate learning. Nominated teachers were not regarded as effective in the narrow sense of being able only to facilitate student achievement on external examinations or within-school tests.

An interpretive research methodology (Erickson, 1986) was used in the study. The data were primarily qualitative and were obtained by direct observation of teaching by participant observers. The data that were collected consisted of observations of teaching for at least eight lessons, interviews with the teacher and students, and examination of curriculum materials, tests, and student work. Interpretation of data occurred at the individual level, within teams, and at the entire research group level. Throughout the study, team meetings were held to facilitate discussion of administrative matters and substantive issues related to interpretation.

PURPOSE

The paper compares two high school chemistry teachers from a case study conducted by Garnett (1987) with two primary science teachers from a case study conducted by Goodrum (1987). The comparison was made as a result of dramatic differences observed in the content knowledge of the secondary and primary teachers and possible implications of such discrepancies for science teacher education. The database for the high school teachers consisted of 20 observations for each teacher, however, in the case of the two primary teachers the results were based on a sequence of two lessons. These lessons may not have been typical of the way that these teachers taught, however, the lessons do serve as an example of what might be expected when teachers teach in a content area which is 'out-of-field'. Results reported by Goodrum (1987) (based on 8 observations of each teacher) are likely to be more representative of the science teaching strategies employed by these teachers when they teach topics for which their content knowledge is stronger.

The final section of the paper discusses the implications of these results for improving the quality of science teaching. The complete results of the EPSME study are reported by Tobin and Fraser (1987).

A COMPARISON OF SELECTED SECONDARY AND PRIMARY SCIENCE TEACHERS

Primary science teaching

The first example concerns Richard, a teacher of a primary grade six class. Richard made an effort to model enthusiasm for participating in science, wondering about science, and applying science to the world outside of the classroom. He regularly used motivating techniques to involve students in science activities in an imaginative way as well as in a substantive way. For example, when students were given their record sheet prior to a materials centred activity, Richard asked them to write their names on top of the sheet. At the top of the mimeographed sheet was the title Professor ———. He asked them to imagine what it would be like to be a Professor. Students clearly enjoyed the introduction to the activity and had a positive mindset prior to commencing work.

At the beginning of the activity, Richard discussed the properties of water. It was raining at the time and he told the class that this was why they were doing this activity rather than the solar energy activity that had been scheduled. Throughout the lesson he consciously manoeuvered from 'classroom science' to 'outside of the classroom science' in a skilful manner.

During the activity, Richard monitored student learning and provided assistance as required. As he moved around the classroom he participated in the activity and demonstrated interest in the results that students obtained. Richard was modelling the behaviours he expected students to exhibit. He did this in the general sense of being polite and friendly and in the specific science sense of inquiring and working with students in an enthusiastic manner.

One major problem emerged during the lesson. Students began to take advantage of the relaxed atmosphere, and as the lesson progressed the amount of off-task behaviour increased. Students began to mess about with eye droppers, coins, and detergent in 'non-scientific' ways. Although the teacher endeavoured to bring the students under control he was unsuccessful, and many students were off-task for more than one-third of the one-hour lesson. While students were off-task they interfered with learning opportunities of others.

In terms of instruction, Richard adopted the plan of engaging learners in a whole-class interactive mode when an investigation was planned and explained, and when the results were interpreted. Whole-class interactive activities were characterized by extensive involvement of several boys in the class. These 'target' students were eager to respond to teacher questions, routinely raised their hands following a teacher question, and occasionally called out a response without waiting to be called to respond. The pattern that was evident in Richard's class was almost identical to that which has been described in studies of high school science classes (e.g. Gallagher, 1985; Tobin and Gallagher, 1987).

Two problems emerged regarding Richard's teaching practices. In small group activities classroom management was problematic, and during whole-class activities, interactions were dominated by a few target students. Improvements in these two areas could result in enhanced learning opportunities for all students.

Graham was a primary school teacher of students in grade seven. He was nominated for the study by several Education Department personnel, teachers, and science educators on the basis of his interest in science education and his active endeavours to promote materials-centred science programmes in the State. When he taught science, Graham was clearly a materials-centred science advocate. However, as was the case with Richard, he had management problems during his lessons. Graham had students involved with materials soon after the commencement of the lesson. For example, in one lesson students were given a handful of drinking straws and a number of pins and were instructed to make a tower that was self supporting. Classroom management was problematic from the outset of this lesson and became more so as the lesson progressed. Students were organized into groups, but generally speaking, the groups were unproductive. Although the teacher monitored student work, an increasing number of students were off-task throughout the lesson.

Graham had other problems as well. Although he monitored student behaviour, he did not monitor student thinking. He moved about the room attending to administrative matters, leaving students to construct their own knowledge without teacher cues or feedback. In some groups certain individuals monopolized the use of materials and prevented others from manipulating the pins and straws. In other groups there was division of labour as the 'architects' supervised the 'workers'. At the end of the data-collecting activity Graham asked students to pack away the equipment. There was no time allowed for discussion of results.

In Graham's class the use of materials appeared to be an end in itself. Although the students were directed to do a particular activity, i.e. build a straw tower, there were no clearly identifiable understandings or skills which the teacher sought to develop. This was apparent both in terms of the type of feedback provided to students during the lesson and also from the lack of discussion after the activity. As a result, many of the potential benefits of this activity were lost.

High school science teaching

Garth and Don were teachers who were exemplary in most respects. Each taught high school chemistry, but at different schools. Garth taught at a comprehensive co-educational high school and Don taught at a girls' private high school.

Garth used groups for most of the time during his lessons. Although he was teaching chemistry to students in grades 11 and 12 he involved students in constructing their own knowledge in a variety of ways during the study. Students worked in self-formed small groups on tasks such as assignment work, laboratory activities or summarizing the text. The students exercised considerable control over the pace at which they moved through the assigned work, and to some extent, over the activities which they selected. For example, following a lively discussion on the reaction between hydrochloric acid and magnesium, his grade 11 class was given the problem of calculating the number of moles of magnesium needed to produce 50 ml of hydrogen at STP. Having calculated an answer the class was expected to confirm the result experimentally. In order to do this they had to calibrate a burette to measure the volume of hydrogen. Once the activity started, Garth monitored student engagement and actively taught students without reducing the cognitive demands of the task. In these small group situations Garth asked students questions which probed their understanding and caused them to think about the work and to reflect on their own thinking. Although students were working in groups there were no obvious examples of students copying work from one another. If a student had difficulties the teacher appeared on the scene and a private conversation ensued.

Of course there were examples of students dealing with their social agendas during group work. However, the teacher did not have to call the class to order, noise levels were never excessive, and engagement levels were high. Garth had established a routine of working with students in groups. If students appeared to be socializing, Garth was there before it became too much of a problem and encouraged students to get back on-task. It was apparent that the students knew what to do and what to expect during the lessons that were observed.

Garth had extensive knowledge about teaching and a strong background in high school science. He believed that students learn best in situations where they structure and take the responsibility for their own learning. Consequently, his knowledge was active in the sense that it could drive behaviour during teaching. During science lessons Garth was relaxed and clearly able to think about instruction and how to better engage individuals in the class.

Don was a contrast to Garth. His teaching was mainly to the whole class and he perceived his role differently from Garth. Whereas Garth was an advocate of students constructing their own knowledge, Don perceived his role as presenting knowledge in a form that would enable students to make the necessary connections. He believed that by linking new material to previous work and by careful explanation he was able to facilitate student understanding and develop the logical framework of the discipline. Don's own academic background in chemistry was considerably stronger than Garth's, although each had a more than adequate background. During class Don used demonstrations effectively and passed around materials so that students could have firsthand experience with the chemicals to which he was referring. Don went to considerable trouble to assess students' understandings of chemistry. He skilfully used questions and short quizzes to establish the extent to which the students had achieved the objectives. As well students were encouraged to ask questions about aspects of the course which they did not understand. In some lessons the students initiated most of the student–teacher interactions which took place. Clearly Don had established a classroom environment in which students were expected to monitor their own understanding. Don attended to the important aspect of relating chemistry to the world outside of the classroom in an effective manner. In fact his general knowledge was impressive as he was able to take current events in the mining industry and interrelate economic and environmental issues with the chemistry that was being discussed.

Don used lectures, whole-class interactive activities, demonstrations, and laboratory work in his teaching. In all these modes the level of student engagement was exceptionally high, typically over 90%. He did not appear to have target students and the students were comfortable asking the teacher questions or responding to the many teacher-initiated questions. On numerous occasions the level of cognitive processing required to answer teacher-initiated questions was quite high. Students were sometimes called upon to explain or justify their answers. However, this was done in a classroom environment which was supportive and free of threat.

DISCUSSION

The examples involving Richard, Graham, Garth and Don are illustrative of the findings of the EPSME study. Some teachers were very good and others were average and had some difficulties. However, the case studies have resulted in models of effective practice which might be used in teacher education courses as a basis for illustrating good science teaching. For example, Richard demonstrated exemplary strategies to increase student motivation to learn, Garth implemented effective small group activities and used procedures to maintain a high level of cognitive demand, and Don showed how science content could be taught in a meaningful way. The study was also useful in providing insights into the reasons why some strategies would not work in particular contexts. What was not clear from the study was how the results could be used to enhance science teaching.

An examination of the relative content strengths and weaknesses of the four teachers involved in this study highlights some salient points. Don and Garth had degrees in science and were able to use their knowledge to stimulate overt learner engagement on high level cognitive objectives. Students in their classes were involved in thinking about science content in an overt way. This was not the case to the same extent in either of the primary teachers' classes. Of course some of the differences could be explained in terms of the relative ages of the students involved. Perhaps older students could be expected to engage in high level cognitive tasks more often and for longer periods than younger students. Although this might be the case, our interpretation is that the two high school teachers facilitated overt student engagement through the strategies that they used. In Garth's case he was able to use questions directed to individuals to promote thinking about content in materials-centred environments. This was possible because he had a firm grasp of the content that he wanted to teach and he knew how to sustain student engagement. His monitoring was effective because he was in the right place at the right time and he had the content knowledge to maintain the momentum of the lesson. He could ask students what they were thinking and could provide feedback on the substance of their thoughts.

Although Don did not use small groups in the same way as Garth, he was able to keep students engaged because of his skills in whole-class interactive activities. He used demonstrations to provide concrete referents for student thinking and he involved students in a systematic manner in answering well chosen questions. Because of his extensive knowledge about the subject that he was teaching he was able to introduce the content in an appropriate manner and assist students to link the concepts within lessons and from one lesson to the next. Don's obvious enthusiasm for chemistry teaching and his tendency to use illustrative examples from real life, provided students with a model of how science ought to be presented and learned.

The two primary teachers provided a marked contrast to the two secondary teachers and to one another. Each of these teachers was certified to teach primary grades and was not a specialist science teacher. Their preparation as science teachers was based on professional courses in their education degrees and graduate work in science education. The focus of all science-related courses they had taken was on teaching science. The emphasis was on curriculum resources and types of activities that were appropriate for teaching and learning of science. In addition, Graham and Richard were enthusiastic science teachers with a conviction about the value of primary students learning science in a 'hands-on' manner.

Our interpretation of the lessons observed is that neither of these teachers possessed sufficient knowledge of science to successfully implement activities of this type. They knew how to arrange students in groups and how to get the activities started, but they were unable to assist students to develop science content from the activities. Richard made attempts to focus student thinking on concepts associated with the properties of water. There was no doubt that he knew how to monitor student engagement and how to probe student thinking. However, he could not ask the crucial questions to focus student thinking on what was to be learned. In fact, there was no evidence that Richard knew what students were supposed to learn from the activity. The data-collecting part of the lesson became an end in itself, and there were no links forged between the activity and the subsequent, discussion of properties of water in the post-lab discussion. Failure to focus on content development during the activity is a possible reason for the increasing incidence of off-task behaviour during the activity.

Graham appeared to have even less content knowledge about structures. The activity was a favourite of Graham's and he had taught sequences of lessons involving structures on many occasions in the past. Unlike Richard, he did not endeavour to monitor student understanding during the activity on structures. His concern was with classroom management. As a consequence, students focused their attention on construction and competing with other groups in the class. During the lesson they were left to their own resources to discuss observations that may have been relevant to the content they were to learn. Undoubtedly each student in the class learned something about construction, but it was apparent that the potential of the learning environment that had been established was not realized because of the relative inactivity of the teacher. His failure to attend to the cognitive needs of students was reflected in their inappropriate behaviour throughout the lesson.

The two sets of science teachers provided an interesting contrast which highlights the importance of teachers having adequate pedagogical and content knowledge. In this study, each of the four teachers had adequate pedagogical knowledge, however, only the two high school teachers had sufficient knowledge of science. The lack of necessary content knowledge has important implications for assisting the two primary teachers to improve their teaching.

Concerns about having sufficient content knowledge to teach science in an adequate manner is not just a problem for primary science teachers. Happs (1987) reported that a high school teacher made many errors while teaching a general science topic which for him was out-of-field. The knowledge limitations were evident in the observed lessons and most likely resulted in students developing or reinforcing misconceptions. Tobin (1987) also reported how an experienced and 'well qualified' high school teacher made numerous errors while teaching grade 10 general science. Although the teacher had an undergraduate major in anatomy and had a graduate qualification in science, his knowledge of nuclear energy was extremely limited and his teaching reflected his inadequacies. Furthermore, when the same teacher taught a vertebrates topic he made almost as many errors. These findings highlight the importance of content knowledge and its impact on science teaching in high school courses as well as primary school courses.

How can a deficiency in content knowledge be redressed? Planning is an obvious way to overcome the problem. But primary teachers, such as Richard and Graham, are required to teach subjects such as mathematics, social studies, English, art, and physical education as well as science. If similar amounts of planning are required in each subject, the time needed to plan a day's lessons would be daunting. The task of building a sufficient knowledge base in all of these subjects and maintaining the currency of that knowledge base may be too large for most primary school teachers. Since two of the best primary school science teachers were involved in this study, it is likely that most primary teachers would encounter problems of greater magnitude than those described in this paper. The challenge of upgrading the science knowledge of all primary teachers to a satisfactory level may be too great to contemplate. Serious consideration should be given to training specialist teachers to implement the science curriculum in primary schools.

The problem of high school teachers possessing the necessary content knowledge also needs close consideration. In most instances, the high school teachers in the EPSME study had more than adequate content knowledge to teach the topics which we observed. As a consequence, they were able to focus on teaching with student understanding as their main focus. These results highlight the importance of ensuring that high school science teachers have the knowledge needed to explain science phenomena, demonstrate science principles, probe student understandings, diagnose partial understandings and misunderstandings from student responses, and expand on student understandings of given science concepts. This type of content knowledge, which Shulman (1986) called pedagogical content knowledge, is the professional knowledge of the science teacher. Priority should be given to research which is focused on understanding how teachers acquire pedagogical content knowledge and how it relates to the professional education of science teachers.

When we began the EPSME study we expected to identify exemplary practices which would serve as models for teachers wanting to improve their teaching. It is now apparent to us that our model for improving teaching was probably too simplistic. There is no doubt that videotapes of any of these teachers in action provide a context in which a change process could begin. Critical instances from a videotaped lesson could be identified and used as a basis for discussion and stimulating reflection on a teacher's personal teaching style. According to Schon (1983), reflective practices can initiate an intention to change, which appears to be an essential ingredient for improvement of teaching.

If improvements are to be sustained, we should realize that teachers will probably need to identify the area in which change is needed and believe that the changes will be worth the effort. Having made the initial commitment, teachers need to acquire the knowledge needed to implement the change and put the changed practices into effect. Unless they are successful or receive encouraging feedback and support, teachers might opt to discontinue the changed teaching practices after an initial trial.

CONCLUSIONS

The EPSME study provided a substantial knowledge base concerning effective teaching practices in science and mathematics classes. One challenging outcome of the study is that no matter how good a teacher might be there will inevitably be some area in which they can improve. However, the best way to effect change is not clear and it is unlikely that there will be only one best way. What is apparent from this study is that both pedagogical and content knowledge are important ingredients for outstanding teaching. While all four teachers described had sufficient pedagogical knowledge to deal with grouping and management concerns, the weaker content knowledge of the primary teachers was a significant barrier to effective teaching, even at the primary level. Without this essential content base teachers are unable to focus student thinking, unable to provide appropriate feedback to students, and unable to discuss effectively the content dealt with in different classroom environments.

The challenge that faces our research group in the wake of EPSME is to identify how teachers can construct knowledge about science content and teaching so that their teaching performance improves. In order to address this task and to learn about the art and craft of teaching it will be necessary to further explore classrooms of exemplary and non-exemplary teachers. It might be that teaching is very hard to change because knowledge of teaching develops over a long period of time and the active knowledge that drives behaviour is difficult to change and to construct. As a consequence, teachers find it difficult to improve. If classroom researchers are to seriously address the issue of improving science teaching and learning we must learn more about the role of different knowledge forms in teaching.

REFERENCES

Erickson, F. (1986) Qualitative methods in research on teaching. In Wittrock, M. C. (ed.) *Handbook of Research on Teaching (3rd Edition)*. NY: Macmillan Publishing Co.

Gallagher, J. J. (1985) *Secondary school science* (Interim Report). East Lansing: Michigan State University, Institute for Research on Teaching.

Gallagher, J. J. and Tobin, K. (1987) Teacher management and student engagement in high school science. *Science Education*, 71, 535–55.

Garnett, P. (1987) Teaching for understanding: Exemplary practice in high school chemistry. In Tobin, K. and Fraser, B. J. *Exemplary Practice in Science and Mathematics Teaching*. Perth: Curtin University of Technology.

Goodrum, D. (1987) Exemplary teaching in upper primary science classes. In Tobin, K. and Fraser, B. J. *Exemplary Practice in Science and Mathematics Teaching*. Perth: Curtin University of Technology.

Happs, J. (1987) Good teaching of invalid information: Exemplary junior secondary science teachers outside their field of expertise. In Tobin, K. and Fraser, B. J. *Exemplary Practice in Science and Mathematics Teaching*. Perth: Curtin University of Technology.

Mitman, A. L., Mergandoller, J. R., Packer, M. J. and Marchman, V. A. (1984) *Scientific literacy in seventh grade life science: A study of instructional process, task completion, student perceptions and learning outcomes*. San Francisco, CA: Far West Laboratory for Educational Research and Development.

Penick, J. E. (ed.) (1983) *Focus on Excellence: Science as Inquiry*. Washington, DC: National Science Teachers Association.

Penick, J. E. and Bonnstetter, R. J. (eds.) (1983). *Focus on excellence: Biology*. Washington, DC: National Science Teachers Association.

Penick, J. E. and Lunetta, V. N. (eds.) (1984) *Focus on Excellence: Physical Science*. Washington, DC: National Science Teachers Association.

Penick, J. E. and Yager, R. E. (1983) The search for excellence in science education. *Phi Delta Kappan*, 621–623.

Sanford, J. P. (1987) Management of science classroom tasks and effects on students' learning opportunities. *Journal of Research in Science Teaching*, 24(3), 249–265.

Schon, D. A. (1983) *The Reflective Practitioner: How Professionals Think in Action*. New York: Basic Books, Inc.

Shulman, L. S. (1986) Those who understand: Knowledge growth in teaching. *Educational Researcher*, 15(2), 4–14.

Stake, R. E. and Easley, J. A. (1978). *Case Studies in Science Education* (Vols. 1 and 2). Urbana: Center for Instructional Research and Curriculum Evaluation and Committee on Culture and Cognition, University of Illinois at Urbana-Champaign.

Tobin, K. (1987) Teaching for higher cognitive learning. Paper presented at the annual meeting of the National Association for Research in Science Teaching, Washington, DC.

Tobin, K., Espinet, M. and Byrd, S. (April, 1987). Impediments to change: An application of coaching in high school science. Paper presented at the annual meeting of the National Association of Research in Science Teaching, Washington, DC.

Tobin, K. and Fraser, B. J. (1987) *Exemplary Practice in Science and Mathematics Teaching*. Perth: Curtin University of Technology.

Tobin, K. and Gallagher, J. J. (1987) Target students in the science classroom. *Journal of Research in Science Teaching*, 24(1), 61–75.

Tobin, K. and Gallagher, J. J. (in press) What happens in high school science classrooms? *Journal of Curriculum Studies*. 19 (6), 549–60.

Yager, R. E. (1984) Searching for excellence. Paper presented at the annual meeting of the American Educational Research Association, New Orleans.

Part 2: Learning Science

Introduction

Eileen Scanlon

The articles in this part contribute to an exploration of the theme 'Learning in science'. Alex Johnstone provides a starting point for this by attempting to answer the question 'What makes science hard to learn?' He discusses the nature of science with references to his own experience in chemistry education and considers features of the way science is taught in schools, such as the nature of science concepts, different levels of representation in the subject matter and the role of learning from experimentation.

Marcia Linn and Nancy Butler Songer provide a wide-ranging review of recent research on psychological theories of learning, concentrating on the topic of how learning in science comes about in children by a process of conceptual change. Focusing on conceptual change in adolescence, the article notes two key threads in this research: namely, that students construct understanding by integrating observations and activities into intuitions, and that learners over-compartmentalize their knowledge into domains, thereby failing to recognize parallels in similar situations. The social context of learning is also stressed in the paper and examples are taken from the 'Computer as Lab Partner' project.

Tim O'Shea and co-workers give a concrete example of an attempt to use research findings on the existence of prior concepts in children and the design of computer-assisted learning to promote conceptual change in a group of eleven- and twelve-year-old children. The computer programme was used with small groups of children and was a key part of a specially designed curriculum combining computer and 'real' practicals.

Philip Adey and Michael Shayer report on their work, starting from the view that the possibility of teaching general thinking skills is worth pursuing, and describe its consequences for teaching science. They describe results achieved by pupils taking special lessons in the science curriculum they call 'Thinking Science'. They present evidence that their intervention led to immediate gains in Piagetian measures of cognitive development and they demonstrate that their programme results in gains in achievement in science, mathematics and English language measured at two and three years after the end of the intervention programme.

In the article by Wynne Harlen the focus is on learning science in primary schools. She provides a review of research in which she discusses participation in primary science and discusses evidence about achievement of goals both on a national level in Britain and also in terms of the individual child's developing ideas in science. She also discusses what she describes as the gap in research at the levels both of school and class planning and teacher–pupil interaction.

These articles combine to form a view of the current research on learning science, providing some commentary on the implications that current psychological perspectives have for teaching.

2.1

Why is science difficult to learn? Things are seldom what they seem

A. H. Johnstone

INTRODUCTION

Was there ever a time when school science was easy to learn and easy to teach? The answer must be a qualified, 'yes'. There was a time when physics was concerned with nothing smaller than a brick, when biology was taxonomic and descriptive and when chemistry dealt with preparations and properties (bulk properties only). Everything came in well designed, closed boxes and the exams explored the contents of each box and never asked the pupils to look in two boxes at once. The halogen question was absolutely distinct from the nitrogen question and nobody seemed to look for similarities or patterns. All of this brought a sense of security to both pupil and teacher, but was it science? The 1960s made us stand back and ask serious questions about science, its concepts, its overarching theories and insights, its consequences, its issues and its place in education and in society in general.

Chem Study, PSSC, BSCS (in all its versions), Nuffield, Scottish Alternative and many, many more schemes were launched at that time, all of which tried to address these questions about science. Books such as *Physics for the Enquiring Mind, Physics is Fun, Chemistry Takes Shape* and *Biology by Enquiry* all began to reflect the new thinking about teaching and learning in science. Many of these innovations were the 'expert' view of science: a view which saw concepts as unifying and emancipating: a view which went in for large universal patterns (remember 'waves' and the 'mole' and 'energetics'?); a view which could 'see' in an experiment things which were far beyond the immediate and the perceptual.

It was all 'good science' and the enthusiasm of the writers infected many teachers, but it is doubtful if the cascade got much further. We perhaps made the serious error of confusing our enthusiasms for those of our pupils (Johnstone, 1974). We did not stop to ask questions about the nature of learning because we were being carried along on the wave of ingenuity which was tied to content and to the 'clever' ways of getting it across. The reader will

From: *Journal of Computer Assisted Learning*, (1991) Vol. 7, pp. 75–83.

remember the linear air track, the ticker tape, the conductivity apparatus, the Wilson Cloud Chamber and the ripple tank and many more ingenious devices. But did these things really 'get it across'?

The fact that many pupils claim that science is hard to learn might suggest that 'it' is not being successfully transmitted. The faults could lie in various places such as with the *transmission system* itself, the methods used and the facilities available or with the *receivers* (the learners) and the nature of their learning or even with the *nature of the message* itself. Almost certainly the problems lie with all three to varying degrees.

A great deal of effort has been expended on the techniques of transmission without asking too many questions about how young people learn. Not enough thought has been given to the message itself and to whether it has any significance at all for young people. This has become even more acute since science has now entered the core of the curriculum and pupils are no longer able to vote with their feet and make their escape.

A LAYPERSON'S VIEW OF FORMAL SCIENCE

It is true that children learn by asking questions, by making observations, by forming concepts and by 'making sense of things'. They do this about things which matter to them and they come up with working hypotheses to meet immediate needs. These hypotheses are usually of short range and are there to serve a purpose. Some are passed on 'ready made' like the danger of walking under a ladder or the necessity for drinking milk to make strong bones. Others come only from experience, such as things to do (or not to do) when riding a bicycle or 'reading the sky' for suitable weather to play football.

Formal science on the other hand is looking for large, long-range theories and hypotheses to 'explain' or systematize the Laws of Motion, the behaviour of tides, the nature of matter and so on. This type of thinking is what makes science powerful, but its significance may be lost on young people who are living perfectly well, despite their ignorance of the grand picture.

So many of the questions which science teachers make children ask may be, for the pupils, non-questions or so-what questions – 'Why is grass green?', 'Why is glass fragile?', 'What is lead doing in petrol?' We can go even deeper into the realm of non-questions by asking 'What is there between the molecules in a glass of water?' Within the molecular model, this is a non-question at any level, but for a pupil it can have no significance. Non-events are often the substance and content of formal school science.

There is no doubt that a knowledge and understanding of science is enriching for those of us who can see the world in this way. It is maybe philanthropic and evangelical on our part to want to share it with our fellow creatures, but it is arrogant to suggest that everybody wants or *needs* a knowledge of science to live happily in a scientific society. Provided people follow the instructions on the label of the tin of paint, on the bottle of lavatory cleaner, on the packet of food or on the lawn mower, they will live happily and safely in our society today.

Where people begin to feel their need (or suspicion) of science is not so much in everyday living, where so much is taken for granted, but in the large issues on which the media thrive; issues such as salmonella poisoning, greenhouse effects, ozone layer, algae in shellfish, and air pollution. Here there is a feeling of helplessness and a desire to get at 'them'. They have no yardstick by which to measure seriousness or to judge rights and wrongs. They are blown about by claims and counter claims without knowing how to separate fact from hysteria. Surely a good grounding in science education would put this right! If for no other reason, everyone should be taught science. This argument is not really tenable.

Most of these issues are highly complex and can be dealt with only superficially in school science. Even competent professional scientists decline to comment on issues which are outside their own immediate area of expertise, if they are prudent. Recent experience of marking A-level chemistry papers showed, even at this level of sophistication, utter confusion between greenhouse effects and the depletion of the ozone layer. What hope is there for a GCSE band X pass candidate?

However, let us get back to the business of science teaching as it occurs in schools at present and readdress the question, 'Why is science difficult to learn?'

SCIENCE AS TAUGHT IN SCHOOLS

1. The nature of science concepts

The common type of concepts with which children and adults are familiar are made up of tangible instances. The concept of 'cat' is built up from seeing a lot of cats, looking for visible and other sensory attributes which they have in common. They are recognized as a subset of the concept animal or even mammal. If a tiger is introduced, the concept may be modified to accommodate something of a different size, but with otherwise similar attributes. Even concepts such as 'kindness' can be exemplified by kind acts, and unkind acts can be seen as non-examples.

But how about the concept of 'element' or 'compound'? There is no immediate sensory way to get at these ideas. Examples of elements may be yellow powders, colourless gases or brown liquids, but so also are examples of compounds. Where are the common factors? Where are the distinguishing marks? They exist only in the mind, unless the compounds can be shown to be broken down into elements experimentally and then to prove that the elementary bits really are elements. This is a long way from school science.

Many scientific concepts are of a similar nature: the electron, bond energy, photons, structures and molecules.

These ideas are all beyond our senses and pupils have little or no experience in constructing such concepts. In the 'good old days' definitions purported to act as anchors for these concepts, but whether they were ever understood is open to debate.

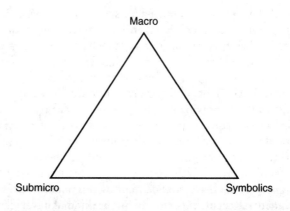

Figure I

2. Multilevel thought (Johnstone, 1982)

In the revolution of the 1960s, curriculum projects had a habit of trying to settle themselves on some conceptual tripod. For example chemistry was supposed to sit on the three ideas of structure, bonding and energy. These were the big unifying ideas which were to permeate the whole course. But lurking almost unseen under this was a triangle (Figure 1) of levels of thought. This can be exemplified from chemistry, but similar triangles exist in all the sciences.

The macrophenomenon (tangible and visible) that salt dissolves in water is 'explained' in terms of its existing in a regular lattice, being attracted to water molecules and being towed off into solution. This is then 'shown' as

$$Na^+Cl^-(s) + H_2O \rightarrow Na^+ (aq) + Cl^- (aq).$$

Almost in one breath the teacher ranges across this diagram, but the pupil can be stranded at the 'macro' corner. So much of teaching takes place *within* the triangle where the three levels interact in varying proportions and the teacher may be unaware of the demands being made on the pupils. There has been a suggestion that worthwhile, 'real' chemistry can be done only when juggling at all three levels, but this is patent nonsense. Perfectly respectable chemistry can be done at the macro level only. After all, it was done there for centuries! Some of the most taxing chemistry is done on *two* levels only, for example, classical thermodynamics uses only the macro and the symbolic levels. Why must we inflict all three levels *simultaneously* on young people?

In physics, there are three similar levels: the macro, the invisible (e.g. forces, reactions, electrons) and the symbolic (maths, formulae etc.). Biology has its three levels: the macro (plant or animal), the micro (cells), the biochemical (DNA etc.). It is little wonder that science is hard to learn.

3. How helpful are experiments?

There is a touching faith among science educators that practical work is, without question, a good thing. It certainly provides the teacher with an

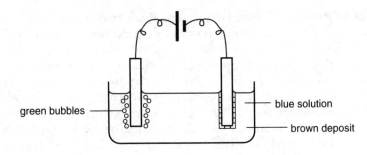

green bubbles
blue solution
brown deposit

Figure 2

increased battery of teaching tools and gives the pupil a welcome break from written work or from listening. But does it really make the learning of science easier? Reports from all over the research literature (Hofstein and Lunetta, 1982) are fairly pessimistic and this is not surprising when the teacher uses macrophenomena to pull the pupil, almost instantly into the middle of the triangle mentioned previously. Let us take an example (Figure 2).

An electrolysis cell is set up with a blue solution being electrolysed between carbon rods. The student observations are as follows: a blue solution, a brown deposit on the carbon attached to the black terminal and sharp smelling bubbles coming off the other electrode attached to the red terminal. The pupil has to take on trust that electrons are being supplied at the black terminal and withdrawn at the red. This is already in the invisible, submicro level. If the teacher names the blue solution as copper chloride the next set of questions are begged. 'What might the brown material be?' 'What might the bubbles be?' Now we plunge into the middle of the triangle if the teacher leads the reasoning as follows. 'If the brown material is copper this shows that, in the blue solution, copper exists as positively charged particles called ions, in fact as Cu^{2+} (aq). When it arrives at the electrode, it collects two electrons to become solid copper metal. This can be shown as:

$$Cu^{2+} (aq) + 2e^- \rightarrow Cu (s)$$

At the other electrode negatively charged chloride ions are arriving, surrendering an electron to make chlorine atoms which pair up to give chlorine gas as shown:

$$2Cl^- (aq) \rightarrow Cl_2 (g) + 2e^-$$

This edifice of reasoning is being built on a very few perceptual clues and piled high with concepts, terminology and representation. It is doubtful if the edifice would have been any less secure if the experiment had not been done at all. The 'results' the teacher wanted are several levels removed from the observations. It is little wonder that electrochemistry is reported by students as one of the areas they find most difficult.

An example from biology will serve to illustrate this further. If a muscle fibre is clamped at one end and attached at the other to a movable lever and then a drop of ATP solution is added to the fibre, the lever twitches. This is supposed to show that ATP is an energy source causing the fibre to contract. But precisely the same effect can be shown by adding a drop of dilute hydrochloric acid. Does this show that hydrochloric acid is an energy source?!

Another factor in experimental work is the presence of both 'noise' and 'signal' in observations (Johnstone and Wham, 1982; Johnstone and Letton, 1988). Unfortunately the pupil cannot tell one from the other. The stray bubble becomes as important as the colour change or the temperature change. Often the vital 'signal' is missed because the pupil has been beguiled by the 'noise'. Free discovery learning is seen for the nonsense it is under these conditions. Guided discovery is just a way of trying to separate 'signal' from 'noise', but no amount of guided discovery could genuinely generate the conclusions required from the electrolysis experiment above. It took the best scientific brains of Europe nearly half a century to do so! How can we expect pupils to do it in 10 minutes?

Pupils are not deceived by practical work. They know that they can splash about, draw the craziest conclusions, but that, at the end, the teacher will tell them what they have seen. A very able sixth former was heard to describe practical chemistry as 'the long way to the sink'!

This is not a blanket condemnation of practical work, but so much of it creates more problems than it solves. If anything in school science needs to be rethought, it is certainly the place and nature of practical work.

4. The language barrier

This would seem to be a very obvious source of difficulty since science is bristling with unfamiliar technical words, but what has been shown to be the case is that the technical terms present few difficulties compared with the familiar non-technical terms which pupils *think* they understand (Cassels and Johnstone, 1983). A pipette is a pipette and a cotyledon is just a cotyledon, but a 'volatile compound' can mean at least *four* things to as many pupils. 'Volatile' has left the realm of science with its meaning of 'easily vaporized' and gone off into common speech where it is applied to markets, people, countries and hostile situations. It then filters back into science with meanings which do not seem out of place in science (to the pupils) but which make a nonsense of a science discussion. A 'volatile compound' is understood as a 'flammable, explosive, unstable and dangerous compound'. If the teacher asks, 'Do you know the meaning of volatile?' he will be assured by his pupils that they do, but the vital check that they are all using the *same* meaning may not be carried out. An alarming number of words are understood as having the *opposite* meaning by 12–14-year-olds in Britain. For example 'contract' is understood by about 50% as 'get smaller' but the other half think it means 'get larger'. 'Abundant' is taken to mean 'plenty' by a half and 'scarce' by the other half. 'Audible' is heavily confused with 'edible' and 'efficient' with 'sufficient'. In recent studies (Cassells and Johnstone, 1985) about a hundred common words of this kind have been found which are transmuted as they pass to and fro across the science/common speech interface.

There is also the clutch of pompous words which scientists use as if they were trying to fend off learners rather than encourage them. There is really no need for 'aqueous', 'incident', 'discrete', 'diaphanous', 'hirsute', 'decussate', 'immiscible', 'pungent' and many more. Of course we have a responsibility for developing our pupils' language, but this type of development seems to be encouraging advancement backwards into the archaic rather than into living language.

If the language, the vehicle for communication, is suspect, no wonder science is hard to learn.

THE CONFLICT OF THE MESSAGE WITH THE NATURE OF LEARNING

In all models of learning there is the idea that the learner can be constrained by limits: Piaget's developmental stages; Ausubel's inadequacy of previous knowledge for meaningful learning; Pascual-Leone's idea of limited space related to age and Information Processing models (Greene and Hicks, 1984) containing something of all of the other models (Figure 3).

If we use Figure 3 as a very much simplified working model to set alongside what has been said above about the nature of the message, it can be seen not only why science, taught as it is, must be difficult, but also how we might see ways of rectifying things. Let us take each of the ideas numbered 1–4 above and examine them in turn.

Many of *the concepts of science* don't present themselves for selective observation. Nothing can be pulled out from long-term memory experience to provide either the means of matching or provide anchorages for the new ideas to be filed away in long-term memory. Probably the best that can be done is by analogy which has to be carefully thought out. We now recognize the pitfalls of water analogies for electricity and two-compartment analogies for dynamic equilibrium. Research is needed here.

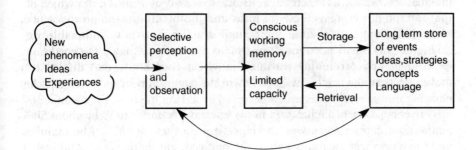

Figure 3

There is also the problem that what is available in long-term memory may distort the selection process and provide, for the working memory, information which is incompatible with what is coming in from outside (Driver *et al.*, 1985). This will interfere with the pupils' ability to construct meaning out of the new information, thus causing distortion or compartmentalization or rejection of the new science. The inability to make sense of science must be demotivating and demoralizing.

The *multilevel thought* problem is partly conceptual as described above, but is also capable of rapidly overloading the Working Memory Space with observation, 'explantation' and simultaneous representation which is calling on symbolism and convention all at the same time. Teachers jump so rapidly from level to level that they can merge them into one 'reality', but this is very much an acquired skill requiring very efficient chunking skills. There is a sense in which science should be taught at a macrolevel only, with 'explanation' available on demand and in doses small enough to be processed. This is the essence of the new Standard Grade Chemistry programme in Scotland (SEB, 1987) in that each topic is dealt with on a macro, observable level and the levels of explanatory thought are available in add-on units at the pupils' request. Software such as Hypercard lends itself very well to this. It means that many pupils would choose never to learn to think on all three levels, but this need not be any kind of disaster as long as good science is available at all levels, in the sense that pupils are allowed to frame scientific questions and find out ways of answering them at all levels.

In the area of *practical work* the same mechanisms must apply. If pupils are really to be allowed to do practical work for themselves they will perceive and observe in a selective way based upon previous knowledge and expectation. There is no guarantee that pupils will 'see' what we 'see'. It is not just a matter of using their sense, but of using them in a guided way. Full, unbridled discovery learning is likely to turn up some strange ideas (at least strange to us) depending upon priorities and interpretations of observations. 'Noise' will rank with 'signal'.

If we give strict worksheet instructions we shall tend to focus attention on the 'signal', but the simultaneous reading of instructions, using techniques and making observations can create a serious overload of working memory such that interpretation, resynthesis of ideas and meaningful learning cannot take place (Johnstone and Wham, 1982). Pupils react to the overload discomfort by taking in only small portions of instructions at a time, thus fragmenting the experiment and precluding learning. However they know that it does not matter because the teacher will give them the results and explain things at the end.

This area of science education needs intensive research to reduce this load. Simulations can go some way to helping this in that 'noise' can be excluded and the worksheet mentality can be discouraged, but there has to come a time when pupils have developed such a well integrated cognitive structure that they can separate 'signal' from 'noise' themselves.

Language fits into this model very well because so much of what goes on in working memory takes place in visual or verbal form. An unfamiliar word or phrase can occupy an inordinate amount of working memory space as we strive to make sense of it from the context. If the context is already complex as indicated throughout this paper, the chance of clarifying the meaning of unfamiliar words is slim. The words may eventually be taken into semantic memory in [an undigested] and unrelated form and later used in an attempt to cover ignorance. It is not uncommon to find undergraduates who trot out words like 'delocalization' or 'surface tension' with only the faintest idea of their meaning. They sound erudite, but cannot stand up to even gentle investigation.

CONCLUSION

We have tried to answer the question 'Why is science hard to learn?' Part of the problem rests with the nature of science itself, but more seems to lie with the ways by which science is customarily taught.

A working model has been proposed against which research hypotheses can be raised and tested to give some hope of doing something about making science less difficult to learn.

REFERENCES

Cassels, J. R. T. and Johnstone, A. H. (1983) The meaning of words and the teaching of chemistry. *Education in Chemistry*, 20(1), 10–11.

Cassels, J. R. T. and Johnstone, A. H. (1985) *Words that matter in Science*, Royal Society of Chemistry, London.

Driver, R., Guesne, E. and Tiberghien, A. (1985) *Children's Ideas in Science*. Open University Press, Milton Keynes.

Greene, J. and Hicks, C. (1984) *Basic Cognitive Processes*. Open University Press, Milton Keynes.

Hofstein, A. and Lunetta, V. (1982) The role of the laboratory in Science Teaching. *Review of Educational Research*, 52(2), 201–17.

Johnstone, A. H. (1974) Evaluation of Chemistry Syllabuses in Scotland. *Studies in Science Education*, 1, 21–49.

Johnstone, A. H. (1982) Macro and micro chemistry. *School Science Review*, 64 (No. 227), 377–379.

Johnstone, A. H. and Letton, K. M. (1988) Is practical work practicable? *Journal of College Science Teaching*, 18(3), 190–2.

Johnstone, A. H. and Wham, A. J. B. (1982) The demands of practical work. *Education in Chemistry*, 19(3), 71–3.

Scottish Certificate of Education (1987) Standard Grade Science, Scottish Examination Board, Edinburgh.

2.2

Research and the development of science in the primary school

Wynne Harlen

INTRODUCTION

Over the past decade the position of science in the primary school curriculum has become established in all countries across the world. A survey of UNESCO Member States in 1984 led to the conclusion that 'there would seem to be universal agreement that science should form part of the primary curriculum' (Morris, 1990, p. 39). This must be interpreted in the context of the provision of primary education in various parts, remembering that while developed countries had reached 100% enrolment in primary education by 1960, this is still not the case in many developing countries (Orpwood and Werdelin, 1987). However, the extension of primary education, where it can take place, invariably includes science and technology, often in the expectation that this will further the cause of a country's economic and social development. To a considerable extent the enthusiasm for science and technology at the primary level has been greater in developing countries than in developed ones, although it must be remembered that there is a considerable difference between national policies reflected in official surveys and what happens in the schools. Indeed, in the UK, until the national curriculum was introduced with the force of law in 1988, there were some schools where little was taught, despite official but non-statutory backing for many years (e.g., DES/WO, 1977; DES/WO, 1982).

It seems, then, that there is no longer a need to agonize over the arguments for teaching science at the primary level, as used to be the case in the early 1980s (for example, the final report of the meeting of experts on the incorporation of science and technology in the primary school curriculum, Paris 1980, in Harlen, 1983), since in principle the arguments have been accepted. However, evaluation of what is happening in schools and of what children are learning as a result would almost certainly reveal, in all countries, a considerable shortfall in providing what is needed to meet the goals which are claimed. Where such evaluation has taken place, very similar types of problem have been identified across different countries. The fact that these problems still exist cannot be

From: *International Journal of Science Education* (1992) Vol. 14, no. 5, pp. 491–503.

blamed entirely on the lack of research into primary science, since they are clearly bound up in the issues which surround the whole of primary education – teachers' own level of education, resources, class size, and so on – but the low level of research attention to science in the primary school, compared with that for post-primary phases, has left decisions about policy and practice to a large extent uninformed about the consequences of different actions.

Some of these problems, and what research where it exists can tell about them, will be considered in the four main sections of this paper dealing with the goals of primary science, the achievement of these goals, what research into children's learning has to offer and implications for practice and for research.

GOALS AND EXPECTATIONS OF TEACHING SCIENCE

In their review of goals for primary science, Orpwood and Werdelin (1987) found a number of key themes. The main groups of goals were the usual ones of knowledge and understanding, skills and attitudes. For each of these, however, there were statements of two different kinds: those relating to *knowing about* science as an enterprise and those relating to *participation in* science during learning. So, for example, the goals included knowledge and understanding of scientific method and of the role of science in society as well as knowledge and understanding of the immediate environment and of basic scientific ideas. Skills included those of using science in the context of 'life problems' (energy, food supply, living and growing up) and the development of scientific skills of investigation and manual skills. Scientific attitudes such as curiosity, respect for evidence and 'search for truth' were less frequently mentioned than attitudes *towards* science and sometimes towards work more generally. Some sweeping expectations were expressed:

> . . . develop the pupil's way of thinking towards a more scientific attitude from an earlier stage in order to be able to solve their social, parental, and everyday life problems by putting possible solutions to face such difficulties . . . a scientific point of view which aims at preparing the new generation to be more responsible, have a better way of thinking scientifically to be able to face difficulties in the future.
>
> (quoted by Orpwood and Werdelin, 1987, p. 84)

Whilst recognizing that goals may well be stated for political as much as for educational purposes, there are dangers in such wide-ranging statements which will never be approached in practice. Primary science is doomed to failure if it is judged by such expectations. Indeed it is possible to see, in those countries which were in the early wave of primary science development, a disillusionment about the changes actually brought about.

Running across these various goal statements are different views of the purpose of science at the primary level. These varying purposes seem to include:

- to teach children about science;
- to teach children science;

- to teach children skills and attitudes applicable to all parts of life;
- to teach children the established science knowledge (the 'truth');
- to start teaching secondary science at an earlier stage;

and running across these, in turn, are different views of the process of learning and of the nature of science.

As understanding of the process of learning has moved away from the notion of behaviourism, in which learning is seen as basically the appropriate response to a stimulus, towards the notion of learners taking a mentally active and creative part in constructing their own understanding, so the view of education has changed from one of presenting information suitably ordered and packaged to one of providing opportunities for the gradual change and development of ideas and skills. The move from learning by rote to learning with understanding has significance for the goals of science education, particularly with regard to the process–content debate.

Ideas which are learned with understanding are identified as those which make sense to the learner in terms of the evidence available, previous experience and his/her ways of reasoning about it. We seek to understand new experience initially by using ideas drawn from past experience. The already existing ideas are tentatively linked to new experience by some similarity, the observation of some feature through any of the senses, possibly by a word which recalls something similar. The tentatively linked idea is then rested, by gathering further information in a more focused way in order to test a prediction based on it (Harlen, 1992). Inevitably, young children have limited experience on which to draw and their naive ideas reflect this (see later). What makes sense to them in terms of their experience will not necessarily match up to the accepted scientific view of the same phenomenon. Subsequent extension of experience will lead to further modification and to ideas which have wider application.

If using ideas and modifying them as experience grows there is an important role for the process skills – observing, hypothesizing, predicting, investigating, interpreting, drawing conclusions. These skills are used in linking existing ideas to new experience, forming hypotheses, and testing predictions against new evidence. But if they are not carried out in a rigorous and scientific manner, then the emerging ideas will not necessarily fit the evidence. Ideas may be accepted which ought to have been rejected, and vice versa. Thus the development of ideas depends crucially on the processes used.

The extent to which process skills develop has been argued by science educators. It is very difficult to determine this matter by research because of the interaction between processes and content on which they are used. This becomes an obvious point if we think of a nine-year-old, say, successfully investigating the relationship between how a paper aeroplane flies and the shape of its wings, while failing to investigate the relationship between the concentration of a solution and its osmotic pressure. Interest plays a similar part in the performance of older pupils (Gott and Mashiter, 1990). The point at issue is whether the skills a child can use actually change or whether the child becomes able, and willing, to deploy them in relation to more complex content. Evidence from the Assessment of Performance Unit (APU) surveys (DES/WO/DENI, 1981, 1988) and work reported by Russell and Harlen (1990) suggests that, at the primary level at least, there are differences among children when dealing with content within their grasp which suggest a hierarchy of development. Young children often observe superficially, looking for confirmation of their ideas rather than being more open-minded in using all the evidence available; we know that their first attempts at prediction are really based on what they already know to be the case rather than being true predictions; the tests they carry out are often far from being 'fair' or controlled; they rarely check or repeat observations or measurements.

The argument that concept development depends on process skills provides an important rationale for emphasizing the development of these skills without appealing to any supposed value in their own right or claim of promoting logical thinking as a general mental ability. Process skills need to be developed because of their value in creating understanding of concepts. Acceptance of the interdependence of process skills and concepts has muted the dispute about whether processes or content should be emphasized. More subtly it has shifted emphasis from *knowing about* process skills to *participation in* using them in developing understanding. This has brought the notion of learning science closer to that of doing science. A parallel movement in the view of the nature of science has brought these even closer.

Influential writers in the philosophy of science (e.g. Kuhn, 1962; Popper, 1959; Toulmin, 1972; Hawking, 1988) have rejected the view of science as 'established truths' which are 'proved' by experiment and have replaced it with a view of science as the construction of explanatory models that encompass wider and wider ranges of phenomena. Thus scientific knowledge is seen as the construction of human minds rather than a set of truths to be discovered (e.g., Conant, 1947); always subject to change, although the mechanism for this has been contested by Kuhn and Popper; and provisional, a feature elegantly expressed by Stephen Hawking, as follows:

> Any physical theory is always provisional in the sense that it is only a hypothesis; you can never prove it. No matter how many times the results of an experiment agree with some theory, you can never be sure that the next time the result will not contradict the theory. On the other hand, you can disprove a theory by finding even a single observation that disagreed with the prediction of the theory.
>
> (Hawking, 1988, p. 10)

Science seen in this way is not all that different from the learning of science seen as the construction by pupils of ideas about the world around and tested against their own experience. Thus these two advances are regarded as connected and as leading towards 'a new science of learning with great import for the learning of science' (Novak, 1988).

ACHIEVEMENT OF GOALS

Surveys at both national and international levels have provided measures of performance in science since the later years of the 1960s. The first survey by the International Association for the Evaluation of Educational Achievement (IEA) surveyed six subject areas at three ages (10, 14 and 17 years) in 19 countries between 1966 and 1972 (Comber and Keeves, 1973). The instruments used were almost entirely multiple-choice items, thus providing little opportunity for pupils' own ideas to be expressed either in the knowledge or science method items. There were many criticisms of the survey items and the accuracy of the background information collected and, not least, the long delay in publishing results. Thus, when the first International Assessment of Educational Progress (IAEP) was carried out in 1988, one of its aims was to publish results rapidly. Although only six countries participated, the results, published in 1989 (LaPointe *et al.*), were promising enough to lead to a second IAEP project in which 20 countries participated in 1991 (Lapointe *et al.*, 1992). This most recent survey, of pupils at ages nine and 13, included some practical tasks for the older age group as well as multiple-choice written items relating, in equal number, to skills and content.

Not surprisingly, because countries had to finance their own surveys, no countries with still developing educational systems have participated in these surveys. Few firm trends emerged from the international comparisons among those countries which did take part; the greatest benefit is probably for each individual country in contemplating its place compared with others on different performance measures. The association of certain home background and school factors with performance varied from country to country, although in the majority, at age 13, time spent on homework and the number of books in the home were positively correlated with performance while time spent watching TV was negatively related. There was no apparent relationship between average national performance and time spent on science; clearly what the time is spent on is more important than small variations in it. At age 13 the participation of pupils in experiments was negatively related to performance for most countries, as it was at age nine for half of the countries. This might be explained partly by low variation within those countries reporting very low participation of pupils in experiments, but it also raises questions (if the validity of the measures is accepted) about how well the time spent on experiments is being used, particularly at age 13 (see Hodson, 1991). At the same time the high proportion of pupils, in all countries except England and Taiwan, who were reported as never doing practical work at the age of nine casts doubt on the extent to which 'hands-on' science is really as widely embraced as policy statements would suggest.

International surveys use multiple-choice items for convenience and reliability in marking. Many items of this type are of questionable validity in relation to the skills and understanding they purport to measure. In the APU surveys carried out in England, Wales and Northern Ireland annually from

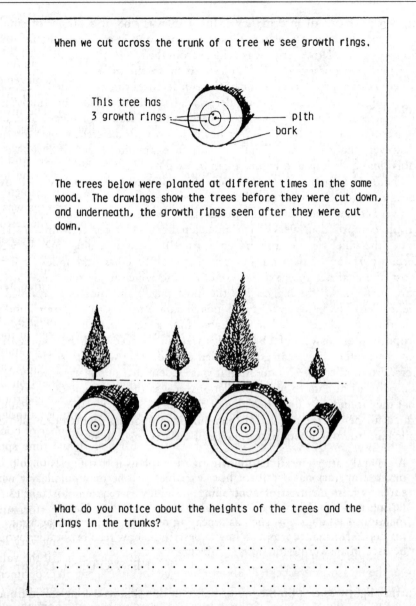

When we cut across the trunk of a tree we see growth rings.

This tree has
3 growth rings ----------- pith
                          bark

The trees below were planted at different times in the same
wood. The drawings show the trees before they were cut down,
and underneath, the growth rings seen after they were cut
down.

What do you notice about the heights of the trees and the
rings in the trunks?

. . . .
. . . .
. . . .

Figure I   Question used to assess 'interpretation of data'

1980 to 1984 much greater regard was paid to the validity of the measures.
Open response and practical items were included where required by the nature
of the outcome being assessed and a matrix sampling model enabled a large
number of items to be used for each category of skill. For example, Figure 1
(DES, 1983) shows a question used to assess 'interpretation of data', where all
the information required about tree rings is presented, thus removing the

burden on recall of information. This item was one of a family of similar questions about situations where patterns exist and in each case the information was given. However, it was evident from the results that pupils responded differently to questions which appear to make the same skills demand but concern different subjects. Some of these differences can be avoided, by choosing subjects which have no gender, social or cultural bias, but individual differences remain. The influence of these on the overall results was minimized by averaging over a large number of questions with different subject-matter. However, there was considerable value in examining types of response to individual questions and Figure 1 can be used to illustrate this.

The open response form of the question allowed pupils to give their own ideas without being influenced by suggested alternatives, and different kinds of answers could be identified and categorized. In the case of Figure 1, the main groups comprised answers which stated a pattern which correctly linked all the data ('the taller the tree the more the rings'), those providing links between certain parts of the data but not bringing it all together ('the tallest tree has most, the next has the next most, etc.'), those which made reference to only part of the data ('the biggest has the most rings') and those which failed to identify any link between the two kinds of data. Answers to all pattern-finding questions could be coded in the same four general categories. The largest proportion of answers of 11-year-olds were in the second of these categories, but the profile across categories varied considerably with the subject of the item. From other types of question it was evident that pupils were well able to *use* patterns in data to make predictions; it was the statement of the pattern that they found difficult. The value of extended-answer questions can be illustrated further by the results for 'planning investigations'; which provided detailed information about performance of different aspects of this skill:

> A general pattern in all 'entire investigation' plans is that pupils have often omitted operational details of how variables will be manipulated or measured, whilst mention of controlling variables as required for fairness in testing was mentioned by a small proportion of pupils. Hardly any pupils mentioned taking steps, such as repeating readings, to increase accuracy of results. Performance was also low in describing how results obtained would be used in answering the initial problem.
>
> (DES/WO/DENI, 1988, p. 83)

Further light was cast on the performance of this skill by asking shorter questions about separate aspects of planning, with the following results:

> Performance was higher in questions where the focus was on the parts of planning which logically came earlier in developing a plan and tailed off rapidly on questions focusing on obtaining and using results. Thus the general trend in results for the 'entire investigations' was confirmed, but there were some important differences. Performance on questions about controlling variables was the highest of all types of question, suggesting that the low performance on the whole plans was less a matter of inability than of

recognising this aspect as something which should be included in the producing of a plan.

(DES/WO/DENI, 1988, p. 84.)

Results of these kinds are clearly of more use than overall test scores in showing what pupils may be able to do at different points in their schooling, and so in guiding the selection of appropriate and realistic goals.

DEVELOPING IDEAS AND SKILLS

The APU surveys, of pupils at ages 11, 13 and 15, provided a wealth of evidence to support the interest which had grown throughout the 1970s in the ideas which pupils hold about the world around and which are found to be in conflict with what they are intended to learn in science lessons. The investigation of what were at first called misconceptions (e.g., Johnstone *et al.*, 1977) and later called 'alternative frameworks' (Driver, 1985) or 'children's ideas' (Osborne and Freyberg, 1985), became a major focus of research in science education in the 1980s. At first the fascination was with the nature of the ideas found and the similarity of findings in different countries across the globe. Attention was subsequently directed at ways of teaching which would enable the development of ideas closer to the accepted scientific view.

Techniques used for investigating pupils' ideas include one-to-one interview, sometimes based on discussion of a series of drawings (Osborne and Gilbert, 1980) or a series of events (Osborne, 1980), and written questions, such as those taken from the APU surveys used by the Children's Learning in Science Project (CLISP, 1987). While this technique may be appropriate for older secondary pupils, who have a wider range of experience and are used to written examinations, it has been argued (Russell *et al.*, 1989) that for primary children it is important for there to be some interaction with real objects and events. Two problems in particular have been identified in using paper-and-pencil procedures with younger pupils: first, the problem of communication both by the pupil of what is written or drawn and by the teacher of what the pupil writes in response; second, that the pupil may not have had the experience of the 'real' thing depicted or recalled in the question and so will give an answer which does not reflect their thinking about it.

It was to minimize such problems that the Science Processes and Concepts Exploration (SPACE) project developed, in collaboration with teachers, techniques for finding out children's ideas in the context of classroom activities. The techniques found most useful include: open questioning; asking children to draw and annotate their drawings (for younger children the teacher might annotate in discussion with them); encouraging children to write about or talk about their ideas; listening to children in discussion with each other as well as with the teacher. For example, Figure 2 shows a response to being asked to draw a picture to show: 'how you think the drum makes a sound, how you think the sound gets from the drum to be heard and how you think you hear the sound' (SPACE Report: Sound, 1990).

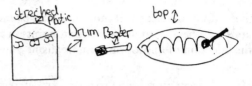

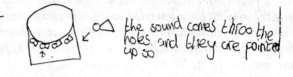

"*When you beat the drum it vibrates and the sound rolls across the drum.*"

(Age 10 years)

"*The sound comes through the holes and they are pointed up so.*"

Figure 2   Response to a question on the sound made by a drum

Figure 3 (from SPACE Report: Evaporation and Condensation, 1990) shows a response of a seven-year-old to being asked to explain what happened to water evaporating from a tank left uncovered for several days.

Discussing the growth of plants from seeds with primary children revealed that most had a notion of the process as being an unfolding of leaves and stem

(Age 7 years)

"*The sun is hot and the water is cold and the water sticks to the sun and then it goes down*"

Figure 3   Response to a question on evaporation of water from a tank

already in the seed. Few had any idea of the process of plant growth as the production of new material (SPACE Report: Growth, 1990).

Many more examples can be found in the SPACE project research reports (SPACE, 1990, 1991, 1992). The overwhelming conclusion from studying children's ideas on a wide range of scientific topics is that they are the product not of childish imagination, but of reasoning. The gap between the children's ideas and accepted scientific ones may arise because of the children's limited experience (e.g., they assume that all wood floats because they have never seen any that does not) or from immature reasoning and selective use of evidence. This underlines the importance of the notion that the goals of science education include both the extension of experience and the development of process skills.

Several strategies have been proposed for changing pupils' existing ideas into more 'scientific' views once they are revealed. An early and still popular approach is to introduce an event or phenomenon which is discrepant or conflicting with the pupils' view in the expectation that this will cause a modification in thinking. At a theoretical level, Piaget's notion of provoking disequilibrium in order to bring about accommodation of the mental framework to encompass new experience suggests that new experiences should challenge existing ideas. However, there has been much discussion of the nature of the dissonance between the pupils' ideas and those required for scientific understanding of the new experience. Too small a gap means that pupils assimilate the new experience into existing ideas (perhaps with minor modifications); too great a gap means that the new experience makes no connection with existing ideas which are left unchanged. Fensham et al. (1981) point out, also, that a situation which may bring about a change in ideas in the context of experimental research may not do so in the normal classroom context. The different ways proposed for using 'discrepant events' in the classroom include following the event with group discussions (Erickson, 1979), brainstorming and then debating ideas (Nussbaum and Novick, 1981), charting all the ideas coming from the class (Shapiro, 1988), and 'interpretive discussion' (Baird and Mitchell, 1986).

However, an important cautionary note about discrepant events is offered by Fensham and Kass (1988). They point out that, since pupils' ideas are often different from scientific ones, what may seem discrepant to the teacher may not be so to the pupil. Moreover, pupils are more tolerant of exceptions to their views than are scientists and so may not see a need to change their ideas simply because an exception has been demonstrated.

An objection raised by Solomon and Simpson (1989) on more ideological grounds is that the notion of conflict between ideas and the subsequent decision as to which one 'wins' is unsound as a basis for learning. Certainly it would not seem to aid pupils' ownership of ideas of the understanding of science as providing theories which are always open to contradiction.

It can be argued that these objections have particular force at the primary level, where it is important to take children's ideas seriously. Finding out what children's ideas are in order to 'confront' them is not the same as requiring children to use and test their ideas, as a result of which the ideas may be modified or perhaps abandoned in favour of ones which they decide are better fits for the evidence available. In response to the need to start from the ideas that children have worked out for themselves, the SPACE project developed techniques for helping children to modify their ideas which do not include presenting conflicting or discrepant events and are intended for use in all cases, whether the idea a child has is 'right' or 'wrong'. They include: enabling children to test their own ideas (essentially through using and developing process skills); encouraging generalization from one context to another; discussing the words children use to describe their ideas; extending the range of evidence available; requiring children to communicate their ideas.

IMPLICATIONS FOR PRACTICE AND FOR FUTURE RESEARCH

A number of points arise from the discussion of the meaning of a constructivist view of learning in practice which serve to underline the enduring problems bedevilling any approach to primary science teaching. Of these only three will be considered here: the role of the teacher, the knowledge the teacher requires and the impact of assessment (for others see Harlen, 1992).

There are profound implications of taking seriously the goal of enabling children to learn with understanding. The teacher's role changes from one of presenting information to one of helping children to use and develop their own ideas. The two basic elements of helping children to learn in this way have been identified as the availability of materials as evidence for testing ideas and discussion (e.g., Harlen and Jelly, 1989). Neither alone is sufficient. Science sessions which are all practical activity to the neglect of discussion and reflection ('hands-on' but not 'minds-on') are as unsatisfactory as learning experiences as lessons which are all talk and no practical activity. To strike the right balance requires careful study of experiences relating to learning goals collectively as well as individually. Research has tended to look at process and concept outcomes separately; what is now needed is a more integrated study of children's reasoning about their experiences and of the various influences on it. This may help to identify more closely the role of the materials, the impact of other pupils' ideas and of social exchanges, the media and books, and of discussion with the teacher.

Recent research (e.g., Kruger and Summers, 1989) has confirmed what was perhaps already too well known about the low level of primary teachers' background knowledge of science. At the same time, we know that a good knowledge of science is not sufficient for a teacher of primary science. Knowledge is also needed of children's learning in science and of how to manage it, of how to handle children's questions, of how to plan and provide appropriate experiences, etc. The role of subject-matter knowledge within all these other aspects of professional knowledge has not been disentangled. Many teachers who have developed confidence in their ability to start from children's ideas feel less concerned about their own scientific knowledge but for others, confidence depends on what they know even if they do not need to use it directly. After two years of compulsory science teaching in England, a large sample of primary teachers surveyed by Bennett *et al.* (1992) expressed significantly higher confidence in teaching science processes but not in teaching certain content areas.

Assessment has a number of roles to play in education. Its role in providing research information about pupils' ideas and skills has been evident in earlier sections of this paper. At this point, however, the concern is with assessment which has a direct impact on teaching.

Teaching through finding and using pupils' ideas implies the ability to assess pupils' existing ideas and skills by means of methods which are part of teaching, not added tests or tasks. This demands considerable skill: skill in planning so that evidence can be obtained about pupils at appropriate times, in collecting the evidence and subsequently in interpreting it in terms of progress towards learning goals. This is far more difficult than administering a quick test and marking it according to a prescribed scheme. Claims are made for the superiority of continuous assessment as part of teaching, but there is much to be understood about how it takes place, its validity in practice and the reliability of teachers' judgements.

Assessment of pupils for summative purposes is already known to have an impact on the curriculum (Corbett and Wilson, 1988; Madaus, 1988). In countries where there is an end-of-primary school examination or where end-of-year tests determine progress within the school, assessment tends to have a high profile and to lead the curriculum rather than follow it. Those subjects *not* assessed are likely to be neglected in all but lip-service and this accounts for some of the divergence between classroom practice and national goals of education. In these contexts the success of any attempt to improve science will be limited by existing procedures for assessment and indeed it had to be accepted, perhaps reluctantly, that the swiftest way to change teaching is to change assessment.

In all contexts, however, the development of assessment procedures and instruments must be continued in pace with curriculum developments in order to preserve the integrity of the latter. Projects such as the APU did much to show that process skills and understanding (as opposed to knowledge of facts) can be reliably assessed. However, since the demise of these projects the development of assessment is no longer taking place. Research into assessment should be keeping pace with the rise of its importance in national policies.

CONCLUSION

Primary science is a poorly researched area compared with post-primary science. This applies particularly to research in implementation at the school level and in classroom practice. Surveys of policies and performance describe the picture of provision and effects at national levels and research into pupils' ideas has shed some light on the learning of individual pupils. Between these extremes, however, at the levels of school and class planning and of teacher–pupil interaction, very little has so far been done. The areas identified in this paper – the role of the teacher in helping children to develop concepts through the use of process skills, the role of teachers' scientific knowledge, the investigation of teachers ongoing assessment and the development of more valid and reliable procedures for summative assessment – are but a small proportion of the large number of areas where there is a need for greater understanding of factors influencing children's science education. As the problem facing primary teachers in relation to science are common to all countries, international co-operation in research could be of particular value in ensuring that the problems are studied in the context of the constraints of human and material resource available in various parts of the world.

REFERENCES

Baird, J. R. and Mitchell, I. (eds.) (1986) *Improving the Quality of Teaching and Learning: an Australian Case Study.* Melbourne, Monash University.

Bennett, S. N., Wragg, E. C., Carre, C. G. and Carter, D. S. G. (1992) A longitudinal study of primary teachers' perceived competence in, and concerns about, National Curriculum implementation. *Research Papers in Education,* 7(1), 53–78.

CLISP (Children's Learning in Science Project) (1987) *Information Leaflet.* Leeds, Centre for Studies in Science and Mathematics Education, University of Leeds.

Comber, L. C. and Keeves, J. P. (1973) *Science Education in Nineteen Countries.* Stockholm, Almqvist and Wiksell.

Conant, J. (1947) *On Understanding Science.* New Haven, CT, Yale University Press.

Corbett, R. and Wilson, B. (1988) Raising the stakes in state-wide mandatory minimum competency testing. In *The Politics of Education Association Yearbook Journal of Educational Politics,* 3(5).

DES (1983) *Science at Age 11,* APU Science Report for Teachers No. 1. London, DES.

DES/WO (1977) *Education in Schools: A Consultative Document.* London, DES.

DES/WO (1982) *Science Education in Schools: A Consultative Document.* London, DES.

DES/WO/DENI (1981) *Science in Schools: Age 11,* Report No. 1. London, HMSO.

DES/WO/DENI (1988) *Science at Age 11: A Review of APU Survey Findings 1980–84.* London, HMSO.

Driver, R. (1985) *The Pupil as Scientist?* Milton Keynes, Open University Press.

Erickson, G. L. (1979) Children's conceptions of heat and temperature. *Science Education,* 63, 221–30.

Fensham, P. J., Garrard, J. and West, L. (1981) The use of cognitive mapping in teaching and learning strategies. *Research in Science Education*, 11, 121–9.

Fensham, P. J. and Kass, H. (1988) Inconsistent or discrepant events in science instruction. *Studies in Science Education*, 15, 1–16.

Gott, R. and Mashiter, J. (1990) Practical work in science – a task-based approach. In B. Woolnough (ed.), *Practical Science*. Milton Keynes, Open University Press.

Harlen, W. (ed.) (1983) *New Trends in Primary Science*, Vol. 1. Paris, UNESCO.

Harlen, W. (1992) *The Teaching of Science*. London, David Fulton.

Harlen, W. and Jelly, S. J. (1989) *Developing Science in the Primary Classroom*. Edinburgh, Oliver and Boyd.

Hawking, S. W. (1988) *A Brief History of Time*. London, Bantam Books.

Hodson, D. (1991) Practical work in science: time for a reappraisal. *Studies in Science Education*, 19, 175–84.

Johnstone, A. H., MacDonald, J. J. and Webb, G. (1977) Misconceptions in school thermodynamics. *Physics Education*, 12, 248–51.

Kruger, C. and Summers, M. (1989) An investigation of some primary teachers' understanding of change in materials. *School Science Review*, 71(225), 17–30.

Kuhn, T. S. (1962) *The Structure of Scientific Revolutions*. Chicago, University of Chicago Press.

Lapointe, A. Mead, N. and Askew, J. (1992) *Learning Science. The Second International Assessment of Educational Progress*. Educational Testing Service.

Lapointe, A., Mead, N. and Phillips, G. (1989) *A World of Differences. An International Assessment of Mathematical and Science*. Educational Testing Service.

Madaus, C. F. (1988) The influence of testing on the curriculum. In L. Tanner (ed.) *Critical Issues in Curriculum: 87th Yearbook of the National Society for the Study of Education*, Part 1. Chicago, University of Chicago Press.

Morris, R. (1990) *Science Education Worldwide*. Paris, UNESCO.

Novak, J. (1988) Learning science and the science of learning. *Studies in Science Education*, 15, 77–101.

Nussbaum, J. and Novick, S. (1981) Brainstorming in the classroom to invent a model: a case study. *School Science Review*, 62(221), 771–8.

Orpwood, G. and Werdelin, I. (1897) *Science and Technology in the Primary School of Tomorrow*. Paris, UNESCO.

Osborne, R. (1980) Some aspects of students' views of the world. *Research in Science Education*, 10, 11–18.

Osborne, R. and Freyberg, P. (1985) *Learning in Science: the Implications of Children's Science*. Auckland, Heinemann.

Osborne, R. and Gilbert, J. (1980) A technique for exploring students' views of the world. *Physics Education*, 15(6), 376–9.

Popper, K. (1959) *The Logic of Scientific Discovery*. New York, Basic Books.

Russell, T. and Harlen, W. (1990) *Assessing Science in the Primary Classroom: Practical Tasks*. London, Paul Chapman.

Russell, T. J., Harlen, W. and Watt, D. (1989) Children's ideas about evaporation. *International Journal of Science Education*, 11, 566–76.

Shapiro, B. (1988) What children bring to light: towards understanding what the primary schools science learner is trying to do. In P. J. Fensham (ed.), *Directions and Dilemmas in Science Education*. London, Falmer Press.

Soloman, J. and Simpson, M. (1989) Contributions as discussants. *Proceedings of the Conference on Adolescents' Thinking in Science*, September 1987, Falmer Press.

SPACE Research Reports: *Evaporation and Condensation*, 1990; *Growth*, 1990; *Light*, 1990; *Sound*, 1990; *Electricity*, 1991; *Materials*, 1991; *Processes of Life*, 1992. Liverpool, Liverpool University Press.

Toulmin, S. (1972) *Human Understanding*, Vol. 1: *The Collective Use and Evolution of Concepts*. Princeton, NJ, Princeton University Press.

2.3

Cognitive and conceptual change in adolescence

Marcia C. Linn and Nancy Butler Songer

Cognitive changes occur during adolescence, both because students assimilate knowledge about previously unstudied phenomena and because ideas are replaced by more predictive, abstract, or robust notions. We look at cognitive change primarily by examining changes in conceptual understanding as well as by characterizing the process of abandoning one view for another. We focus on serious intellectual tasks such as understanding evolution or interpreting Faulkner's novels.

Furthermore, we recognize the powerful influence of the social context in which learning occurs. This social context gains importance during adolescence in conjunction with the increased awareness of social relationships and social influences. Although cognitive and social factors interact to yield conceptual changes, we discuss these factors somewhat separately to make the task more manageable.

Researchers investigating cognitive change have offered theories (a) at the level of information processing (i.e., positing changes in working memory (Case, 1985)), (b) in terms of abstract reasoning strategies (i.e., positing transitions from concrete to formal reasoning (Inhelder and Piaget, 1958)), and (c) in terms of domain-specific reasoning strategies (i.e., positing development of expertise (Brown *et al.*, 1989; Chase and Simon, 1973)). As Keating and Crane (1990) argue, the dichotomy between domain-general and domain-specific reasoning strategies has proved unproductive for analysing problem solving in exactly the complex situations we consider most important for adolescents and poses unanswerable questions for developmentalists. Keating and Crane (1990) and Sternberg (1989) call for an integrated perspective. Keating and Crane advise researchers to respect the creative tension between domain-specific and domain-general views of the developmental process yet to acknowledge their joint role in cognitive change. Following this lead, we take an integrated perspective and focus on how students develop the ability to

From: *American Journal of Education* (1991) Vol. 99, no. 4, pp. 379–417.

reason about complex situations. We discuss the implications of research on conceptual change for cognitive theory after providing a synthesis of the recent findings.

In this article we provide a theoretical perspective for examining conceptual change. Then, we discuss research on conceptual and cognitive changes in adolescence. In this section, we focus primarily on a case study of students' ability to understand scientific concepts. This focus is chosen in part because of the rich array of research available on students' understanding of scientific concepts. We believe that the implications of this research extend beyond science and discuss parallels in other disciplines. Next, we discuss mechanisms of cognitive change. We then discuss research on how the social context interacts with conceptual change during adolescence. In the Conclusions section, we discuss the implications of this research for education and make suggestions concerning future research on instruction, conceptual change, and cognitive change.

THEORETICAL PERSPECTIVE

We take a constructivist perspective on cognitive change consistent with the theoretical perspectives of Piaget (Inhelder and Piaget, 1958) and Vygotsky (1962) and focus on conceptual changes in complex domains. This perspective is also consonant with a vast array of research on student understanding of complex phenomena (e.g., Eylon and Linn, 1988; Glaser, 1984).

This perspective draws special attention to the ideas that students bring to the learning situation, their initial understandings, and the mechanisms that determine the pace of the constructive process. Eylon and Linn (1988) recently reviewed the four main research perspectives in science education by analysing how investigators view initial understanding and how they describe the mechanism governing cognitive change. Although virtually all researchers document the process of cognitive change, there is considerable disagreement concerning the mechanisms guiding this process and the levels of description (e.g., information processing vs. conceptual understanding) appropriate to the task.

In offering a perspective on conceptual change in adolescence, we are guided by Piaget's description of the process of reflective abstraction, in which he argues that adolescents combine information available to them by reflecting on commonalities and inconsistencies, as well as by Piaget's assertion that adolescents develop the ability to represent their knowledge in formal systems. In addition, we are informed by the work of Vygotsky, who places emphasis both on the initial understandings that students have and on the interaction between those understandings and the learning environment. Vygotsky (1962) describes what he calls the 'zone of proximal development', which is the range of possible cognitive changes that might result for students with a given set of initial understandings and a particular learning environment. By focusing on this zone of proximal development, we suggest that the learning environment, and indeed the nature of instruction, can foster or inhibit the speed of conceptual change.

Conceptual changes

During adolescence, students gain understanding of a staggering array of topics. They attest to the Piagetian view that they are capable of formal reasoning by learning about formal systems such as Euclidian geometry and calculus and dealing with complex, interwoven, and incomplete bodies of knowledge in history, literature, and science. They grapple with fields that are in formation and have the opportunity to recognize the distinctions between what is known, what is being understood, and what is not yet understood. As they develop, learners gain knowledge and have the opportunity to construct understanding. We discuss the course of knowledge acquisition as well as the process of knowledge integration.

Knowledge acquisition

We assert that the process of knowledge acquisition begins with action and observation. We refer to the initial, unreflective responses that students make to events that they encounter in their lives as 'action knowledge' starting with simple reflexes. Students develop action knowledge from experience. They say, for example, 'Bigger things are heavier' or 'Boys hate girls.'

We argue that students combine action knowledge by autonomously using the process of reflective abstraction, or as a result of specific experiences, into what we call 'intuitive conceptions'. These conceptions are the conjectures students make to explain events they have observed or experienced in the world. Students conjecture, for example, that 'objects move in the direction they are pushed' or that 'objects slow down' because these intuitive ideas are consistent with their observations. To achieve these ideas, students need to put together a series of observations. Sometimes this process of combining observations into intuitive conceptions is supported by instruction featuring multiple representations of the same idea. By presenting an idea in a visual format, a verbal format, and a dynamic format, instructors may support the process of abstraction and encourage students to integrate ideas. For example, Songer (1989) demonstrated that students gain better understanding of insulation when they have a concrete integration aid in the form of a continuum line, as well as representations gained from experiments and from verbal formulations.

We hypothesize that effective instruction can help students organize their intuitive conceptions into 'principles' consistent with those held by experts. For science, we define principles as abstract general rules about the operation of the scientific world that subsume a large number of related events and can be applied broadly. Examples include 'energy is conserved' or 'objects in motion tend to remain in motion'. These principles are often difficult to infer from direct observation but can result from effective instruction. In the Research section, we will discuss some of the features of this effective instruction.

Thus, during adolescence, students develop intuitive conceptions and scientific principles. How does this development proceed? Researchers differ in their perspective on the qualitative and quantitative changes in students' understanding. Some believe that students undergo 'revolutions' in their thinking as they develop more sophisticated intuitive conceptions and scientific principles (Carey, 1985; Wiser and Carey, 1983). Others suggest that learning is more 'evolutionary' – that students select promising ideas and neglect ideas that lack predictive power, but that few notions are directly supplanted by new contradictory viewpoints (see, e.g., Keating and Crane, 1990; Linn, 1986). Similarly, researchers differ in their views on whether these developmental accomplishments reflect gains in domain-general or domain-specific reasoning (see, e.g., Linn *et al.*, 1983). Those focused on domain-general strategy acquisition also expect qualitative changes in reasoning. In this article we are primarily concerned with describing the course of cognitive development in complex domains. We briefly examine whether these changes are revolutionary or evolutionary, domain specific or domain general.

At the same time that students develop intuitions and principles about specific scientific, mathematical, and other phenomena, they also develop views about the nature of knowledge itself. For example, in mathematics and science, some students come to expect the information that they encounter to 'make sense' while others seem to abandon the notion of sense making and instead rely on a process of memorization (Schoenfeld, 1985). What is clear is that students take a view on how knowledge progresses, and, as will be discussed in the Research section, this view of the nature of knowledge influences the development of understanding.

Knowledge differentiation and integration

During adolescence, more than previously, students differentiate their knowledge into ideas they view as relevant to each other and ideas they view as uninfluenced by each other. This differentiation can be into domains such as mathematics or science, concepts such as motion or temperature change, or sets of actions such as the motion of objects on inclined planes and the motion of cars. In many cases, as these examples suggest, students select boundaries between knowledge domains that are too narrow and as a result lead to the development of isolated ideas. Ideally, students' understanding should move toward more integrated views of knowledge and involve a process of seeking relevant information in seemingly diverse domains.

This overspecialization by students is reinforced by instruction that provides fleeting coverage of a massive number of topics (see, e.g., Linn, 1987). When information is presented but not fully understood, it is easier to view it in isolation than to try to integrate it into already-existing conceptual structures. For example, it is easier to assume in science class that objects in motion tend to remain in motion while, on the soccer field, objects in motion tend to come to rest than to try to find some kind of integration of those two incompatible views.

When instruction encourages students to develop isolated ideas rather than integrate relevant information, it reinforces a view of the nature of knowledge as idiosyncratic and even perverse. Students bombarded with information about science, or mathematics, or history, or English, may be forced to abandon the goal of understanding this information and instead adopt a policy of memorization. Once that decision has been made, students are reinforced in the view that knowledge is isolated and incommensurate.

This perspective on knowledge and on learning through memorization may result from information overload rather than from a natural propensity to avoid knowledge integration. If there is insufficient time for reflection, students will be pressed to form superficial constructions that are likely to be fragile and easily forgotten. In fact, it may well be that students engage in greater knowledge integration when learning on their own than for topics that are taught in school.

Thus, students may develop boundaries between knowledge topics based not so much on the affinity of these phenomena as on the conditions under which learning takes place. If in school they encounter far too much information and spend short periods of time on each topic, they may identify school learning as different from out-of-school learning. Clearly, this is undesirable and deserves serious attention in our efforts to improve education.

An important factor in the development of domain boundaries by students concerns the cognitive goals selected for instruction. If instruction focuses on cognitive goals that cannot readily be achieved using the constructive process, students may abandon the constructive process and simply try to memorize some information about that topic. For example, when instruction in mechanics begins by describing frictionless universes, students, whose total prior experience has been in a friction-filled environment, often cannot see the relevance between their experience and the goal of instruction. To rectify this problem, they may simply declare these to be two different topics rather than trying to integrate them. Minstrell (1982), Clement *et al.* (1989), and others suggest the importance of benchmarks, anchoring, bridging, and other processes to fill in the gaps between the students' views and an idea more closely aligned with the views of scientists. We argue that another approach is also worthy of consideration: namely, that of choosing goals that are more compatible with student needs and closer to the knowledge students bring to science courses. This point will be illustrated in the case study section.

In summary, we take a constructivist perspective on knowledge development and conceptual change in adolescence. We identify action knowledge, intuitive conceptions, and principles as characterizing the progression of knowledge construction during adolescence. Furthermore, we point out that students construct idiosyncratic topic boundaries and are unlikely to integrate understanding across those boundaries; thus, the constructive process involves both developing understanding of events and phenomena and then integrating that information. We note that this process applies not only to topics such as history, mathematics, and science but also to the students' view of knowledge itself. In the next section we look at how students' constructions of their social context influence conceptual change.

Social context

During adolescence, the social context of learning plays a larger and larger role in cognitive change (Dewey, 1920; Vygotsky, 1978). In adolescence, status differences among individuals become more pronounced and have a broader impact on educational attainment (Eckert, 1990). In addition, societal norms become more predominant, and these create a different social context for students from different population groups (Coleman, 1961).

During adolescence, students elaborate and extend their views of themselves as learners. They understand something about their own style of learning, which disciplines are more interesting to them, and which disciplines are more appropriate to their population group (see, e.g., Gilligan, 1982). Students develop a view of themselves as succeeding or failing in a particular discipline or under particular learning conditions. For instance, some believe they could succeed on a timed test but fail when creating an integrated perspective in a term paper.

In adolescence, males and females start to construct quite different views of themselves as learners. Males see maths and science as male domains (Hyde *et al.*, 1990). Females do not agree with males concerning the nature of maths and science, but they do report feeling unwelcome in domains that have been constructed by males and are perceived by males as having more of a male orientation. Interests are differentiated along sex lines during adolescence as well (Eccles, 1985).

In addition, during adolescence, students' views of themselves as learners interact with their beliefs about the nature of science. If they view themselves as participants in the scientific or mathematical process, they are also more likely to believe that science and mathematics are disciplines that are continuously being improved and that social processes influence the progress of science.

The social context of learning during adolescence also influences conceptual change through the choices that students make for course enrolment and interest. During adolescence, many students choose to avoid science. Students make choices about enrolment in advanced mathematics, science, history, and English courses. The students who do not enrol in these courses are less likely to master the information in the discipline.

Many factors contribute to course selection and persistence in mathematics and science and other domains, but the social context of this decision-making process is a primary factor (see, e.g., Linn, in press). Families, teachers, and counsellors offer opinions that are likely to influence adolescents. Peers and peer-group norms are extremely important in these decisions (Coleman, 1961; Eckert, 1990). Subtle influences, such as the well-documented phenomenon that teachers are more likely to call on male students than on female students, probably contribute to decision making at this point (Brophy and Good, 1986, 1974).

In summary, the social context of learning influences both the decisions students make about the material that they have an opportunity to learn and their views of themselves as learners. This social environment interacts with the cognitive activities of adolescents.

RESEARCH ON COGNITIVE CHANGE: A CASE STUDY

In this section, we elaborate our view of cognitive change and provide evidence to support our perspective on the constructive process primarily from a case study of the 'Computer as Lab Partner' project. We focus on the nature of action knowledge, intuitive conceptions, and scientific principles. We draw on this research and that of others to characterize and illustrate with examples what we mean by action knowledge, intuitive conceptions, and scientific principles. We rely on experimental and longitudinal studies of changes in students' understanding of elementary physical science concepts to discuss both cognitive and conceptual change.

We have designed the Computer-as-Lab-Partner (CLP) curriculum to help middle school students integrate knowledge in elementary thermodynamics (Linn and Songer, in press; Linn *et al.*, in press). The CLP curriculum emphasizes experiment-based instruction that utilizes powerful computer software and features both interactive real-time experiments and simulated investigations of naturally occurring problems. Students are asked to make predictions before experimentation, choose experimental parameters, run experiments, summarize their findings, and generalize and extend their results. Students integrate their ideas by constructing scientific principles common to many experiments and applying each experiment to a familiar natural-world instance of the same principle, or prototypic situation. The curriculum requires 12–14 weeks to communicate integrated and relevant understandings of elementary thermodynamics. We have substantially altered the cognitive demands of this curriculum as a result of our research on cognitive change. The first version of the curriculum resulted in 30 per cent of the students gaining understanding of heat energy and temperature. The current version imparts this level of understanding to close to 70 per cent of the students. Thus, we feel this project is an excellent case study for illustrating both conceptual change and interventions that foster conceptual change.

We draw on our investigations of this curriculum to characterize how students develop action knowledge, intuitive conceptions, principles, and beliefs about the nature of science. We discuss our interventions and how they influence conceptual change.

Action knowledge

The development of adolescents' scientific knowledge begins as a result of experience with the world around them. Knowledge of experience is represented first as initial unreflective actions or responses to situations in the world.

These actions are constructed in isolation often by imitating the actions of others (Baldwin, 1894; Piaget, 1952).

Action knowledge tends to summarize actual experiences, not more general consequences. We have identified examples of action knowledge in students' initial predictions about a natural-world experiment concerning heat energy and temperature concepts. Students are asked to make predictions and answer the question, 'Which material would be best to wrap a hot potato if you want to keep it hot? The potato has been in a 200°C oven for an hour.' The students choose from four options of insulating materials and respond as follows:

> Student (S): Our predictions are that for the aluminium one, the temperature would decrease a little and stay the same. The wool one would cool a little faster and decrease in temperature to room temperature. The reason we predict this is aluminium doesn't let the heat escape as quickly as the wool napkin does. The heat escapes through the fabric of the wool because it is not as solid (dense) as aluminium foil.

Another example comes from a pretest question that asked students to distinguish the concepts heat energy and temperature.

> S: The coffee was so hot, it burned my tongue.

This student reports a natural-world action associated with temperature but makes no attempt to relate the action to the distinction between the concepts as asked in the question.

The presence of action knowledge and its discontinuity with much of the material presented in science classes also influences the beliefs students develop about science learning and the nature of science. In initial interviews with students, several mention that the material they are learning in their eighth-grade science class is 'new' material – in other words, has no connection to any other material they have encountered, either in a previous science class or outside of class.

> Interviewer (I): Why do you think it [science] is so confusing?
> S: I think because it is like that stuff that we haven't learned before, and it is just . . . I just memorize the stuff and I just never really understood [sic] it. And so that is probably why.

When students view each subject as 'new', they are unlikely to seek similarities with prior experiences. This leads to confusion and a lack of general principles governing several situations. Thus, the earliest conceptions held by students are unreflective descriptions of the actions they observe or perform. These ideas are next combined to form more general 'intuitive conceptions'.

Intuitive conceptions

We hypothesize that students intentionally organize their action knowledge to make sense of the world. We call these constructions 'intuitive conceptions' because they are firmly grounded in observation and personal experience and they are consciously formed. Intuitive conceptions combine action knowledge and observations into larger, more general views of the world than those described by action knowledge alone. Students consciously identify ideas that apply to several actions and related observations and subsume these into their own intuitive conceptions. These intuitive conceptions allow students to make predictions about related scientific events. Often, these intuitions imply some explanation or mechanism, but, at other times, they are solely descriptive.

Examples of intuitive conceptions

Researchers have described many intuitive ideas in life science (Brown *et al.*, in press; Carey, 1985), mechanics (Champagne *et al.*, 1982; Clement, 1982; di Sessa, 1982), heat and temperature (Linn and Songer, in press; Tiberghien, 1980; Wiser and Carey, 1983), and electricity (Gentner and Stevens, 1983). Researchers characterize these intuitive ideas as derived largely through natural-world experiences. They show how these ideas are used for prediction making despite their inability to provide compelling explanations for outcomes. For example, di Sessa (1987) calls students' fragmented, experience-based knowledge in physics 'phenomenological primitives', or 'p-prims'. An example of a p-prim is 'dying away'. This refers to the dying-away or fading sound (amplitude) after a bell is struck. Like intuitive conceptions, p-prims are generalized conceptions with little or no explanation or mechanism. They are based on a collection of experiences and are therefore compelling because of their frequency of occurrence in everyday situations.

The construction of intuitive conceptions

We hypothesize that students actively organize their experiences to reduce the complexity of their world. The constructive process is mediated by language (Bruner, 1977; Piaget, 1926; Vygotsky, 1962) and is driven by the desire to develop conceptions that are consistent across several instances and contain predictive power for new cases. The process involves identifying consistencies in experiences and observations and conferring status on a set of observations and action knowledge that appears consistent.

For example, students may generate an intuitive conception that says it is necessary to have a source of heat in order to maintain a particular temperature. They reach this conception by combining actions such as turning on the stove to warm water in a pot or turning up the furnace to warm a room. This intuitive conception is arrived at consciously and is therefore more accessible to analysis and reflection than are actions. It is also more general than action knowledge. Intuitive conceptions may or may not be consistent with scientists' conceptions of the same phenomena.

Interventions to encourage the development of intuitive conceptions

Classroom activities can foster the development of intuitions by encouraging students to combine observations. For example, in the CLP curriculum, one

successful intervention requires students to make predictions about the outcomes of experiments they have designed by drawing on results of previous
investigations and on observations (Friedler *et al.*, 1990; Linn and Songer, in
press). Students work in groups of three or four led by a 'prediction coordina-
tor'. This format encourages students to combine information. For example,
before experimentation, we ask the groups of four students to make predictions concerning equal volumes of hot water cooling in a Styrofoam cup and a
paper cup. One group predicts,

> S: At the end of fifteen minutes, we believe the difference in temperature will
> be approximately 10°C. The reason we predict this is . . . that Styrofoam
> has a porous surface and thus traps heated molecules and retains heat for
> a longer period of time. Paper works well also, but from our previous
> experience, Styrofoam has proved to be a superior insulator, although we
> have never compared the two directly.

A second group of students states,

> S: Our predictions are that . . . the cup with 80° of water will cool faster
> than one with only 50° water. The reason we predict this is . . . because
> the cup with 50° of water is closer to room temperature. Nothing can get
> cooler than room temperature and in past experiments we have witnessed
> that as the water gets closer to room temperature the rate at which it
> cools is slower.

Individual interviews illustrate students grappling with the problem of constructing an explanation. Here we see firsthand how action knowledge and
observations are combined to form intuitions. This student is asked to make
predictions about equal volumes of hot water cooling to room temperature in
identically sized glass or Styrofoam containers.

> I: Which one stays hot longer?
> S: I think the Styrofoam, but I don't remember why.
> I: Any reason why?
> S: Because of the material and because glass, I don't know what the dif-
> ference is between glass and Styrofoam . . . I guess because Styrofoam is
> thick so that heat energy can't pass through the Styrofoam as quickly.
> Well, it can't pass through the glass either except through the lid. I know
> that Styrofoam is probably better because . . . I don't know. Because of
> experience.
> I: Have you had other experiences that convinced you that that is the right
> answer?
> S: I don't know. Well, I think that if you want to keep warm you wouldn't
> put glass around it.
> I: Why doesn't that seem right?
> S: I am not really sure but just Styrofoam seems to always work but I don't
> know why.

One necessary step to the construction of powerful and generative conceptions is that the scientifically correct ideas be shown to be predictive of new

natural-world situations. If textbook ideas appear to hold less predictive power for natural-world situations than students' experience-based intuitions, students will often stick to intuitive conceptions that are descriptively accurate but flawed from the standpoint of scientists (see, e.g., Eylon and Linn, 1988). Students even contort new evidence to defend the ideas that they have developed (see, e.g., Linn and Pulos, 1983). For example, consider this interview with a student in the CLP curriculum,

I: You had two things that you wrap Coke in.
S: I remembered that aluminium foil is a good conductor but see . . . we used aluminium foil and wool and it turned out on the graph . . . we predicted that aluminium foil was going to be the better conductor but they are almost similar.
I: Why do you think that aluminium foil is going to be better?
S: Because what it is made of or something. For the Coke can you already have the aluminium surrounding so the aluminium just keeps the cold inside.
I: Is that what you got?
S: Yes, aluminium was better but not by far.
I: Better than wool?
S: Yes.

This was not the result shown on the graph generated by these students. However, the student wished to make their experimental results compatible with their intuitions, so the recollection of the experiment was altered to be consistent with intuitive ideas. Instruction must capitalize on the sense of worth that students acquire from making predictive conjectures while at the same time encouraging students to develop their own rules of evidence and to be appropriately sceptical of new scientific ideas. As discussed below, our interventions have been improved to help students build more predictive beliefs.

Language confusion

Carey (1985) and others confirm that the construction of intuitive conceptions is a process that is made difficult by confusion over language and its application to situations in natural-world or scientific contexts. Often terms such as 'heat' and 'temperature' can hold meanings in natural-world contexts that are quite different from their scientific definitions. This confusion leads students to conclude that heat and temperature are either alternative names for the same phenomenon or measures along the same scale, with temperature being the whole scale and heat referring to only the higher temperatures. Students express heat energy and temperature as along the same scale when they mention,

S: Heat energy is what makes the temperature of an object. If an object is cold, there is not heat energy, but the cold object still has a temperature.

In addition to differences between natural-world and scientific uses of the same terms, single terms can hold different meanings in different natural-world contexts. The term 'temperature' is used in many confusing contexts; for example, we say, 'The baby has a temperature', referring to a body temperature above 98.6°F, or we say, 'The temperature, with the windchill, is 35° below zero', referring to how the weather will affect a human. How does that compare to the temperature measured by a thermometer placed outdoors? These complicated and disjointed uses of the term 'temperature' contribute to students' confusion when trying to construct meaning for a scientific term.

In our interviews, students frequently show evidence of confusion over scientific term usage as they struggle to reach greater understanding of scientific concepts. In trying to find evidence for experimental results, the student in the following example latches onto 'convection' but is not really sure what the term means.

> I: Talk about your predictions and results.
> S: We predicted that the larger bowl will cool quicker than the smaller bowl because the smaller bowl uses less convection than the larger bowl.
> I: What is convection?
> S: The heat that goes into. More heat goes out of the larger bowl than the smaller bowl.

Another student confuses properties of heat exchange with temperature and states,

> S: Foil keeps baked potatoes hot when you barbecue and a soda cold when refrigerated because the foil attracts the temperature and locks it in.

This last example involves both an intuitive idea and a confused use of language.

Other aspects of thermodynamics also pose both language and conceptual difficulties. For example, thermal conductivity is poorly captured in language. Students from the CLP curriculum say,

> S: If you put a Coke can in a freezer and a wooden spoon in a freezer, the Coke can would be a lot more colder than the wooden spoon would be.

In this case the students are probably confusing how an object feels with what temperature it is. So they confound the rate of heat transfer from metals and woods when they are touched with their temperature. Objects that 'feel' like they have different temperatures could register the same temperature on a thermometer if they were in the same room. Here, lack of a clear meaning for a term plus an unpredictive intuitive idea creates real confusion. This sort of language confusion makes classroom discourse about scientific concepts very imprecise. As a result, our interventions have focused on helping students develop agreed-upon 'principles' to explain observed events (Linn *et al.*, in press). Even with this assistance, however, it is important to help students recognize when their efforts to understand are successful.

Misconceptions versus intuitive conceptions

Often, scientists' conceptions differ from students' conceptions because students base their conceptions on personal observation and experience rather than on a broader range of investigations. The process of unguided discovery that governs much of the formation of intuitive conceptions means that many students (and adults as well) develop ideas that are viewed by scientists as flawed. Often, scientists label these intuitive conceptions 'misconceptions'. We note instead the similarities in the constructive process and the difficulty of completely overcoming intuitions.

Our interventions emphasize the positive nature of the developmental accomplishments of students. The process of constructing these ideas often parallels that of scientists constructing knowledge. Intuitive conceptions form the basis of much of adult scientific thought (see, e.g., Burbules and Linn, in press). Even if these conceptions are not consistent with ideas held by scientists, they are 'intuitive conceptions' rather than 'misconceptions'.

Thus, our interventions focus on the productive ideas held by students, rather than attempting to eradicate unpredictive ideas. Even scientists often revert to unpredictive intuitions rather than applying more abstract principles when solving problems in familiar situations. For example, Lewis and Linn (1989) found that even those with Ph.D.'s in chemistry sometimes use observational data to predict the best material for wrapping a drink in order to keep it cold. Since intuitive ideas persist even after training for the Ph.D., clearly, massive amounts of instruction do not completely counteract these ideas. Often, the productive ideas of students differ substantially from those of scientists. An important part of any intervention is to determine the goals for students. We have addressed this issue in some depth.

Scientific principles

Scientific principles are primarily acquired as a result of schooling because they depend on integrating such a broad range of information and because they are often based on hidden mechanisms. These principles took scientists centuries to develop and are often inaccessible to unguided discovery. An important consideration in designing science curricula is to carefully identify the goals for students in terms of principled understanding of scientific concepts. Instructors need to pick scientific principles that students can use to make predictions about their own experiences, and that they can integrate with their other ideas using the construction process.

Most science textbooks rely on microscopic mechanisms such as molecular kinetic theory to explain scientific phenomenon; for example, the following passage appears in an eighth-grade science textbook:

> The temperature of a substance is a measure of the average kinetic energy of the atoms or molecules that make up that substance. Temperature is measured in degrees Celsius. As the atoms or molecules of a substance move faster, the temperature of the substance increases. Similarly, when the atoms or molecules of a substance slow down, the temperature decreases. . . . On a hot day (30°C) the average speed of the molecules in air is about 440 m/s.

On a very cold day (–20°C) the molecules average about 400 m/s. At a low enough temperature (–273°C), the average speed would be almost 0 m/s. There would be only slight vibrational motion. Since –273°C is the lowest possible temperature, it is called absolute zero. Scientists have been able to create temperatures close to absolute zero.

(Nolan and Tucker, 1984, p. 256)

Scientists generally defend this choice by saying that students should learn the principles of scientists. They also point out that the microscopic models are often more elegant and richer in detail than macroscopic models. In contrast, we have found that macroscopic models are more accessible to students. Furthermore, Lewis and Linn (1989) report that scientists often use macroscopic rather than microscopic models to explain natural-world events concerning thermodynamics, especially when the macroscopic models map sensibly onto their experiences and observations.

An unanticipated consequence of many science curricula, then, is that they discourage knowledge construction because there is too large a gap between intuitions and the scientific principles in the textbook. Students need help in selecting their most productive ideas. If inaccessible principles are presented, students may abandon construction and turn to memorization. Effective science courses guide students to construct principles. Appropriate guidance is crucial to the production of successful scientists and requires intervention that is cognizant of the nature of knowledge construction among adolescents. Our investigations of students' views of schooling suggest that current instruction falls miserably short of this goal.

What scientific principles should students acquire? Scientific principles can provide abstract explanations or mechanisms for scientific events at a variety of levels. In thermodynamics, the eighth-grade textbook features molecular kinetic theory. A macroscopic model would feature heat flow.

Often, students cannot apply abstract principles because the conditions never exist. They rarely encounter frictionless surfaces or vacuums. Thus, more accessible principles might help. Even with more colloquial principles, however, students comment that the words used in the construction of scientific principles are often incomprehensible. To help students learn scientific principles, we taught what we call 'pragmatic' principles based on heat flow and consistent with student experience rather than 'expert' principles based on molecular kinetic theory. One version of the principles we have used is given in the Appendix. The contrast between these principles and the textbook material quoted above is quite dramatic. These pragmatic principles are close to the ideas held by scientists in about 1750. The major difference is that the pragmatic principles do not postulate that heat has mass. Many students found these principles appropriate for summarizing classroom experiments as well as their own experiences.

One student in the CLP classroom who used the colloquial heat-flow principles in the Appendix commented that these principles were useful but would be difficult to create.

S: The principle is like I guess, just harder words that we don't quite understand. . . . Some people might not understand the words [in scientific principles] but they may understand the idea of it. . . . They could understand the concept of it but not how to word it.

Other CLP students view principles as the foundational knowledge that summarized concisely the main aspects of the experiment. For example,

I: What is a principle and does it help you understand the experiment?
S: Yes it does because when we first learned about principles, I didn't know what it was about at all and really actually it is just a definition of what we are all trying to figure out and about the results and experiments, it is just a whole big definition.
I: How did that help you understand the experiment?
S: It helps me a lot because if I don't understand the experiment or what we are trying to look for, it is all explained in the principle. It is something that I can refer back to.

Thus, the nature of a student's prior knowledge as well as the character of the principle influence access to principled understanding. Careful selection of instructional goals is key to the success of science instruction emphasizing principles. In the case of the CLP curriculum, pragmatic principles were more accessible to students than were expert principles. When effective, these principles help students identify appropriate boundaries between domains. We turn to a discussion of principles and domains before returning to the issue of knowledge integration and considering how prototypic examples help students integrate their knowledge.

Knowledge boundaries and principles

Students develop intuitive conceptions that confer status on certain actions. Ideally, we would like students to develop a few intuitive conceptions that can serve as a foundation for the development of a few scientific principles to account for a wide range of observations and experiences. These principles would be consistent with the beliefs of scientists. However, often, students' efforts to organize action knowledge and observations result in the compartmentalization of knowledge in categories unified by surface characteristics. These knowledge boundaries are different and more narrow than those of scientists. For example, in the context of heat and temperature, students initially believe that the scientific principles that apply to the heating of objects are distinct from those that apply to cooling objects (Clough and Driver, 1985; Linn and Songer, in press). When asked before CLP instruction, 'Do containers or wraps that help hot objects stay hot also help keep cold objects cold?' many gave a negative response. A few students gave examples such as

S: Thermoses keep soup warm in lunches. Foam holders that hold soda cans keep them cold.

Frederiksen and White (1988) report an instance of classroom presentation encouraging artificial boundaries within a content area scientists see as governed by the same principles. In learning about electricity in a traditional introductory high school physics course, students are presented with two types of electricity problems. They are given a causal, qualitative model for electrostatic problems and an algebraic, noncausal problem-solving technique for solving circuit problems. As a result, students come to view these problem situations as completely distinct from one another. Clearly, this presentation encourages artificial boundaries and also discourages organizing knowledge into more powerful and encompassing intuitions and principles.

An example of students grouping intuitions and experiences into a more powerful scientific principle can be found in the student interviews during the CLP curriculum. In this example, a student has used the process of the construction of scientific principles about a group of experiments to realize the importance of scientific principles for making predictions about a whole set of new situations. The student comments.

> S: I mean the principle is just like anything. If you just have [any] two objects that only differ in mass that are placed in the same surrounding you just keep on going. You know the temperature of the object with the lesser mass will change more quickly.
> S: Ordinary kids don't understand important concepts.
> S: Learning science is a chore because I don't know any of the scientific words.
> S: When I drink orange juice, I don't break down the chemicals or minerals, I just drink it [implying scientific information is not needed for everyday activities].

Students who hold such unproductive beliefs about the nature of science are less likely to achieve integrated understanding, in part because they see the development of complex understanding in science as running counter to their goals for science learning (Songer, 1989). Students may abandon their goal of understanding science events, or they may conclude that their intuitive beliefs should govern the decisions they make in familiar situations, while the information in the science textbook should be recalled only to answer questions posed in science courses. They may then turn their intellectual efforts to other domains.

We hypothesize that students who develop predictive beliefs about the nature of science will be ready to build their intuitive ideas into scientific principles more easily than those students who hold unpredictive beliefs that are incongruent with their other ideas. On balance, if they encounter scientific principles while holding a set of beliefs that do not support integrated science learning, they will resort to either memorization and segregation of knowledge or rejection of the principles presented.

We suggest that the goals of science courses should be altered to include recognition of student beliefs about the nature of science and should focus on activities that encourage building productive beliefs and strong intuitions, rather than on those that encourage discontinuity and memorization of abstract principles. Thus, choosing effective representations for scientific ideas fosters development of scientific principles. Furthermore, these selections need to respond to the differing entering characteristics of students.

Summary and implications for other disciplines

In summary, the CLP case study illustrates the nature of action knowledge, intuitive beliefs, and scientific principles, suggests how these are constructed, and indicates the success of several types of interventions. In particular, we found that encouraging students to actively predict the outcomes of experiments and then reconcile these outcomes with their predictions leads to more powerful understanding. In addition, we found that students benefited when encouraged to integrate their ideas around a principle or prototype. We also learned that the focus for knowledge integration needed to be matched to the knowledge of the student. In general, pragmatic principles were better than expert principles, and some students found prototypes more accessible than pragmatic principles.

What are the implications of these findings for development and instruction in other disciplines? Researchers exploring such diverse disciplines as literature (Bereiter and Scardamalia, 1986; Spiro and Jehng, 1990), geography (Downs and Liben, in press), mathematics (Cognition and Technology Group at Vanderbilt, 1990; Schoenfeld, 1985), computer programming (Linn and Clancy, in press), and biology (Brown *et al.*, in press) report consonant findings. In all these disciplines students bring action knowledge and intuitive beliefs to the learning situation and often find little reason to abandon these ideas. For example, in literature classes many students develop the belief that they should process information at the sentence level rather than look for themes in paragraphs, much less in whole stories or novels. School experience often reinforces this view. Many assessments of 'comprehension' rely primarily on information that could be acquired by treating such sentence as an isolated entity.

Interventions that succeed in helping students develop more powerful and predictive ideas support the constructive process. For example, Collins *et al.* (1989) summarize successful interventions for literature, writing, and mathematics in terms of what they call 'apprenticeship'. They argue that this approach succeeds because it features (a) careful analysis of the beliefs students have about the domain, (b) clear statement of the goals for students, and (c) explicit support for the constructive process. Other successful programmes, such as the ACCESS (American Culture in Context: Enrichment for Secondary Schools) project at Brown University that teaches students about the nature of historical events using a hypermedia database, provide further evidence for the need to support students as they construct understanding and to set sensible goals for knowledge construction.

A variety of successful programmes indicate that students can construct more powerful and predictive beliefs with appropriate instruction. What cognitive mechanisms explain these accomplishments?

MECHANISMS OF COGNITIVE CHANGE

We have discussed a progression of understanding from action knowledge to intuitive conceptions and scientific principles. Although many have provided rich descriptions of conceptual changes in a variety of content areas, there is controversy surrounding cognitive mechanisms responsible for such changes. While some (Carey, 1985; Inhelder and Piaget, 1958; Kuhn, 1970) argue that conceptual changes occur in a revolutionary manner, many researchers and theorists support more evolutionary changes. In a somewhat parallel manner some argue that revolutionary changes occur as a result of acquisition of domain-general strategies (e.g., Inhelder and Piaget, 1958), while others stress the gradual acquisition of domain-specific knowledge as the key to cognitive change (e.g., Anderson, 1983). At the information-processing level, some, including neo-Piagetian researchers, posit growth in working memory capacity as the mechanism governing revolutionary change (see, e.g., Case, 1985) while others argue that students compile information into more efficient chunks as they develop and therefore can do more with the same basic capacities (see, e.g., Greeno and Simon, 1986).

In this section we summarize the mechanisms proposed to explain conceptual change. These theories range from descriptive to prescriptive.

Conceptual change

The most descriptive theories of conceptual change characterize students as acquiring new domain-specific knowledge and reflecting on their learning. As a result of this reflection, change occurs. Carey (1985), in her descriptions of children's understanding of 'living things', states that, from the ages of 4 to 10, students acquire a great deal of information about the internal functions of all living things. As a result of an understanding of how these internal systems work, students come to have more 'adult-like' understandings of eating, drinking, and breathing. Reflection on which animate and inanimate beings are capable of these functions leads to a clearer understanding of the term 'living thing'. The impetus for change is 'prediction based' – students reject earlier notions that do not provide the predictive power consistent with their new knowledge about the internal workings of human bodies and other living things. Eventually the inability of the old knowledge to make adequate predictions about new cases leads to the abandonment of one set of conceptual understandings for another. This change is motivated by the build-up of knowledge and the reflection on that knowledge; the mechanisms for change could be referred to as 'the force of knowledge' combined with a 'goal of consistency within a knowledge topic'.

A second class of theories explains conceptual change as the result of events that motivate reflection, such as conflict. In the work of Piaget (1952), Doise et al. (1975), and others, the presentation of conflict between conceptual understandings provides the impetus for the abandonment of one set of understandings for another. Obviously, alternative conceptions must exist for this approach to work. However, numerous instances of conflict between student intuitions and formal classroom concepts testify that the presence of conflicting ideas by no means guarantees change. In some cases, students hold alternative intuitive conceptions and apply each within a different context without concern about controversy. In other cases, as illustrated earlier, potential conflicts are contorted to support intuitive views.

Many researchers describe change as fostered by supportive instruction, while others attempt to separate learning and development (e.g., Liben, 1987). Clement *et al.*'s (1989) 'anchoring conceptions' identify student intuitions that are compatible with scientists' conceptions and therefore help students select or promote knowledge, which enables change with appropriate guidance and feedback. Minstrell's (1982) 'benchmarks' serve a similar function, helping students build useful, generative scientific principles that are also compatible with productive intuitions. In the CLP curriculum, prototypes help students select productive intuitive conceptions that serve as a foundation for the integration of action knowledge and link intuitions with scientific principles.

Finally, some theories emphasize the process of guidance and scaffolding for the enabling of conceptual change. In their work with students learning about animal adaptation and endangered species, Brown *et al.* (in press) emphasize the process of reciprocal teaching to effect change. They stress that students need knowledge as a basis for change, and they clearly define the goal state for students. The key idea is to encourage learning and reflection by modelling the process and helping students work in groups to sustain the modelled behaviour.

Similarly, the CLP curriculum emphasizes the process of guidance and scaffolding to achieve change. Integration among experiments is emphasized through students' construction of scientific principles and finding applications for prototypes after each experiment. In addition, students work with an 'Integration Card'. In this activity, students identify four results, principles, or prototypes from different experiments that they find similar. After choosing these components, they must justify their similarity and differences. This activity has proved to be a successful, direct way to encourage students' generalizations beyond individual experiments. Students are also encouraged to reflect by using results of one experiment to predict the outcome of a new experiment and by reconciling results with predictions following experimental investigations. Finally, this project makes distinct efforts to define the goal state clearly for students and to encourage the integration of intuitive ideas leading to appropriate scientific principles.

Strategy acquisition

One mechanism postulated to account for conceptual change in adolescence is the acquisition of 'formal' reasoning strategies as defined by Inhelder and Piaget (1958). This view describes adolescents as capable of more hypothetical

and abstract reasoning than younger individuals, postulates that students acquire domain-general reasoning strategies involving causal and correlational
reasoning during adolescence, and suggests that students can apply these strategies in any domain. Researchers who endorse this position also acknowledge
the role of domain-specific knowledge in reasoning and as a result make it
difficult to isolate the potential impact of acquiring new, powerful strategies
from the gradual increase in domain-specific understanding. For example, how
should we interpret the behaviour of students who believe that metals have the
capacity to impart cold and therefore assert that aluminium foil is a good thing
to wrap around a drink to keep it cold when they misinterpret experiments
showing the opposite outcome? Should this failure to use evidence be attributed to the lack of the abstract ability to interpret experiments or to confusion generated by unpredictive domain knowledge? In interpreting behaviour
in any complex domain, the role of abstract reasoning strategies is difficult to
isolate. As long as theories define a role for both domain-general and domain-
specific knowledge acquisition, it is always possible to explain observed data in
terms of either gains in domain-general strategies or gains in domain-specific
knowledge.

Information processing

The most powerful information-processing argument for revolutionary change
is the neo-Piagetian theory that postulates an increase in working-memory
capacity (processing capacity) during adolescence (see, e.g., Case, 1985). The
neo-Piagetian researchers suggest that the Piagetians may be wrong about the
acquisition of new strategies during adolescence. Research tends to show that
the strategies conjectured to develop in adolescence were already in place at
younger ages. What adolescents develop is the ability to apply these strategies
to complex problems (Case, 1985).

With a larger working memory, these researchers argue, students can engage
in the more complex reasoning found in adolescence. For example, a larger
working memory permits students to keep track of more variables in an experiment and therefore to solve more complex problems without gaining more
powerful strategies. An alternative argument is that students, as they become
more familiar with a domain, can combine information that they previously
treated separately and therefore use their processing capacity more efficiently.
Thus, students might be able to integrate more intuitive ideas as a result of an
increase in processing capacity, or they might use the same working memory
more efficiently by synthesizing a few intuitions around a prototype and then
combining the synthesized ideas into a scientific principle. It is difficult to
differentiate the separate effects of these two potential influences on reasoning.

While all these approaches to cognitive change offer promise, specifics of the
cognitive change mechanism are not clearly defined. Studies examining student
learning in complex domains are coming increasingly closer to identifying
aspects of the elusive mechanisms of conceptual change. Whether conceptual

change is revolutionary or evolutionary, it is clear that studies of the development of reasoning about complex events will contribute to a powerful view of cognitive change.

Summary

In summary, although the observed changes in student understanding proceed by fits and starts, the explanations for these behaviours are difficult to establish. Students acquire a massive amount of information during adolescence. Most commonly, students hold several different views about a scientific event and eventually come to prefer the view that is most predictive. Occasionally, students abandon one view and dramatically replace it with a more predictive or robust view. Over time and under supportive instructional conditions, students' views become more robust and predictive and, as a result, closer to those of scientists. This may occur as a result of acquisition of strategies, increases in working-memory capacity, or reflection on related domain knowledge.

Knowledge boundaries become major issues during adolescence, often compartmentalizing information and discouraging integration of related concepts. In response, effective instruction should set reasonable goals for students, build on and emphasize the positive nature of students' action knowledge and intuitions, and encourage students to develop and refine more comprehensive scientific principles. Indeed, curricula often encourage memorization by emphasizing theories held by scientists without providing the scaffolding needed to ensure that students construct the views of scientists or encourage students to develop some very general reasoning strategies that do not help them understand everyday events.

Clearly, both the beliefs that students develop about the scientific enterprise and the views that they construct of themselves as learners contribute to cognitive change. We address these issues in the next section.

COGNITIVE CHANGE AND THE SOCIAL CONTEXT

Cognitive change occurs in a social context. A long history of research illustrates the power of the social context in shaping learners (e.g., Coleman, 1961; Dewey, 1920). Key features of this context include the peer group that the student chooses, the normative groups that students belong to, and the beliefs that students develop about learning.

Eckert (1990) aptly characterizes typical peer groups in American high schools. She differentiates a group of students labelled 'dropouts' who construct views of themselves and their learning as largely separate from the institution called 'school'. These students do not conform to the expectations of their teachers or of the school authority in general. If they learn, it is in spite of, and not because of, the institution in which they are enrolled. In contrast and at the other extreme, Eckert describes what she calls 'jocks', who have also created a social structure that is more powerful than that of the school structure; however, this group behaves in a way largely compatible with the expectations of teachers and of school authorities, while perhaps at the same time constructing a view of knowledge acquisition that is in opposition to the purposes of school. This group, for example, places popularity (the ability to be elected to office or to participate in an athletic event) above mastery of school subjects. Eckert notes that many schools cooperate with this group of students and also may place these activities at least on par with intellectual pursuit. Thus the social norms in schools have a profound impact on the cognitive development that occurs during schooling.

Adolescents are constructing a view of themselves and a view of the group to which they belong that fundamentally influences their progress and their accomplishments. This process is particularly powerful during adolescence because students at the same time develop greater awareness of sex-role stereotypes and status differences and are more responsive to the views of their peers. Elkind (1967) describes adolescents as constrained by the perception of an 'invisible audience' of their peers judging their performance. Maccoby (1990) charts the early sex differences in peer-interaction patterns, their continuing influence on behaviour, and their interaction with status differences during adolescence. Eccles (1985) demonstrates that sex-role stereotypes become more pronounced during adolescence. These and other aspects of the social context during adolescence help determine the views adolescents construct of themselves.

Adolescents construct views, for example, of 'appropriate' intellectual interests that reflect the perceptions of their peer group and their normative groups. These views tend to reflect past practice. Thus, literature and dance are viewed as appropriate for females while mathematics and science are viewed as appropriate for males. In mathematics and science, both peer expectations and societal perceptions emphasize the maleness of these domains. Sex-role stereotypes found in advertisements, and especially predominant in situation comedies on television, communicate that women are less successful in mathematics and science and are also less likely to participate in these disciplines. Recently, these views have been reinforced when scholarships have been awarded more commonly to males than females because performance on potentially biased tests is among the criteria used in selecting recipients.

These societal perceptions are particularly important given that a large amount of data, recently subjected to meta-analysis, indicates that the gender gap in cognitive ability has essentially closed in the last twenty years (Linn and Hyde, 1990). Meta-analyses of verbal ability show that this once-female domain is now neutral with regard to gender differences (Hyde and Linn, 1988). In mathematics, over the past twenty years, there has been a similar decline in the gender differences, and this once-male domain is now neutral on measures of computation, general problem solving, and mathematics applications (Hyde et al., 1990). However, differences are still found on the Scholastic Aptitude Test's (SAT) mathematics section, a measure of complex problem solving.

These differences are particularly pronounced among the most able students. Among those scoring at the very top of the distribution, there are many more males than females. These somewhat anomalous findings will be addressed shortly. In spatial ability, as in verbal ability and mathematical ability, the trend is toward no gender differences on standardized tests. Thus, in the last 20 years, there has been a substantial decline in gender differences on a variety of cognitive measures. Participation of females in domains such as mathematics, science, and engineering, however, remains extremely low.

Clearly, these trends in cognitive gender differences are best attributed to changes in the social context of learning. It would be unreasonable to assume that genetic changes had occurred over such a short period. Given this dramatic change in cognitive gender differences, it is important to analyse why there are some tests for which the gender gap is closing more slowly, or perhaps not closing at all.

The most prevalent anomaly is the SAT scores for mathematics. In contrast, national tests given in England, Norway, and other countries show either no gender differences or perhaps slight differences favouring females on complex mathematical problem-solving tests. One difference between American tests and European tests is the reliance of the American tests on the multiple-choice format. It has been hypothesized that this format may advantage males much more than females. Testing programmes are now moving to include constructed response items that will address this potential difficulty. In addition, it has been hypothesized that gender differences on complex problem solving in mathematics might more aptly be attributed to the domain in which the problems are set than to fundamental differences in problem solving. Some have argued that these problems are commonly presented in a sports domain, which is more familiar to males. This issue has also been addressed, and national testing organizations are moving to reduce or eliminate the number of items in which the context is likely to interact with gender. Other factors that may contribute to this anomaly include greater interest and course participation in mathematics and science among males than among females. For performance at the high end of the distribution, it seems likely that the greater experience with mathematics and science characteristic of those students may contribute to this gender difference. More subtle factors may also be at work. Feminists postulate that the male domination in mathematics and science may have resulted in fields that are constructed to favour those who participate in them. Clearly, how adolescents view themselves as learners is crucial to their ultimate achievements.

Although women and men perform similarly on measures of cognitive skills and earn similar grades in mathematics and science courses, women are less confident of their ability to perform in mathematics and science (Linn, in press). In mathematics, for example, Hyde et al. (1990) report that males are about one-quarter of a standard deviation more confident of their mathematical abilities than females. In science, a similar situation arises (National Assessment of Educational Progress, 1988).

In spite of the societal norms and anomalies that discourage women in mathematics and science, by far the most serious issue with regard to the social context of learning in America today is that far too few students altogether are being attracted to mathematics, science, and technology. Advanced courses in these domains are optional, and a small number of students are choosing them. In assessing the nature of conceptual change, it seems imperative that we look at why it is that students are choosing to limit the development of their understanding of these domains. We have argued that the current courses in mathematics and science, with their fleeting coverage of a large number of topics, discourage integrated understanding (Linn, 1987). These courses may ultimately discourage students from participating altogether. Certainly, national assessments of young adults' understanding of mathematics and science reveal that our society as a whole has limited understanding of these important topics. Attention to the process of conceptual change seems imperative in order to improve understanding in all disciplines.

Changing the context of classroom learning is an important starting point for influencing the views students construct of themselves and of schooling. Subtle changes such as taking care to call on women as often as men rather than maintaining the status quo of calling more frequently on men can help. Our experience with the CLP curriculum suggests that both males and females view themselves as more competent in science when they extend their scientific ideas beyond classroom experiments. For example,

> S: Before we did everyday life examples I thought I would hardly use any of this but now I think I will use almost everything I learned in this class in my everyday life.

Both male and female students in the CLP programme make substantial gains in integrated understanding of scientific concepts and of graphing of scientific relationships. On post-tests given to 10 different cohorts of students we have never detected gender differences in scientific understanding. On our measures of beliefs about the scientific enterprise we find that female students are more aware than male students that science is a socially constructed enterprise, perhaps because they also realize that women have contributed less than men to the construction of these fields.

In summary, the construction of cognitive understanding is closely entwined with the social context of learning. In adolescence, sex-role stereotypes, peer-group influences, and status differences become particularly pronounced. As a group, adolescents avoid mathematics, science, and technology. Unless both social and cognitive factors are addressed, a large number of students will construct the view that they do not need to understand mathematics and science. This trend may extend to other important domains as well. At the same time that our society demands greater intellectual accomplishments from its members and offers fewer career opportunities for those who lack understanding of mathematics and science, it seems imperative to address these dual concerns.

CONCLUSIONS

In conclusion, we argue that conceptual change is governed by a constructive process and that the pace of this construction as well as the direction of construction are influenced by a wide range of important factors. We argue that schooling is of primary importance in governing students' ability to achieve principled understanding of mathematics, science, literature, and other topics. Principled understanding rarely arises as a result of unguided discovery. It is even more unlikely to arise if students choose to avoid advanced courses.

Second, we argue that the pace of constructed understanding is influenced by the view that students construct of themselves as learners. If students view active engagement in the constructive process as an important component of their own understanding, then they are far more likely to construct new understanding than if they see themselves as passive memorizers of information with little possibility of integrating and synthesizing the knowledge in their environment. We argue that students are more likely to become active integrators of their own knowledge if their prior efforts at integration are rewarded, and if instruction fosters and encourages this process.

Students' efforts to understand complex events are sometimes labelled as 'misconceptions' rather than 'intuitive conceptions'. By labelling students' ideas as misconceptions, we discourage learners from viewing the constructive process as a positive accomplishment. Unless learners are encouraged to recognize their initial efforts in developing intuitive beliefs as drawing on the processes that will ultimately lead them to more sophisticated understanding, they are less likely to continue engaging in the constructive process throughout their lifetime.

Even if students become convinced that the constructive process is a valuable one, they may fail to engage in it in school settings because of the nature of instruction. If students cannot actively integrate the information presented, and instead resort to less generative but nevertheless satisfactory resolutions of the problems, they will achieve less. If students perform satisfactorily on tests as a result of memorization or sentence-level understanding, they will not strive for integrated understanding. Thus, a primary factor in creating effective understanding and fostering conceptual change is to match instruction and assessment to the nature of the constructive process.

We have argued that instruction must take into consideration the initial state of the learner. When learners come to classes with action knowledge, they need considerable assistance to integrate that knowledge into intuitive conceptions and ultimately gain principled understanding of a domain. We have suggested that those designing educational programmes seek to identify appropriate intermediate levels of understanding, such as heat flow rather than molecular kinetic theory in thermodynamics. This approach has equal promise for complex domains such as literature and philosophy. What are intermediate levels of understanding for the interrelated themes in one of Faulkner's novels? How might instructional practices such as providing serious coverage of several themes rather than listing endless themes help? Would the goal of relating themes in these novels to social structures in schools or communities familiar to students help students integrate their understanding? If instruction aims to move students farther than the zone of proximal development, as characterized by Vygotsky (1962), then again the constructive process breaks down – the students turn to other means for dealing with the task at hand. Research suggests that one can dramatically extend the zone of proximal development with appropriate educational programmes (Collins *et al.*, 1989). Thus, attention to initial state and to final state can be tempered with the possibility that improved instructional methods will extend the span of comprehension for students.

As students develop understanding, they can identify broader knowledge domains and integrate information in these broader domains. To avoid the common problem of students identifying large numbers of tiny domains rather than recognizing the commonalities of information in broader knowledge areas, it is important again to pay attention to the constructive process. Students need assistance in identifying commonalities across domains, and they may need integration aids to be clear on the similarities between those domains. For example, as students develop an understanding of elementary thermodynamics, they frequently differentiate heating and cooling. Integration aids that place insulators along a continuum help students to recognize that heating and cooling are similar phenomena and ought not to be separated into different domains.

The problem of domain differentiation is particularly important when students think about information relevant to out-of-school experiences. If in science, for example, students study only simply laboratory events, they will be unable to extend their knowledge outside the classroom. Instead, with the advent of technology, students can investigate complex and ambiguous situations using simulations and then more readily extend their understanding to experiences that they encounter in their lives. A similar argument can be made for literature when augmented with videodisc depictions of relevant historical events.

We argue that cognitive change takes place in a complex, social environment and that the social context influences, in particular, the pace of conceptual change as well as the locus of knowledge integration. We argue that students construct views of themselves as learners, influenced importantly by their social context, and that these views determine the enthusiasm with which they attack the process of understanding. These views may interfere with conceptual change because they result in students constructing a view of knowledge as static and inaccessible to understanding, rather than dynamic, constructed by individuals, and in the process of being reconstructed. Students' views of the nature of knowledge are part of the process of constructing views of themselves as learners and affect the pace of their understanding. In addition, factors such as sex-role expectations, status differences, and peer-group norms influence the domains that students choose to address.

As a result, we argue that the goal of attracting a broader constituency to domains such as mathematics and science requires reform of the instructional approaches to these domains such that the constructive process is supported. It also requires reform of the views that society holds for these domains such that individuals have generative views of the nature of mathematics, of science, and of literature or other disciplines. In addition, it probably requires reform of the nature of the environments in which male-dominated careers take place. Currently, mathematics and science are largely male dominated, and we see that one of the major differences between males and females is their perception of math and science as male domains. To encourage the participation of individuals who are not perceived to be members of these domains requires a change in these perceptions.

We argued that research on conceptual change sheds light on cognitive change and, furthermore, that theories of cognitive change should inform those concerned with improving conceptual understanding. We have illustrated conceptual changes that need explanation. In particular, during adolescence students experience an information explosion and come to organize this information in much more abstract principles than are typical of younger students. Students go from action knowledge to intuitions in a broad range of fields and gain principled understanding of many important domains. Research evidence suggests that in virtually all areas students explore they hold multiple intuitions that may be contradictory or at least incongruous and that these unintegrated views are not fundamentally disturbing to students. Instruction, then, encourages students to integrate information that could be viewed as inconsistent. A major difficulty in attempting to achieve these integrations is that students may have differentiated this knowledge into separate domains and therefore find it easy to view the knowledge as isolated rather than contradictory. It may be that a key to differentiating an evolutionary from a revolutionary view of knowledge development requires disentangling the domain-boundary issue from the general understanding that students achieve. One way to determine whether students undergo revolutionary changes in their views is to examine whether these changes occur as a result of integrating information that was previously viewed as belonging to separate domains, or whether these changes occur as a result of modifying views about the same domain.

In adolescence, students make real progress in conceptual understanding. This change is consistent with cognitive theories that pose increases in working memory, those that posit development of domain-general strategies, and those that focus on reflective abstraction. Research applying cognitive explanations to conceptual change offers considerable promise both for understanding the process and for fostering cognitive growth. It is clear that greater understanding of this important area will have far-reaching impact on the nature of instruction as well as on the level of societal understanding of important concepts and principles.

APPENDIX

EXAMPLES OF CLP PRINCIPLES

Flow Principles:
   Heat-Flow Principle: Heat energy flows only when there is a temperature difference.
   Direction-of-Heat-Flow Principle: Heat energy flows only from objects at higher temperature to objects at lower temperature.
Rate Principles:
   Surface-Area Principle: When only surface area differs, heat energy will flow faster through the larger surface area.
   Mass-and-Rate Principle: When only mass differs, the temperature of the larger mass will change more slowly. Initially, heat energy will flow at the same rate from both objects to a cooler surround.
   Material-and-Rate Principle: When only material differs, the temperatures of the two objects will change at different rates. Initially heat energy will flow at the same rate from both objects to a cooler surround.
   Temperature-Difference Principle: The greater the temperature difference between objects and their surround, the faster heat energy flows.
   Conductivity Principle: A good conductor allows heat energy to flow faster than a poor conductor.
Total-Heat-Flow Principles:
   Thermal-Equilibrium Principle: Eventually all objects in the same surround become the same temperature unless an object produces its own heat energy.
   Mass-and-Total-Heat-Flow Principle: When only mass differs, more heat energy flows from the larger mass to a cooler surround.
   Material-and-Total-Heat-Flow Principle: When only material differs, more heat energy flows from one material than the other to a cooler surround.
Integration Principle:
   Heat-Energy-and-Temperature Principle: When each part of an object has the same temperature, more heat energy will flow to a cooler surround from the whole than from each part.

NOTES

This work draws on the research of the 'Computer as Lab Partner' project. We appreciate the contributions of the other group members, including Doug Kirkpatrick, Eileen Lewis, Jacquie Madhock, and Judith Stern. We would like to thank Evelyn Shapiro and E. Darragh Perrow for producing this manuscript. This material is based on research supported by the National Science Foundation under grants MDR-88-50552 and MDR-89-54753. Any opinions, findings, and conclusions or recommendations expressed in this article are those of the authors and do not necessarily reflect the views of the National Science Foundation.

REFERENCES

Anderson, J. R. (1983) *The Architecture of Cognition*. Cambridge, Mass.: Harvard University Press.

Baldwin, J. M. (1894) *The Development of the Child and of the Race*. New York: Macmillan.

Bereiter, C., and Scardamalia, M. (1986) *The Psychology of Written Composition*. Hillsdale, N.J.: Erlbaum.

Brophy, J. E., and Good, T. L. (1974) *Teacher-Student Relationships: Causes and Consequences*. New York: Holt, Rinehart & Winston.

Brophy, J. E., and Good, T. L. (1986) 'Classroom Organization and Management.' *Elementary School Journal* 83, 265–85.

Brown, A. L., Campione, J. C., Reeve, R., Ferrara, R. A. and Palincsar, A. C. 'Interactive Learning and Individual Understanding: The Case of Reading and Mathematics.' In *Culture, Schooling and Psychological Development*, edited by L. T. Landsmann. Hillsdale, N.J.: Erlbaum, in press.

Brown, J. S., Collins, A. and Duguid, P. (1989) 'Situated Cognition and the Culture of Learning.' *Educational Researcher* 17, 32–41.

Bruner, J. S. (1977) 'Early Social Interaction and Language Acquisition.' In *Studies in Mother-Infant Interaction*, edited by H. R. Schaffer. New York: Academic Press.

Burbules, N. C., and Linn, M. C. 'Science Education and the Philosophy of Science: Congruence or Contradiction?' *International Journal of Science Education* (in press).

Carey, S. (1985) *Conceptual Change in Childhood*. Cambridge, Mass.: MIT Press.

Case, R. (1985) *Intellectual Development: Birth to Adulthood*. Orlando, Fla.: Academic Press.

Champagne, A. B., Klopfer, L. E. and Gunstone, R. F. (1982) 'Cognitive Research and the Design of Science Instruction.' *Educational Psychologist* 17, no. 1, 31–53.

Chase, N., and Simon, H. A. (1973) 'Perception in Chess.' *Cognitive Psychology* 4, 55–81.

Clement, J. (1982) 'Students' Preconceptions in Introductory Mechanics.' *American Journal of Physics* 50, no. 1, 66–71.

Clement, J., Brown, D. E. and Zietsman, A. 'Not All Preconceptions Are Misconceptions: Finding "Anchoring Conceptions" for Grounding Instruction on Students' Intuitions.' Paper presented at the annual meeting of the American Educational Research Association, San Francisco, 1989.

Clough, E. E., and Driver, R. (1985) 'Secondary Students' Conceptions of the Conduction of Heat: Bringing Together Scientific and Personal Views.' *The Physical Educator* 20, 176–82.

Cognition and Technology Group at Vanderbilt. (1990) 'Anchored Instruction and Its Relationship to Situated Cognition.' *Educational Researcher* 19, no. 5, 2–10.

Coleman, J. S. (1961) *The Adolescent Society*. Glencoe, Ill.: Free Press.

Collins, A., Brown, J. S. and Newman, S. E. (1989) 'Cognitive Apprenticeship: Teaching the Craft of Reading, Writing, and Mathematics.' In *Cognition and Instruction: Issues and Agendas*, edited by L. B. Resnick. Hillsdale, N.J.: Erlbaum.

Dewey, J. (1920) *The Child and the Curriculum*. Chicago: University of Chicago Press.

di Sessa, A. (1982) 'Unlearning Aristotelian Physics: A Study of Knowledge-based Learning.' *Cognitive Science* 6, 37–75.

di Sessa, A. (1987) 'The Third Revolution in Computers in Education.' *Journal of Research in Science Teaching* 24, no. 4, 343–67.

Doise, W., Mugny, G. and Perret-Clermont, A. (1975) 'Social Interaction and the Development of Cognitive Operations.' *European Journal of Social Psychology* 5, 367.

Downs, R. M., and Liben, L. S. 'The Development of Expertise in Geography: A Cognitive-Developmental Approach to Geographic Education.' *Annals of the Association of American Geographers* (in press).

Eccles, J. S. (1985) 'Sex Differences in Achievement Patterns.' In *Nebraska Symposium of Motivation*, edited by T. Sonderegger. Lincoln: University of Nebraska Press.

Eckert, P. (1990) 'Adolescent Social Categories, Information and Science Learning.' In *Toward a Scientific Practice of Science Education*, edited by M. Gardner and J. G. Greeno. Hillsdale, N.J.: Erlbaum.

Elkind, D. (1967) 'Egocentrism in Adolescence.' *Child Development* 38, 1025–34.

Eylon, B., and Linn, M. C. (1988) 'Learning and Instruction: An Examination of Four Research Perspectives in Science Education.' *Review of Educational Research* 58, no. 3, 251–301.

Frederiksen, J. R., and White, B. Y. (1988) *Mental Models and Understanding: A Problem for Science Education*. Cambridge, Mass.: BBN Laboratories.

Friedler, Y., Nachmias, R. and Linn, M. C. (1990) 'Learning Scientific Reasoning Skills in Microcomputer-based Laboratories.' *Journal of Research in Science Teaching* 27, no. 2, 173–91.

Gentner, D., and Stevens, A. L. (1983) *Mental Models*. Hillsdale, N.J.: Erlbaum.

Gilligan, C. (1982) *In a Different Voice: Psychological Theory and Women's Development*. Cambridge, Mass.: Harvard University Press.

Glaser, R. (1984) 'Education and Thinking: The Role of Knowledge.' *American Psychologist* 39, 93–104.

Greeno, J. G., and Simon, H. A. (1986) 'Problem Solving and Reasoning.' In *Steven's Handbook of Experimental Pschology*, rev. ed., edited by R. C. Atkinson, R. Hernstein, G. Lindzey, and R. D. Luce, New York: Wiley.

Hyde, J. S., Fennema, E. and Lamon, S. J. (1990) 'Gender Differences in Mathematics Performance.' *Psychological Bulletin* 107, 139–55.

Hyde, J. S., and Linn, M. C. (1988) 'Gender Differences in Verbal Ability: A Meta-Analysis.' *Psychological Bulletin* 104, no. 1, 53–69.

Inhelder, B., and Piaget, J. (1958) *The Growth of Logical Thinking from Childhood to Adolescence*. New York: Basic.

Keating, D. P., and Crane, L. L. (1990) 'Domain-general and Domain-specific Processes in Proportional Reasoning: A Commentary on the Merrill-Palmer Quarterly.' *Merrill-Palmer Quarterly* 36, no. 3, 411–24.

Kuhn, T. S. (1970) *The Structure of Scientific Revolutions*. Chicago: University of Chicago Press.

Lewis, E. L., and Linn, M. C. (1989) 'Heat Energy and Temperature Concepts of Adolescents, Naïve Adults, and Experts: Implications for Curricular Improvements'. Paper presented at the annual meeting of the National Association for Research in Science Teaching, San Francisco, April.

Liben, L. S., ed. (1987) *Development and Learning: Conflict or Congruence?* Hills-dale, N.J.: Erlbaum.

Linn, M. C. (1986) 'Science.' In *Cognition and Instruction*, edited by R. Dillon and R. J. Sternberg. New York: Academic Press.

Linn, M. C. (1987) 'Establishing a Research Base for Science Education: Challenges, Trends, and Recommendations.' *Journal of Research in Science Teaching* 24, no. 5, 191–216.

Linn, M. C. 'Gender, Mathematics, and Science: Trends and Recommendations.' Mystic, Conn.: Summer Institute for the Council of Chief State School Officers (CCSSO), in press.

Linn, M. C., and Clancy, M. J. 'Can Experts' Explanations Help Students Develop Program Design Skills?' *International Journal of Man-Machine Studies* (in press).

Linn, M. C., Clement, C. and Pulos, S. (1983) 'Is It Formal If It's Not Physics?' *Journal of Research in Science Teaching* 20, no. 8, 755–70.

Linn, M. C., and Hyde, J. S. (1990) 'Trends in Cognitive and Psychosocial Gender Differences.' In *Encyclopedia of Adolescence*, edited by R. M. Lerner, A. C. Petersen, and J. Brooks-Gunn. New York: Garland.

Linn, M.C., and Pulos, S. (1983) 'Male-Female Differences in Predicting Displaced Volume: Strategy Usage, Aptitude Relationships and Experience Influences.' *Journal of Educational Psychology* 75, 86–96.

Linn, M. C., and Songer, N. B. 'Teaching Thermodynamics to Middle School Students: What Are Appropriate Cognitive Demands?' *Journal of Research in Science Teaching* (in press).

Linn, M. C., Songer, N. B., Lewis, E. L. and Stern, J. 'Using Technology to Teach Thermodynamics: Achieving Integrated Understanding.' In *Advanced Technologies in the Teaching of Mathematics and Science*, edited by D. L. Ferguson. Berlin: Springer-Verlag, in press.

Maccoby, E. E. (1990) 'Gender and Relationships: A Development Account.' *American Psychologist* 45, no. 4, 513–20.

Minstrell, J. (1982) 'Explaining the "At Rest" Condition of an Object.' *The Physics Teacher* 20 , 10–14.

National Assessment of Educational Progress. (1988) *The Science Report Card: Elements of Risk and Recovery: Trends and Achievement Based on the 1986 National Assessment.* Princeton, N.J.: Educational Testing Service.

Nolan, L. M., and Tucker, W. (1984) *Physical Science.* Lexington, Mass.: Heath.

Piaget, J. (1926) *The Language and Thought of the Child.* London: Routledge & Kegan Paul.

Piaget, J. (1952) *The Origins of Intelligence in Children.* New York: National Universities Press.

Schoenfeld, A. H. (1985) *Mathematical Problem Solving.* Orlando, Fla.: Academic Press.

Songer, N. B. (1989) 'Promoting Integration of Instructed and Natural World Knowledge in Thermodynamics.' Ph.D. dissertation, University of California, Berkeley, Department of Science and Mathematics Education.

Spiro, R. J., and Jehng, J. C. (1990) 'Cognitive Flexibility and Hypertext: Theory and Technology for the Nonlinear and Multidimensional Traversal of Complex Subject Matter.' In *Cognition, Education, and Multimedia,* edited by D. Nix and R. Spiro. Hillsdale, N.J.: Erlbaum.

Sternberg, R. J. (1989) 'Domain Generality vs. Domain Specificity: The Life and Impending Death of a False Dichotomy.' *Merrill-Palmer Quarterly* 35, 115–29.

Tiberghien, A. (1980) 'Modes and Conditions of Learning. An Example: The Learning of Some Aspects of the Concepts of Heat.' In *Cognitive Development Research in Science and Mathematics,* edited by W. F. Archenhold, R. H. Driver, A. Orton, and C. Wood-Robinson. Leeds: University of Leeds Printing Service.

Vygotsky, L. S. (1962) *Thought and Language.* Cambridge, Mass.: MIT Press.

Vygotsky, L. S. (1978) *Mind in Society: The Development of Higher Psychological Processes.* Cambridge, Mass.: Harvard University Press.

Wiser, M., and Carey, S. (1983) 'When Heat and Temperature Were One.' In *Mental Models,* edited by D. Gentner and A. L. Stevens. Hillsdale, N.J.: Erlbaum.

2.4

Twenty-nine children, five computers and a teacher

Tim O'Shea, Eileen Scanlon, Malcolm Byard, Steve Draper, Rosalind Driver, Sara Hennessy, Roger Hartley, Claire O'Malley, Conroy Mallen, Geoff Mohamed and Daz Twigger

INTRODUCTION

This article describes a three-year project on promoting conceptual change in science. The aim of the project was to understand better the process of conceptual change and to develop and test ways in which such change can be promoted by using computer tools in classroom situations. This article describes the development and classroom evaluation of an experimental curriculum designed to teach mechanics concepts to twelve- and thirteen-year-olds. (Children from the ages of nine to fifteen were involved in the testing of prototypes.) The curriculum, which occupies thirty hours of class time, has several interesting features. Some of these are:

- the identification of the prior conceptions which influence children's learning in mechanics;
- the design of four scenarios which underpin the sequencing of the material taught, the use of specially created software designed round these scenarios;
- the integration of the computer experiments with real practical experiments.

The classrom evaluation which we describe later in the article produced some interesting results which have implications for teachers of science.

THE RESEARCH COLLABORATION

The Conceptual Change in Science project was funded in response to a call for proposals made under the auspices of an Economic and Social Research Council (ESRC) research initiative on information technology in education. A research consortium was formed of staff from the psychology department of the University of Glasgow, from the computer-assisted learning research group of the Institute of Educational Technology, The Open University, and from the School of Education and the computer-based learning unit of the University of Leeds.

The work of the project was to clarify and describe the processes of change in learners' conceptual understandings of natural phenomena, and to change them using computer simulations. The research proposal suggested that the project would aim at working with pupils aged nine to thirteen on one or two areas in physics, force and motion and energy transfer, particulate theory of matter and conservation of matter. These are areas where children's conceptualizations and the process of conceptual change are particularly important (Driver and Scanlon, 1989).

STARTING POINTS

Our intention was to use software to explore and develop pupils' ideas, and to study which intervention strategies worked. We aimed to design and use software tools based on two previous pieces of work – the Alternate Reality Kit (ARK), designed by a physicist in California (Smith, 1990), and the work on modelling tools like STELLA, a modelling package for the Macintosh (High Performance Systems, Inc., USA). One particular feature of the software which we felt would be important was how the interface worked and whether it was easy to learn and use. The work on ARK was based on a notion of direct manipulation and so is premised on the idea that there should be no language for the pupil to learn but that the pupil should control the software by carrying out actions using a mouse-controlled simulated hand. These actions might be pressing buttons or moving sliders and should resemble as far as possible the physical manipulation of the objects themselves. Our desire to use such interfaces led to the choice of machines that we used – Apple MacIIs. Another important feature of the research was the testing of these intervention strategies in real classroom settings, rather than in the laboratory.

We planned two types of computer tools. One was a simulation package which could be used for pupils to conduct experiments. The other was computer modelling software which children could use to express their ideas about the concepts being studied. Our research hypothesis was that using these computer tools would promote conceptual change in science for a variety of reasons. It might be that such tools require children to make their reasoning explicit or that they enable them to visualize the consequences of that reasoning. Another possibility is that the computer provides representations to be used as bridging analogies, or devices to follow the progress of interactions, for example simultaneous recordings of experiments which could be replayed and studied. We believed three features of our simulations would be particularly important:

- the use of alternate realities, or the ability to perform experiments where students could see the effect of the laws of physics being 'broken';
- their use of direct manipulation software as described before; and
- their integration of these computer experiments with real experiments.

As well as these starting points taken from contemporary research in information technology we had the benefit of an extensive amount of work on children's prior conceptions (Driver, 1984; Driver *et al.*, 1985). Children construct mental models of how the world behaves. The problem for science educators is that while these models evolve, the children gain more experience with physical phenomena in the world and the children's models often conflict with the Newtonian ideas which teachers are struggling to present. There is considerable evidence that conventional teaching at school and college is unsuccessful at changing children's prior conceptions. In certain domains such as mechanics, informal theories can persist even in university students (Viennot, 1979). This has led to the redescription of science learning as a process of conceptual change (Hewson and Hewson, 1983).

Two examples of attempts to promote conceptual change are documented by Brown and Clement (1987) and Heller and Hungate (1984). Brown and Clement investigated the solving of statics problems and looked at which analogies were used as bridges to new concepts by students. Heller and Hungate (*op. cit.*) looked at how university students were able to analyse mechanics problems from a Newtonian perspective through coaching. We decided also to focus our study on mechanics (force and motion), so that we could build on such previous work. We also focused on the early years of secondary education, which increased the ease with which we were able to have access to classrooms as children of this age are not involved in externally moderated tests.

OVERVIEW OF THE PROJECT

The project ran for three years from October 1988 till December 1991. We initially conducted 'clinical' interviews and paper and pencil studies with thirty children with the aim of identifying common *prior conceptions* in children's ideas about horizontal and vertical motion. This involved children whose ages ranged between ten and fifteen, so that we could investigate whether these prior conceptions were age dependent (Twigger *et al.*, in press).

Next we had to *design* and implement the *software environment*. This involved the construction of prototype screens and subsequent testing of these prototypes with groups of children to remove any problems with their use of either the interface or the representations used on the screen (Hennessy *et al.*, 1990). The next stage was the *design of the computer curriculum*. We chose four scenarios which addressed specific concepts identified as problematic in the interview study, and included these together with associated worksheets and test items. These computer simulations were then pre-tested with groups of twelve-year-olds, before the final stage of the project. The curriculum materials were designed as an integrated whole containing worksheets for both the simulations and conventional classroom laboratory experiments. The final stage, the whole-class evaluation, allowed us to test whether this approach was successful. The curriculum was used over a seven-week period by the teacher of a class of twenty-nine twelve-year-olds, using five computers. The rest of the article describes the work of each of these stages in more detail.

PRIOR CONCEPTIONS

Students are known to have prior conceptions about aspects of force and motion which differ from Newtonian theory and various workers have produced reviews of the research in this area (McDermott, 1984; Gunstone and Watts, 1985; Halloun and Hestenes, 1985). Much of this work had been done with university students rather than secondary pupils, so we decided to investigate the dynamics reasoning of students aged ten to fifteen with the aim of identifying their prior conceptions. The question we focused on was what were the common prior conceptions about aspects of vertical and horizontal motion, and were these conceptions age dependent. We devised seven tasks which covered the range of dynamical contexts of interest to the project. The contexts included motion on the horizontal as a result of an impulsive force, constant motion on the horizontal with friction, accelerated motion on the horizontal, free-fall motion (with air resistance) and projectile motion. We then interviewed pairs of students. The interviews lasted an hour and as a stimulus used either equipment to manipulate, or a video or drawings of simple scenes. Individual students then wrote answers on their own personal response sheets. The audiotape records of these interviews led to the identification of a number of features of students' conceptualizations of forces and motion. Twigger *et al.* (in press) describe these as follows:

Object moving on a surface with friction after impulse (pebble, carriage):

Most . . . say a moving object stops because it runs out of energy. The underlying reasoning is that a push given to the object keeps it going till the push is used up. Friction . . . and air resistance . . . are also given as explanations for the object stopping. In some cases these are seen as external agents acting in addition to the running out of the 'push'. In other cases they are the only agents which cause the slowing down. Even when students identify friction as an agent it tends not to be seen as a force opposing motion.

Objects moving with no friction (pebble in space):

About half the students suggested that an object would keep on going forever in space. About a third had a notion that an object would float or wander around in space. Others assumed the object would stop eventually (because it runs out of energy).

Constant motion on horizontal surface with friction (carriage, girl on cycle):

All students recognize that a constant driving force is required to maintain motion but nearly all (over 80 per cent) state that this must be greater than resistance if the motion is to be maintained. Otherwise they argue if they were equal the object would stop.

Accelerated motion on horizontal surface with friction (carriage, cart):

All students predicted that a steadily increasing force is needed to produce accelerated motion. This is in keeping with the view that a constant force is required to maintain motion. In addition bodies may be thought to go on accelerating briefly after an impulsive force stops acting.

Vertical motion – falling (parachutist):

All students recognized that objects tend to accelerate during free fall. When resistance is increased, e.g. when a parachute is opened, most students aged thirteen and over recognize that the object will then fall at constant speed. In the constant speed case the downward force is seen by nearly all students as being greater than the resistance (in keeping with the horizontal motion case). In a minority of cases air was seen as acting down on an object in free fall yet also acting to oppose motion where air resistance is significant.

Vertical motion – up/down (projectile):

This reveals a combination of issues identified previously. There is a general lack of speed symmetry – the downward motion is seen as faster. The explanation for the motion generally involves the push getting used up as the object goes up and then gravity taking over. There is again a tendency for students to consider that the ball speeds up after it is thrown.

We were particularly interested in the possibility of any age-related trends in these results, either in students prior dynamical conceptions or in their use of representations. In fact these were not much in evidence.

The only age-related feature suggested by our results appeared to be the introduction of friction in students' reasoning around age eleven to twelve. . . . This lack of change is notable since students in the upper age groups had been taught Newtonian dynamics in their science lessons. . . . Notions that have been identified in this study are likely to have developed as a result of a great deal of experience of living in a world with friction and will require carefully designed teaching if they are to change.

Another feature was an age-related change in students' graphical representation of motion,

with older students representing phases in motion more completely and making more distinctions in their representations using speed-distance sketch graphs.

(Twigger *et al.*, in press)

So pupils have the idea of a force which is given to an object when it is pushed or thrown. As an object moves along, this 'force' is used up, and when it is completely used up the object stops. Most pupils do not seem to consider friction as a force opposing motion, though some have the idea of 'grippiness' between surfaces. This grippiness makes it harder to get some things going than others and is related to weight.

Twigger *et al.* (in press) noted three kinds of problem with pupils' predictions:

- Pupils make incorrect predictions based on their alternative models of phenomena, e.g. they predict that an object continues to speed up in situations where it wouldn't.

- Pupils predict events correctly but explain them incorrectly by using their alternative models, e.g. they reason that a forward force must be greater than friction when an object is moving at constant speed (embodying the 'motion requires force' model).
- Pupils have problems with symbolic representation (e.g. graphs).

Given these problems with children's preconceptions and alternative models it is unsurprising that students find it difficult to accept a Newtonian perspective. Students need to be able to explain the motion of a body in terms of the forces acting on it and to be able to predict future motion when forces are known. We summarize in Table 1 the set of commonly occurring prior conceptions, together with goal conceptions which are as specified by Newtonian dynamics. So Table 1 has represented in it the conceptual reconstructions that are required for students learning dynamics.

Table 1   Key reconstructions in dynamics (from Twigger *et al.* (in press)

Prior conception	Goal conception
In space an object drifts about	Objects continue in constant motion in a straight line when no force acts on them
A moving object has a 'force of motion' in it; the object stops when this force 'runs out'	Force opposing motion slows down
Friction not identified as a force	Friction is a force which acts in a direction opposing motion
Driving force must be greater than resistance for object to move at constant speed	Driving force equals resistive force when object moves at constant speed
Heavier things are harder to get going and stop going because of weight pressing them on to the surface	It is harder to get things going than to keep them going; heavier things are harder to get going and to stop going because of greater inertial mass (in addition to any frictional effect)
Heavier objects fall faster than lighter objects	Objects of different weights fall with the same acceleration (ignoring air resistance)

DESIGN OF THE SOFTWARE AND CURRICULUM

The curriculum: four scenarios

Our analysis of the prior conceptions data led to the construction of a curriculum based on four scenarios, which the children were to use both in an informal way and as part of structured experiments. Each scenario is designed to address particular prior conceptions. The basic learning goal concerned Newton's first two laws, revealing what is meant by force, mass and acceleration. Even simple instances of everyday mechanics require the following extra

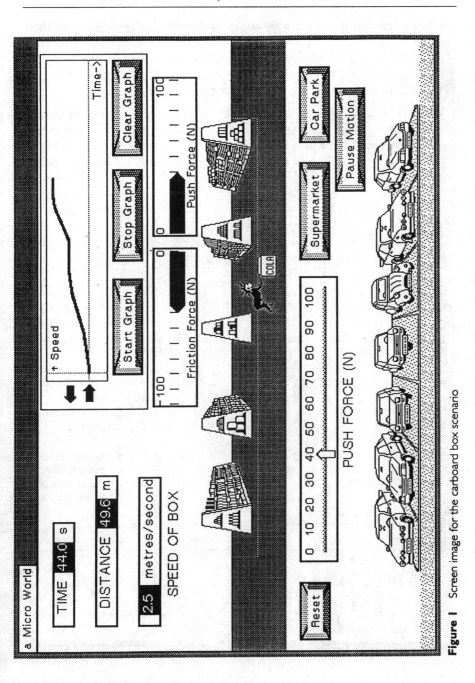

Figure I Screen image for the carboard box scenario

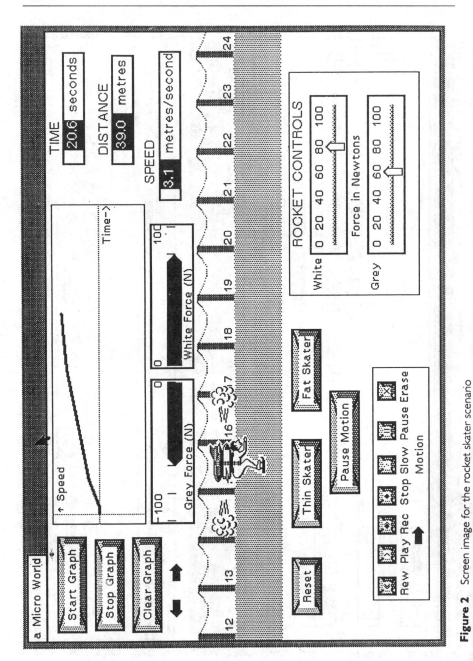

Figure 2 Screen image for the rocket skater scenario

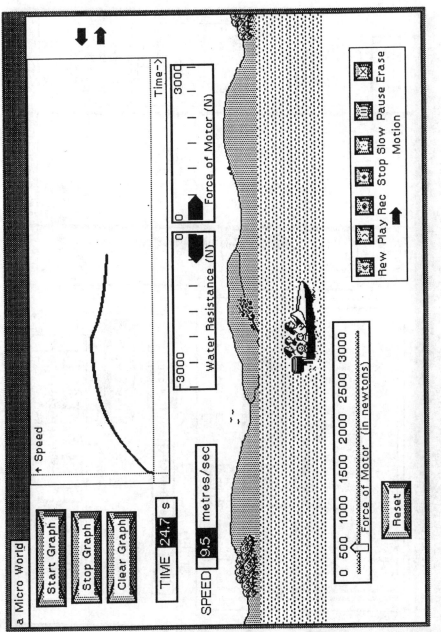

Figure 3 Screen image for the speedboat scenario

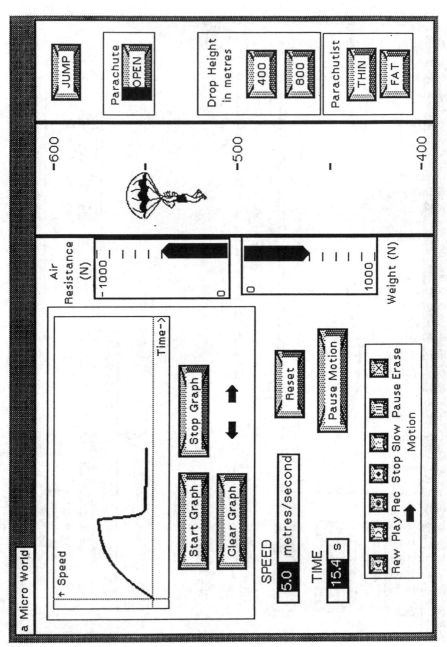

Figure 4   Screen image for the parachutist scenario

features: sliding friction to explain why things slow down when you stop moving them, and fluid friction (to explain why, for example, feathers don't fall as fast as ball bearings). Everyday cases like motion at constant speed as when someone walks, pushes a trolley, or drives a speedboat were included. The screen images for the scenarios are shown in Figures 1–4. The scenarios are as follows:

The cardboard box scenario

This illustrates horizontal motion with friction and consists of an object moving horizontally. The object can be accelerated by a force applied by a human figure and decelerated by sliding friction. Two values of frictional constants, related to the floor of the supermarket and to the rougher surface of the car park, respectively, were available.

The rocket skater scenario

This illustrates horizontal motion without friction. A human figure, which can have two values of mass on frictionless ice, can be propelled by two opposing rockets. The rockets are mounted on the skater's back and can be impulse or continuous rockets.

The speedboat scenario

This illustrates horizontal motion with speed-dependent resistance and consists of a speedboat moving horizontally with the application of a variable continuous force. Its speed settles down to some constant value, the terminal velocity.

The parachutist scenario

This illustrates vertical motion under gravity. A human figure falls vertically under gravity and against air resistance. With the opening of the parachute, the air resistance increases and the figure attains a terminal velocity.

We designed experiments based on these scenarios to enable children to collect empirical data about prototypical motions, and to identify relationships between variables. Computer experiments based on the scenarios combine with support materials such as worksheets and real practical experiments to form an integrated teaching package. The practical work requires pupils to make predictions about the outcomes of either type of experiment, giving the reasons behind their predictions and then to check the outcome.

Part of the approach was to provide counter evidence to their faulty predictions – evidence from experiences either in the 'real' or computer world. In other research projects students have been observed not to believe evidence, to consider it faulty or to forget it quickly and revert to previous beliefs. We believe that learners need an alternative way of conceptualizing the problem before being prepared to reconsider their current ideas. The scenarios provide opportunities for pupils to construct a Newtonian set of rules for force and motion in a supported software environment, through observation of patterns of events and data on the screen. Performing and discussing experiments in the real world gives learners the opportunity to assess the truth of their new conceptions so we incorporated 'real' practicals with computer practicals. The predict/observe/explain methodology (see, for example, Gunstone, 1988) was adopted in the design of worksheets for pupil use so as to fit in with this style of promoting conceptual change.

Two design features of the scenarios are a gradual increase in complexity, and the use of linked scenarios. Therefore in each experimental situation we could add factors one at a time to allow the effect of varying them to be easily explored. Also, the parachutist and speedboat scenarios were linked in a sequence of activities. One of the prior conceptions identified by Twigger *et al.* (in press) had been that students saw some related cases as unrelated, for example pupils intuitively treat vertical and horizontal motion as subject to unrelated rules. Further details of these types of design decision are given in Hennessy *et al.* (in press a).

The software

A software environment called DM^3 – Direct Manipulation of Mechanical Microworlds (Twigger *et al.*, 1991; Draper *et al.*, 1991) was designed for the construction of these scenarios. It is an interactive simulation of mechanical motion under forces, implemented in Smalltalk-80 (as was our inspiration, ARK). This environment allows scenarios, such as the four described above to be constructed easily. Also implemented in Smalltalk-80 is Varilab (Hartley *et al.*, 1991), a qualitative modelling system through which students can express their reasoning and explanations. It is icon based, distinguishes between objects having properties (such as mass and speed) and agents that can cause changes to their attributes. It allows students to build explanations as qualitative models, and it provides both an animated and graphical output of the behaviour of the object as predicted by the student. The research project involved some experiments with Varilab, but it was not included in the large classroom experiment which concentrated on a curriculum based on the scenarios. Further details of the results with Varilab are given in Hartley *et al.* (1991) and will not be discussed further here.

THE CLASSROOM: WHOLE-CLASS EVALUATION

Our curriculum (software, worksheets and experiments) was then tested in a piecemeal way, with small groups of children, and refined. All that remained was to try it out in a classroom. Our purpose was to see whether we could promote conceptual change and to make some inferences about the role that the computer software could have in effecting that change when used in a real school setting. We believe strongly that promoting conceptual change in a real school setting is the appropriate challenge for researchers in this area to accept. We were fortunate to obtain the help and co-operation of an experienced classroom teacher in a local comprehensive school who was prepared to incorporate the curriculum materials we had prepared into the work of twenty-nine children aged twelve and thirteen for seven weeks and to allow us to observe the classroom work in progress. She was able to review the instructional material we had prepared and discuss it with us.

It was a mixed-ability class of thirteen boys and sixteen girls who spent five hours per week working on our curriculum with approximately one hour of homework per week. The children worked in triads, assigned by the teacher. We were able to equip the classroom with five MacII computers, and work was organized so that pupils worked half the time on practical work and half the time on our computer programmes. Each session started with a brief introduction from the teacher. Once both halves of the class were working the teacher circulated round the groups. All of our subjects had prior experience of microcomputers and using a mouse. The pupils had studied an integrated science foundation course for one term previously but had had no science instruction in mechanics or physics since starting secondary school. The data collected involved tests given to all the pupils that could be scored numerically. These data were based on a paper and pencil diagnostic test, a pre-test called 'your ideas about motion'. This was also given as an immediate post-test and again one month later as a delayed post-test. Figure 5 gives an example of one of the test items. We also collected and scored the pupils' answers to the questions in the worksheets that structured their work and their homework assignments.

In addition to collecting these quantitative data we also collected qualitative data to help us interpret the test data and to provide a way of tracking any

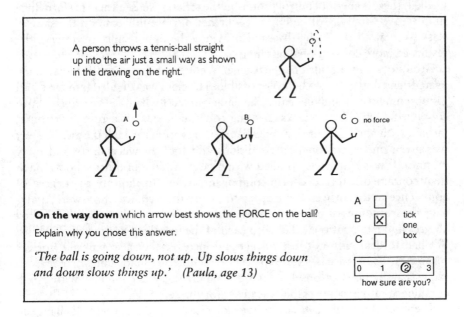

Figure 5 Extract from test on 'your ideas about motion'

processes related to conceptual change. Three triads were chosen to be target groups for the collection of qualitative data. The members were interviewed individually about their understanding of the mechanics curriculum before and after the experimental term. The interviews were conducted by experienced physics teachers who were not part of the research project team. The three interviewers taped private discussions using a series of pictures of situations of objects in motion to prompt discussion of students' reasoning in each of the key areas where we were trying to promote reconstructions. One of the triads was videotaped during all their sessions in the classroom and two other triads were tape-recorded and observed. All three triads seemed at ease with this level of observation. In addition another observer made notes of the way the different triads dealt with each other and the way that the teacher talked to, helped and guided the different triads. All whole-class discussions were also videotaped. Fortunately the lessons took place in quite a large classroom and the pupils and teacher did not seem inhibited by the various forms of monitoring. For example, the videotaped triad chatted quite happily about friendships and fashions between the experiments they carried out.

Naturally we wanted to compare the results of our efforts with results obtained when our tests were done by similar class groups with no access to our curriculum. We also used three control groups: one that was following a different curriculum with a different teacher in the same school, and two other control groups from the Leeds area, one following a more practically based curriculum. Since these classes were all taught by different teachers and we did not attempt to standardize the length of study or content of the material studied, these were not control groups in the strictest sense. Their performance simply gave us a way of finding out whether our pre-test data on the sample class were at all representative, and provided the opportunity to observe the results of more conventional teaching.

Groupings were decided by the teacher in collaboration with the researchers, using friendship groups wherever possible. The class was divided into ten small groups: nine triads and one pair. The diagnostic test which we described above contained a set of fifteen tasks covering twelve contexts concerning horizontal motion with and without friction, and vertical motion through the air. The test was given under examination conditions and took between thirty and forty minutes. It was extensively trialled with ninety children in other schools. Each item contained a forced choice component, a box to indicate the degree of confidence in the answer and a space to justify their choice of answer. Analysing the responses involved looking for particular combinations of forced choices and explanations relating to each of the identified key reconstructions. We had to deal with not just correct and incorrect but also partially correct responses. These are cases were correct predictions are made but where reasoning was ambiguous or loosely expressed. Where this was combined with a high confidence rating, some credit was given for the response.

The most thorough method we used for measuring the conceptual change in the pupils was the series of clinical interviews conducted before and after the intervention. We also looked at how prevalent the identified prior conceptions were in the class, as well as the degree to which the goal conceptions were achieved.

HOW IT WORKED OUT

We have obtained some interesting results. In a relatively short time a significant amount of conceptual change was detected, which showed up on various measures we used. We found that the number of correct responses and explanations based on correct Newtonian theories increased significantly between the pre-test and post-test and the delayed post-test. We found that the pupils' confidence ratings for their correct answers had also increased. However, we also found that students gave more partially correct answers and were also better able to provide explanations for their incorrect responses. The findings about increased confidence are interesting as is the increase in explanations. It suggests pupils are becoming more articulate about their choices. We had been concerned that the pupils might have simply become confused or irritated when the answers provided by our simulations were different to those they expected but this didn't happen.

In our experimental class we found a decrease in two kinds of prior belief: first, fewer explanations asserting that motion implies a force were found, that is fewer explanations excluded the possibility that friction was a force opposing motion; and, second, there was evidence for a greater understanding of resistive forces being directional. More pupils used the concept of friction as a force opposing motion and the idea that the magnitude of friction depends on weight. However, we found that children expressed some new incorrect conceptions in the post-test, which they had not had prior to our intervention. Two kinds of prior conceptions, in particular, became more prevalent over time: 'forward force must be greater than a retarding force in order to maintain motion' and 'an object has force in it'.

These results mostly came from an examination of the test data. The analysis of the transcribed interviews provided clear confirmatory evidence in support of this, suggesting that the written test data provide an accurate picture of the pupil's understanding. In a number of cases the tests seem to have provided an underestimate of the degree of conceptual change in the desired direction in individual pupils, with discussion in the pre-interview showing appropriate vocabulary being used without understanding (for example 'force' used in contradictory ways in different parts of the interview), while explanations in the post-interviews show consistent correct description and use of concepts. This was also shown by the change in the actual vocabulary that pupils used, with a general shift to appropriate vocabulary such as friction force, balanced forces, and an increase in confidence shown by the use of qualifiers like 'I'm sure'. We are currently charting the learning trajectories of some children in the group (Twigger et al., in preparation).

Pupils rarely appealed to the result of a particular remembered experiment or simulation. Our interview data also showed that both pupils and teachers valued the combination of computer and real practicals. One surprising finding from our classroom observation was that we saw little evidence of a classroom computer culture developing. While the pupils were engaged by the simulations and able to use them, we found no informal cross-fertilization between groups, no tips on what worked and no appeals to classroom colleagues when things went wrong. We do not believe that there was any significant Hawthorne effect either, as the pupils very quickly settled into the routine of computer experiments and did not find them at all glamorous. We also found the children's agenda differed from that of both the teachers and the researchers. We did not detect any particular desire to grasp Newtonian concepts.

A substantial amount of conceptual change showed up in only one other class – one of our control groups did show a significant increase in the number or correct responses on the post-test, although the pupils were one year older. This group did not show any decline in any of its incorrect prior conceptions. Further details of the results are given in Hennessy et al. (in press b).

CONCLUSIONS

We are satisfied that the evaluation results indicate that our computer-based curriculum works in a real classroom and that the direct manipulation interface eases problems for computer novices. We also believe that a significantly greater appreciation of Newtonian theory emerges, although some prior conceptions were in fact strengthened. We believe this successful outcome was because our curriculum of experimentation and discussion helps pupils to make their beliefs explicit. The pattern of student learning observed by us leaves us with the hope that if more time were allowed for this curriculum component, students could complete the process of conceptual growth and emerge with secure Newtonian conceptions.

The project reviewed above was an expensive one which used a substantial research grant (£255,000) for equipment and full-time researchers (including a seconded teacher) as well as much additional 'donated' staff resource from four universities and three schools. We do not think it would be possible to have come to the conclusions above with fewer resources and it seems clear that three years was about the shortest period for such a project and that five years would have allowed further refinement of the instructional materials and more detailed tracking of long-term conceptual change. The project findings have implications for current practice in the design of curriculum materials for science education and also help set the agenda for future research and development work on the use of information technology in science education.

Some of the implications for current practice are depressing. Our work on prior conceptions matches other studies and shows a low level of understanding of the fundamental concepts of physics which is almost impossible to relate to the much higher implicit and explicit assumptions of understanding to be found in secondary-school curricula and schemes of work for pupils of this age. Another challenging implication is the large amount of structured pupil activity and study time needed for appropriate conceptual change. It does not seem possible to 'fix' general misunderstandings with single explanations or experiments. The main positive implication is that it is possible to use simulated computer experiments to augment usefully conventional classroom experiments. Moreover such computer use can be a fully integrated part of a modern approach to science instruction, involving spiral exploration, group work, the testing of predictions against observations, written individual explanations and open whole-class discussion. Obviously we cannot argue that computer use is essential to support successful conceptual change in physics understanding. However, given the current position in schools, any workable route has to be welcomed.

The general implications for research and development work in science education include the value of identifying and targetting very particular prior conceptions and the utility of having a progressive series of tests of the instructional innovations, starting with informal prototyping and finishing with a formal evaluation using qualitative and quantitative pre-tests and post-tests. The computer specific findings include the ease of use of direct manipulation interfaces, the value of familiar contexts or scenarios for simulations, the utility of object-oriented computer languages such as Smalltalk-80 for constructing simulations and the need to support collaborative group work rather than isolated individuals. The final methodological conclusion is that the identification of pupils' conceptions of science and the development and testing of new instructional techniques is best done by a partnership of teachers and researchers.

ACKNOWLEDGEMENTS

We wish to thank the science and other staff and the headteacher at Lord Grey School, Milton Keynes, whose co-operation made this investigation possible. We are especially grateful to the teacher (Margaret Marangos) and twenty-nine children who took part in our classroom experiment, and to their counterparts in the three comparison classes. We are also grateful for the participation of all of the children and adults who took part in the extensive pilot studies. The three-year Conceptual Change in Science project was funded by the Economic and Social Research Council through the InTER (Information Technology in Education Research) Programme. We would also like to thank Elaine Brown and Becky Graham for particularly helpful comments on drafts of this article.

REFERENCES

Brown, D. and Clement, J. (1987) Overcoming misconceptions in mechanics. Paper presented at American Educational Research Association (AERA), Washington, DC.

Draper, S., Driver, R., Hartley, R., Hennessy, S., Mallen, C., Mohamed, R., O'Malley, C., O'Shea, T., Scanlon, E. and Twigger, D. (1991) Design considerations in a project on conceptual change in science, *Computers and Education*, 17, no. 1.

Driver, R. (1984) Cognitive psychology and pupils' frameworks in mechanics. International Conference on Physics Education: The Many Faces of Teaching and Learning Mechanics, Utrecht.

Driver, R., Guesne, E. and Tiberghien, A. (eds.) (1985). *Children's Ideas in Science*, Milton Keynes, Open University Press.

Driver, R. and Scanlon, E. (1989) Conceptual change in science. *Journal of Computer Assisted Learning*, 5, (1), pp. 25–36.

Gunstone, R. F. (1988) Learners and science education, in P. Fensham (ed.) *Development and Dilemmas in Science Education*, Lewes, Falmer Press.

Gunstone, R. F. and Watts, D. M. (1985) Force and motion, in R. Driver, E. Guesne and A. Tiberghien (eds.) *Children's Ideas in Science* Milton Keynes, Open University Press.

Halloun, I. and Hestenes, D. (1985) Common sense concepts about motion, *American Journal of Physics*, 53, pp. 1056–65.

Hartley, R., Mallen, C. and Byard, M. (1991) Qualitative modelling. Proceedings of the First International Conference on the Learning Sciences, 31 May–2 June, Illinois, Laurence Erlbaum Associates.

Heller, J. and Hungate, H. (1984) Theory based instruction in description of mechanics problems. Paper presented at American Educational Research Association (AERA), New Orleans.

Hennessy, S., Spensley, F., O'Malley, C. E., Byard, M., Driver, R., Hartley, R., Mallen, C., Mohamed, R., O'Shea, T. and Scanlon, E. (1990) A direct manipulation microworld for vertical motion, in A. McDougall and D. Dowling (eds.) *Computers in Education*, Amsterdam, Elsevier.

Hennessy, S., Twigger, D., Byard, M., Draper, S., Driver, R., Hartley, R., Mohamed, R., O'Malley, C. E., O'Shea, T. and Scanlon, E. Design of a computer-augmented curriculum for mechanics, *International Journal of Science Education* (In press a).

Hennessy, S., Twigger, D., Byard, M., Draper, S., Driver, R., Hartley, R., Mohamed, R., O'Malley, C. E., O'Shea, T. and Scanlon, E. A classroom intervention using a computer-augmented curriculum for mechanics, *International Journal of Science Education* (In press b).

Hewson, M. and Hewson, P. (1983) The effect of instruction using student's prior knowledge and conceptual change categories on science learning, *Journal of Research on Science Teaching*, 20, (2), pp. 731–43.

McDermott, L. C. (1984) Research on conceptual understanding in mechanics, *Physics Today*, Vol. 37, July, pp. 24–32.

Smith, R. B. (1990) The Alternate Reality Kit: an animated environment for creating interactive simulations, in O. Boyd-Barrett and E. Scanlon (eds.) *Computers and Learning*, Wokingham, Addison Wesley.

Twigger, D., Byard, M., Draper, S., Driver, R., Hartley, R., Hennessy, S., Mallen, C., Mohamed, R., O'Malley, C. E., O'Shea, T. and Scanlon, E. (1991) The 'Conceptual Change in Science' project, *Journal of Computer Assisted Learning*, 7, (2), pp. 144–55.

Twigger, D., Byard, M., Driver, R., Draper, S., Hartley, R., Hennessy, S., Mohamed, R., O'Malley, C. E., O'Shea, T. and Scanlon, E. The conceptions of force and motion of students aged between 10 and 15 years: an interview study designed to guide instruction, *International Journal of Science Education* (In press).

Twigger, D., Byard, M., Draper, S., Driver, R., Hartley, R., Hennessy, S., Mallen, C., Mohamed, R., O'Malley, C. E., O'Shea, T. and Scanlon, E. (in preparation) A microgenic study of conceptual change in dynamics.

Viennot, L. (1979) Spontaneous reasoning in elementary dynamics, *European Journal of Science Education*, 1, (2), pp. 205–21.

An exploration of long-term far-transfer effects following an extended intervention programme in the high-school science curriculum

Philip Adey and Michael Shayer

BACKGROUND

During the late 1960s and 1970s there was considerable interest in the Piagetian model of stage-wise cognitive development. Educationalists used it both to seek explanations for the difficulties encountered by students in learning, and as a basis for the design of more effective instruction (e.g. Karplus, 1979; Renner *et al.*, 1976; Lawson, Blake and Nordland, 1975; Shayer, 1978). At the same time, academic psychologists were questioning the mechanisms of cognitive development and both the construct and empirical validity of domain-general stages proposed by the Genevan school (Brainerd, 1978; Brown and Desforges, 1979). This is not the place to review whether the change in fashion against the Genevan model was justified. We merely note our opinion that the British version of the critical position (Brown and Desforges, 1977) was shown to be selective in its use of the literature, and empirically unjustified – see Shayer (1979) and the reply by Desforges and Brown (1979). Whatever one's position is in this debate, it is relevant to recognize that the work to be reported here grew out of results obtained at Chelsea College London in the 1970s based on a broadly Piagetian paradigm.

At that time we conducted a national survey to determine levels of cognitive development using a large representative sample of the adolescent population (Shayer, Küchemann and Wylam, 1976; Shayer and Wylam, 1978). At the same time, we developed an instrument for the analysis of curricula in terms of the cognitive demands made on learners (the 'Curriculum Analysis Taxonomy', in Shayer and Adey, 1981) and applied it to curricula then in use. The co-ordination of these two pieces of evidence provided some explanation for what had been the empirical experience of many science teachers, that the demands made by much of the material then in use in schools was beyond the reach of the majority of pupils.

We thus came to the question that had been bothering American instructors theoretically for some years: can cognitive development be accelerated? In 1975 Niemark wrote:

From: *Cognition and Instruction* (1993) Vol. II, no. 1, pp. 1–29.

One of the more surprising gaps in the reported research concerns what Piaget has called 'The American Question': the possibility of accelerating cognitive development through specific training. . . . When more is known about the course of normal development and the variables which affect it, it is quite likely that sophisticated training research will begin in earnest. Piaget's prediction would be that all such attempts are doomed to failure.

In 1980, following discussion with the Clarkes, who had earlier surveyed the whole field of intervention studies (Clarke and Clarke, 1968), Shayer worked with a number of studies using different intervention models, summarized in Shayer (1987). One of these was a small-scale replication of Feuerstein's Instrumental Enrichment programme (Feuerstein, Rand, Hoffman and Miller, 1980). The reported effect-sizes in relation to controls (Shayer and Beasley, 1987) were large, including a figure of 1.2σ on a battery of individual interview Piagetian tasks, and 1.1σ on Raven's Matrices. However, with this intervention model teachers found it difficult to relate the improved thinking skills of the students, achieved in the context of subject-free intervention lessons, to the specifics of the school curriculum. No effects on school achievement were found at immediate post-test.

At the same time there was something of a rush of cognitive acceleration studies reported from North America and Australia (e.g. Case, 1974; Kuhn and Angelev, 1976; Rosenthal, 1979; Lawson and Snitgen, 1982), reviewed in Adey (1988) and Goosens (1989). Now, when the Piagetian star has waned somewhat and the majority of cognitive psychologists are emphasizing domain-specific skills rather than a general underlying cognitive structure, the question of cognitive acceleration may seem meaningless, or at best irrelevant. Nevertheless, there remain some who continue to dig for the possibility of general thinking skills which are amenable to influence and enhanced development. Nickerson, Perkins and Smith (1985) expressed the search in a form of Pascal's wager:

> If [teaching thinking] cannot be done, and we try to do it, we may waste some time and effort. If it can be done, and we fail to try, the inestimable cost will be generations of students whose ability to think effectively will be less than it could have been. So we are better advised to adopt the attitude that thinking can be taught, try hard to teach it, and let experience prove us wrong if it must.
>
> (p. 324)

We started from both this viewpoint that the possibility of teaching general thinking skills was worth pursuing, and that what have recently come to be referred to as Higher Order Thinking Skills (Resnick, 1987) are well characterized by Inhelder and Piaget's descriptions of formal operations. Again this is not the place to reopen debates on validity of the Inhelder–Piaget account of formal operations, but it is worth noting that the characteristic performance of children on the Inhelder tasks has always replicated the original findings, and can be regarded as a fact requiring explanation.[1] Further, while Piaget's propositional calculus can be handled in a general form, his use of it as an explanatory model is invariably contextualized. While this may infuriate logicians (Parsons, 1960) it does lead to a consistent descriptive model of thought, as Papert (1961) has demonstrated. If further justification for pursuing the Piaget model is required, it may be found in a challenge thrown out to Shayer by Alan Clarke. 'If you want to go on using the Piagetian model,' he said, quoting from Hull, 'bear in mind that one of the best ways of studying a phenomenon is to try to change it.' If the intervention model is incoherent, no successful change can issue from it. Thus by acting on the belief that the Piagetian account of formal operations is a satisfactory description of general higher order thinking skills, the best test is to look for evidence that both in terms of the model (Piagetian tests) and inferred consequences if the model is true (school achievement in science and other subjects), the results are in accord with prediction.

Funding was obtained in 1980 from the Social Science Research Council (SSRC) to investigate the possibility of promoting formal operational thinking in eleven- to fourteen-year-olds. A pilot study conducted in one school led to further SSRC funding to involve teachers in a sample of ordinary state high schools in Britain. The Cognitive Acceleration through Science Education (CASE) projects were based at the (then) Chelsea College Centre for Science and Mathematics Education, University of London.

The results of the experiment, especially as they relate to science education, have been reported piecemeal as they occurred (Adey and Shayer, 1990; Shayer and Adey, 1992a, 1992b, 1993). Here we will provide more detail of the instructional strategies employed, summarize these results in a uniform manner, try to fill in the overall picture which emerges and, by looking especially at the language development, draw implications for models of the mind.

CONTEXT

In approaching a high-school principal with a proposal to introduce a set of activities which might, or might not, help pupils to develop higher-order thinking skills there are (at least in Britain) two stopping answers: (1) 'it will interfere with preparation for external examinations' and (2) 'I am not going to rewrite the timetable to provide a new space for thinking lessons'. The riposte to (1) is to offer to work with the younger pupils, before they get near the end-of-school examination. That to (2) is to embed the new activities in an existing subject. In any case, if an intervention model can be interpolated within the context of an existing body of widely used teaching skills and content, then both students and teachers are immediately helped to apply new thinking skills to that context. Given successful application within such a context, accompanied by an emphasis on the generalizable skills, chances should be much increased of the students' improved cognition subsequently affecting performance in other contexts. Although it has been shown that the Piagetian account of concrete and formal operations can usefully be applied to the context of history (e.g. Hallam, 1967 and Jurd, 1973) and English comprehension and social studies (Fusco, 1987), the field of science learning was chosen for micro-political reasons. These include our own familiarity with the foundations of science teaching, and the fact that in the UK it is the science teaching fraternity which has shown greatest interest in the application of learning theories to the curriculum. It also seemed that, whether or not Inhelder and Piaget (1958) intended the schemata of formal operations to be free of domain constraints, they do look very scientific and are initially easier to 'sell' to science teachers than, say, to language teachers.

THE BASES OF THE INTERVENTION ACTIVITIES

We thus set about designing a set of activities, set in a scientific context and using the schemata of formal operations as a guiding framework. We considered that the chances of achieving domain-general improvements in higher-order thinking skills would be maximized by addressing all ten of Piaget's schemata. Reviews of the literature (Adey, 1988; Goosens, 1989) on cognitive acceleration suggested certain features which should maximize an intervention programme's chances of bringing about long-term effects on the general ability of learners. These include:

- the introduction, through concrete activities, of the terminology of relationships and the context in which a problem will be presented. Goosens (1989) refers to this as *perceptual readiness* but we now prefer the term *conceptual readiness* (suggested by an anonymous review of an earlier version of this paper);
- the presentation of problems which induce *cognitive conflict*;
- the encouragement of *metacognition*;
- the *bridging* of thinking strategies developed within the context of the special lessons to other areas.

We may say that conceptual readiness is the 'set-up', cognitive conflict the 'sting', metacognition makes the thinking process conscious in the learner, and bridging provides a wide range of applications.

The set of activities developed is called 'Thinking Science' (Adey, Shayer and Yates, 1989). Each of the features above will now be described in more detail and illustrated with examples.

Conceptual readiness

Formal operations only operate on a situation that has first been described by the subject in terms of descriptive concrete models. Thus conceptual readiness involves establishing that students are familiar with the technical vocabulary, apparatus and framework in which a problem situation will be set. The first few activities concentrate on the key ideas of *variables* and *relationships between variables*. The terms are introduced in a way that requires only concrete

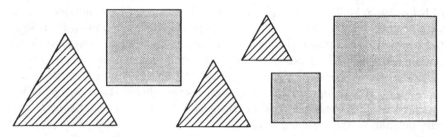

Figure 1 What are the variables here?

operational processing. For example, the teacher displays a selection of books on the table: 'In what ways are these different from one another?' she asks. Answers typically include 'colour', 'size', 'hard- or softback', and so on. 'These are ways in which the books *vary* from each other. We call colour, size, etc, *variables*.' Pupils are now shown a collection of shapes (Figure 1).

'What are the variables here?' Typically eleven-year-olds have no difficulty in establishing that shape, colour, and size are variables. Now we move on: 'Can you see any way in which any of these variables go together?' Some more probing questions and verbal or non-verbal prompting leads pupils from specific statements ('the triangles are red, the squares are blue') to the more general recognition that 'colour goes with shape'. After further similar examples, the term 'relationship' is introduced. There is a relationship between the variables colour and shape. Cartoon examples give practice in recognizing relationship between variables in terms such as 'as the number of sausages goes up, their size goes down' (see Figure 2).

Within the same sequence, it is important also to recognize when there is *no* relationship. For example, with a set of loaded but opaque coloured jars there is a relationship between colour and size (big ones are blue, small ones are red), but pupils find that the weight of the jars bears no relationship to either colour or size.

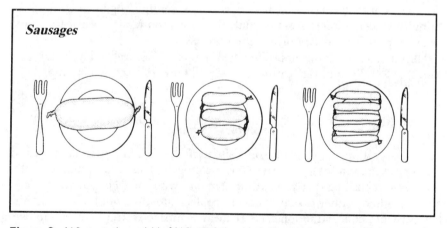

Figure 2 What are the variables? What relationship is there between them?

Where there is a relationship, pupils can be encouraged to use the relationship to make predictions. In the squares and triangles activity, the teacher may ask 'now, if I produce another triangle which follows the same pattern, what colour will it be?' Where there is relationship, no prediction can be made. Knowing the colour of the jar does not help you to decide what its weight is.

Other terms introduced early in the scheme are *input variable* and *outcome variable*, which are used instead of the more formal terms 'independent' and 'dependent' variables respectively.

The examples given illustrate some CASE activities which provide conceptual readiness for the whole 'Thinking Science' scheme. In addition, almost every activity starts with a conceptual readiness phase for that particular activity, as will be seen below. Note that the strategy here is to give the student confidence in the use of the technical vocabulary in a situation requiring only concrete modelling, before she needs to apply it in a context requiring formal modelling.

Cognitive conflict

This is the term used to describe an event or observation which the student finds puzzling and discordant with previous experience or understanding. All perceptions are interpreted through the subjects' present conceptual framework. Where current conceptualization fails to make sense of an experience, constructive mental work by students may lead to accommodation and a change in their conceptual framework. Kuhn, Amsel and O'Loughlin's (1988) investigation of the co-ordination of new evidence with existing cognitive schema confirms that instances of cognitive conflict do not automatically produce a 'Road to Damascus' conversion to a new conceptualization. Younger and less able pupils often seem not to see that there is a conflict, or at least not to be bothered by it. But if there is no conflict, then there is no chance of accommodation. In Vygotsky's (1978) words:

> learning which is oriented toward developmental levels that have already been reached is ineffective from the viewpoint of a child's overall development. It does not aim for a new stage of the developmental process but rather lags behind this process. . . . The only 'good learning' is that which is in advance of development.
>
> (p. 82)

Here are two examples of activities designed to induce conflict:

1. **Floating and sinking jars:** Two sets of jars are prepared. Five jars, A to E, are all the same size but are loaded to have different masses. Six jars, 1 to 6, are each successively smaller than the one before but they all have the same mass. Jar 1/A is common to both sets. The jars are opaque, and labelled only with their number or letter. Pupils have worksheets showing the jars arranged in a matrix. They are invited to weigh each jar, and then drop it in a large bowl of water. On the worksheets, they record each jar's

weight and whether it floats or sinks. The discussion centres first on jars A–E. What conclusions can be drawn? Only two variables are involved, weight and buoyancy, so students can develop a simple concrete model relating the two: 'heavy things sink, light things float.' Similarly, a focus on jars 1–6 leads to another concrete model: 'small things sink, big things float.' (Well, pins sink and ships float, so this accords with experience – albeit rather selected experience.) Now, jar X is produced. It is established that it is the same size as jar 3, a floater, and the same weight as jar C, also a floater (Figure 3).

Students must predict what they think will happen when it is put in water. Application of the two concrete models already developed leads to the prediction that jar X will float. When it is put in the water, it sinks.

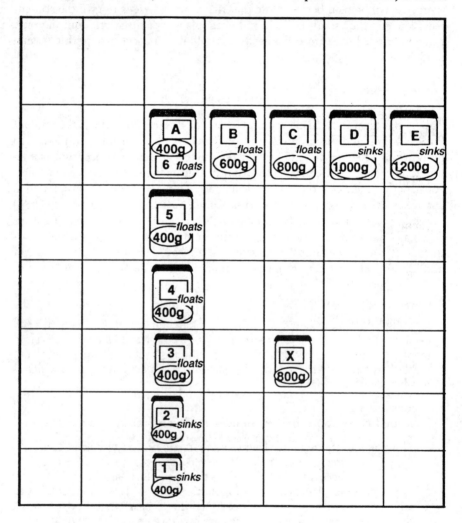

Figure 3   Will jar X float or sink?

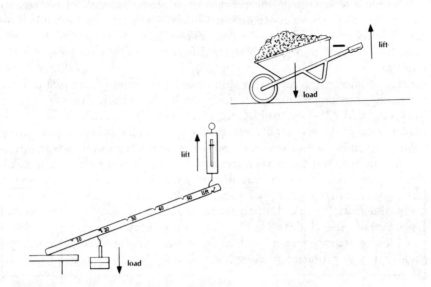

Figure 4   The wheelbarrow as a lever system

Thus there is conflict between perceptual experience and the concrete operations used thus far. Concrete operations will not provide an explanation for the sinking of jar X. A three-variable, formal, model is required employing the notion of 'weight-for-a-certain-size'.

2. **Wheelbarrow:** Introductory discussion and demonstration (the conceptual readiness phase) establishes the parallel between a notched stick and the wheelbarrow as lever systems (Figure 4).

   Students record and tabulate the force at the 'handle' as successive loads are added. With about six pairs of values completed, they draw the straight line graph relating the two on a given grid. From this they are asked to make predictions about what the force would be with extra loads, which are not available. The first predictions can be read off by simple extrapolation of the graph. But then the graph paper runs out. A concrete strategy is no longer available. This is the point of conflict, where a more sophisticated view of the relationship – that involving the constant ratio of load to effort – has to be invented. They have to go beyond the conceptual support of the graph and construct a more general mathematical model through which they can extrapolate. Cognitive operations on the data must become formalized to achieve a successful solution to the problem.

We aimed to maximize the permanent effect on subjects of conflict situations by (a) effective conceptual readiness (illustrated above) and (b) repeated, sometimes small, doses of conflict over an extended period. Note that these 'small doses' were given in many different contexts with the underlying implication that such treatment would lead to accelerated development of a general cognitive structure. This is in contrast to the conflict situations presented by curriculum materials founded in the Alternative Conceptions Movement (ACM) – see for instance CLISP (1987). An ACM-style teaching sequence devotes considerable time to setting up and, it is hoped, to resolving cognitive conflict about one concept. Their aim is the development of that concept rather than the development of general thinking skills. The CASE aim was less specific, and potentially more widely generalizable. Our expectation was not that after the floating and sinking activity pupils would have a grasp of density (some did, some did not), but that they would develop their repertoire of general ideas – in this case that of compound variables – which provide explanatory power. Such higher-order thinking skills are developed such that new problems in completely different contexts could be treated effectively.

Metacognition

It is now widely accepted (Nickerson *et al.*, 1985; Perkins and Salomon, 1989) that students are more likely to develop wide-ranging thinking skills if they are encouraged to think about their own thinking, to become aware of the strategies of their own thinking and actions. This is what is meant by metacognition. In a 'Thinking Science' lesson, the teacher asks pupils to talk about difficulties and successes they have with problems, both with the teacher and with each other – not just 'that was difficult' but 'what was difficult about it, and how did I overcome the difficulty?' Students become accustomed to reflect on the sort of thinking they have been engaged in, to bring it to the front of their consciousness, and to make of it an explicit tool which may then be available for use in a new context. Using the words to describe reasoning patterns is another aspect of metacognition. The aim is that CASE students should not only be better equipped to recognize, say, a proportionality problem when they see one but that they should be able to say 'That's a proportionality problem!' and so open the door to a particular set of solution strategies. This is a special application of what Vygotsky (1978) describes as the use of language as a mediator of learning. The language of reasoning mediates meta-learning.

It is not easy to illustrate this metacognitive element from 'Thinking Science' activities, since it is more a feature of the teacher's strategy introduced through INSET than of the printed materials. One example illustrates how a worksheet can act as a starting point for metacognitive speculation, although in prosecuting the activity the teacher plays an essential role in building on this starting point:

Classification

Students go through a set of simple exercises such as putting animals into groups (according to their own criteria), arranging a variety of foodstuffs on the shelves of a larder, sorting chemicals by colour and by solubility, and so on.

Finally (Figure 5) they are asked to consider the classifications that they have done and to reflect on which was the most difficult for them, and why, and which was the easiest, and why. They compare their feelings with other groups, and discuss why some groups found some activities difficult and others found the same ones easy.

Bridging

The explicit bridging to other contexts is the final link in this chain of developing, abstracting, and generalizing reasoning. During in-service introductions to 'Thinking Science', teachers engaged in exercises to develop their own links between the 'Thinking Science' activities and their regular science curriculum and pupils' experiences in everyday life. During on-service visits by members of the project team to schools, further opportunities for bridging were explored in the context of each school's curriculum and environment. This can be illustrated with one activity concerned with probability:

---

6. Thinking Back

Put a tick by the classification activity you found easiest.
Put a cross by the one you found most difficult.

Why was the one you ticked the easiest?
Why was the one you crossed the most difficult?

Has everyone ticked and crossed the same ones as you?

Write a sentence about a friend, using the word *characteristic*.

Why do you think that it is useful to be able to classify things?

Figure 5   The last of a series of classification activities

Tea tasting

Some people think that tea tastes different if you put the milk in before or after the tea. One student volunteer goes out of the room while five cups of tea are prepared, some with milk first, others with tea first. She returns and tastes each cup, reporting 'tea first' or 'milk first' on each. The problem in front of the class is, how many does she have to get right, out of five, before we believe that she really can tell the difference? (American readers may like to substitute Coke *vs*. Pepsi, although that is much easier.) Typically eleven- and twelve-year-olds may consider that three out of five, or four out of five would be convincing. Now everyone spins five coins, many times, so that a large number of spins soon accumulates. In a concrete way, they discover the percentage of times all five coins show heads, just by chance. The conflict arises as they realise that there is no simple answer to the question 'how many rights is convincing?' Even 100 out of 100 could occur by chance. There is no deterministic answer, only a probabilistic one. The bridging occurs through discussion of, say, smoking and lung cancer. Not everyone who smokes will certainly get lung cancer. Not everyone who does not smoke will avoid it. The idea of a probabilistic relationship between a cause and effect is given meaning.

DEVELOPMENT OF THE INTERVENTION, EXPERIMENT AND TESTS

Activities were drafted and taught by the research team (the authors and Carolyn Yates) themselves to two classes of twelve-year-olds in an ordinary London comprehensive secondary school. A total of thirty such activities, each designed to last about sixty to seventy minutes, were thus devised, pre-trialled, revised, and duplicated.

Nine schools representing a variety of environments in England were chosen in consultation with local education authorities' science advisers who were asked to recommend what they considered to be ordinary mixed comprehensive schools typical of their locality. In some cases advisers directed us to schools which they felt would 'do a good job' for us, and in others to schools which they felt were in need of some help. A total of twenty-four classes of pupils of average ability[2] in these schools were selected and randomly assigned to experimental and control conditions such that there were experimental and control classes in each school. Some control classes were taught by the same teacher as the experimental classes, others were taught by different teachers. Four classes were of the eleven-plus age group (UK Year 7, US Grade 6), eight of twelve-plus (UK Year 8, US Grade 7). These separate cohorts will be referred to simply as the '11+' and '12+' groups.

The twelve experimental classes started in 1985 to receive a 'Thinking Science' lesson in place of a regular science lesson about once every two weeks. Typically classes in this age group would receive a total of two or three science lessons per week, so the 'Thinking Science' lessons could have taken as much as 25 per cent of the normally allotted science time. The 'Thinking Science' activities were introduced to teachers through a series of one-day workshops followed up by visits to the schools during which lessons were observed and discussed with the teacher. We did not expect the physical foundation of the proposed teaching strategies to become readily accessible to teachers through the printed material alone.

One school withdrew after two terms and another, working under especially difficult circumstances, failed to deliver the intervention even approximately as planned. Results will be reported here for the ten experimental classes (four 11+ and six 12+) in seven schools that continued with the programme, more or less as intended, for a period of two years (Figure 6).

After the two-year intervention programme, students were no longer maintained in identifiable 'experimental' and 'control' groups, but mixed together as they chose options for the subjects they would continue with. In the case of three of the 11+ classes, the end of the intervention coincided with the end of the middle-school period, and pupils were dispersed to a number of different high schools.

Testing occasions were *pre-test*, before the intervention began; *post-test*, immediately after the two-year intervention; *delayed post-test*, one year after the end of the intervention; and the General Certificate of Secondary Education

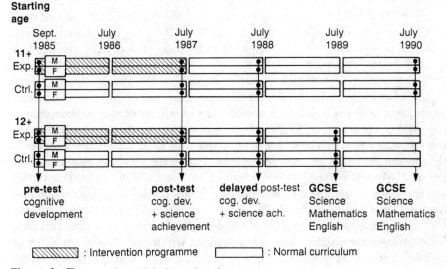

Figure 6 The experimental design and testing programme

(GCSE) taken two (for those who started as 12+) or three (for those who started at 11+) years after the end of the intervention. We have no reason to suppose that those who moved from the schools in which we were able to trace them for testing, or who missed particular tests, were in any way systematically related to whether they had been 'experimental' or 'control' pupils.

The tests of *cognitive development* used were demonstrated group Piagetian Reasoning Tasks (PRTs). These tasks were developed as Science Reasoning Tasks (Shayer, Wylam *et al.*, 1978) in the 1970s for the Concepts in Secondary Science and Mathematics project's large-scale survey of the school population, and have been widely used since. Information on the validity and reliability of PRTs is available in Shayer, Adey and Wylam (1981) There were originally six PRTs which yielded scores within a common scale from 1 (preoperational) through 2A, 2B, . . . to 3B (mature formal operational). Since their development, and before the analyses to be reported here, PRT data were re-analysed using Rasch scaling to give a finer mesh estimate of person-level. Now the total number of items correct on a given PRT can be converted directly into a decimal score on the scale 1 (early preoperational) to 10 (mature formal operational) with a standard error of about 0.4. Table 1 shows some PRT titles, including those used in this experiment, and the ranges within which each operates. Where two PRTs were used, the mean was taken.

Table I　Some Piagetian reasoning tasks

Name of task	Range	Use in CASE experiment
1. Spatial relations	1–5	Not used in CASE
2. Volume and heaviness	2–7	Pre-test
3. Pendulum	5–10	Pre-test and post-test
8. Probability	3–10	Post-test and delayed post-test

Science achievement was assessed at post-test by a common achievement test agreed by the teachers to be a fair test of the objectives of their science curricula for the previous year. At the delayed test, each school's end-of-year science test or mean-of-module test was used. These tests thus, by definition, covered the objectives of each school's curriculum. They were converted to percentages before further treatment.

The General Certificate of Secondary Education (GCSE) is now the examination taken in England and Wales by most sixteen-year-olds as a school-leaving examination and/or as a selection test for further education. There are four different regional examining boards, and within each board a number of syllabus options. Schools may choose the regional board they wish to use for each subject. For instance, a school may decide to enter some pupils for one, two, or occasionally three out of chemistry, physics or biology, others for double-certificate general science, others again for single general science, and these examinations may be set by the same or by different regional boards.

Norm-referenced grades are awarded in all GCSE examinations on a scale A – G and unclassified, eight grades in all, moderated across boards to ensure equivalence of standards. For the purpose of treatment here they were mapped on to an equal-interval scale with values 7 down to 0.

TREATMENT AND PRESENTATION OF RESULTS

Post and delayed cognitive development scores could be reported simply as raw gains over pre-test scores, comparing control and experimental groups. The common science achievement test could be reported as a comparison between experimental and control means, although this would ignore any difference between starting ability levels as assessed by the pre-test. However, the variety of tests amongst different schools used for the delayed achievement measures and for the GCSE made it impossible to make such simple comparisons. For these measures, the method of *residualized gain scores* was used (Cronbach and Furby, 1970).

The method depends on the fact that PRT scores are fair predictors of subsequent academic success. We compute, for each particular achievement test or GCSE exam, the predictive relationship between pre-PRT score and achievement (regression of achievement test score on pre-PRT) for the control group that took that particular test. Then, for each corresponding experimental subject, we use the same regression equation to predict from their pre-PRT score what achievement test score they would obtain, if there were no difference between the experimental and control groups. Finally, we compare the experimental subjects' scores predicted on this assumption with the actual scores that they obtained. The difference is the residualized gain score (rg score). For any group of students the mean rg score is a measure of the extent to which their development or learning has been different from the initially matched control group.

For convenience of comparisons, all results will be reported in terms of rg scores. Note the rg scores build in comparison to controls and that, by definition, the mean rg score of a control group must be zero.

Results will be presented separately for the two groups, 11+ and 12+ (as explained above these represent the ages at which pupils *started* the intervention programme). Results will be broken down further by gender. For each experimental group, the number of subjects (N), their mean residualized gain score (M), the standard deviation of the rg (σ), and the probability that the mean score is significantly different from that of the corresponding control group (p<) will be shown. For significant differences, the effect size (e) is also shown in units of standard deviation of the control group (σ_c). The distribution of the rg scores for the experimental group is shown as a histogram.

In many of the distributions we claim evidence of bimodality. This is based on computing the cumulative χ^2 values for the numbers occurring at each interval compared with those expected on the basis of normal distribution. A

Table 2 Pre-test scores

		Boys		Girls	
		Experimental	Control	Experimental	Control
11+	N	39	55	31	35
	M	6.04	5.94	6.26	6.00
	σ	0.88	1.06	0.69	0.57
12+	N	65	76	59	64
	M	6.09	6.20	6.01	6.10
	σ	0.75	1.06	0.89	0.93

sharp rise in the significance of the χ^2 value indicates that a second peak in the distribution is significant.

RESULTS

1985 pre-tests

Pre-test scores for each group are shown in Table 2. There are no significant differences between any of the subgroups within an age range, but it will be seen that the 11+ group were generally more able than the 12+ group, since the mean scores of the two age groups are similar despite their age difference.

1987 immediate post-tests

PRT post-tests

These are the tests of cognitive development given immediately after the end of the two-year intervention programme. The results are summarized in Figure 7.

It is clear that the 12+ boys have made highly significant gains in levels of cognitive development compared with controls. Further analysis reveals that for this 12+ boys group the distribution of gain scores is bimodal – that is, there is one group who make little or no better gain than the controls, and another group whose gains are far greater than the controls. There is evidence also that the distribution of scores for the 11+ girls is bimodal, although overall their gain is not significantly greater than that of the corresponding control group.

Science achievement post-test

This was the common science achievement test taken by many of the schools immediately after the intervention. At this point, no significant differences emerged between any of the experimental and control groups, although it should be noted that the experimental group lost about 25 per cent of its science curriculum time to the 'Thinking Science' intervention lessons, so it

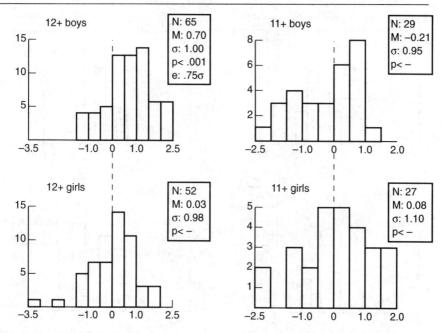

Figure 7 Post-PRT residualized gain scores for experimental groups: means, etc., and distribution

may be considered a virtue that their achievement remained at the same level as that of the controls. Reflection on this and other experience shows that it is not reasonable to expect an intervention programme which addresses underlying cognitive functioning to show an immediate effect on academic achievement. It is only after the completion of the intervention that the subjects have the opportunity to apply their newly acquired thinking skills to new learning. Thus measures of achievement should not be expected to show improvement until some time after the end of the intervention.

1988 delayed post-tests

PRT delayed post-test

This was the measure of cognitive development given one year after the end of the intervention programme. Data from this test are summarized in Figure 8.

One year after the end of the intervention, none of the experimental groups shows any overall difference from the control groups in these measures of cognitive development. The gains that were apparent immediately after the intervention seem to have dissipated. There is, however, some evidence of bimodality in the distributions of the 12+ boys and the 11+ girls, very marked in the former group. It will be seen later that this particular result seems to be anomalous in the whole pattern of data that emerges.

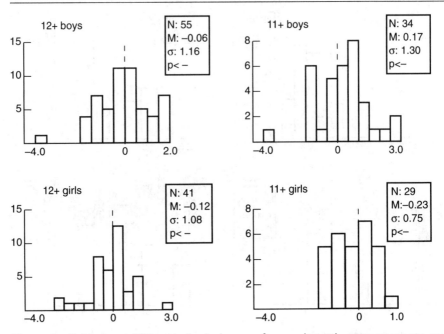

Figure 8   Delayed post-PRT residualized gain scores for experimental groups: means, etc., and distribution

Delayed science achievement

These were the schools' own tests, very different in nature from the Piagetian measures already reported. At this point the CASE intervention was over, and the schools had been asked to provide end-of-year examination results which tested what science the students had learned during the following year. In most cases the students were no longer in classes which could be identified with previous experimental and control groups, but were mixed and taught by different teachers. In the case of most of the '11+' groups, pupils had actually moved from middle to high schools and so were in a completely different environment. Here then is a direct comparison between ex-CASE and control students of their ability to benefit from the same instruction. Results are shown in Figure 9.

The 12+ boys again show a very strong effect, and the bimodality noted previously. The 11+ girls also show a significant effect, confirming the suspicion raised already about an effect with this group. Note that all groups show positive effects, although it does not reach statistical significance for 12+ girls or 11+ boys.

1989/90 GCSE examinations

The group of six 12+ classes completed their Year 11 (US Grade 10) at secondary school and took the GCSE examinations in June 1989, two years after the

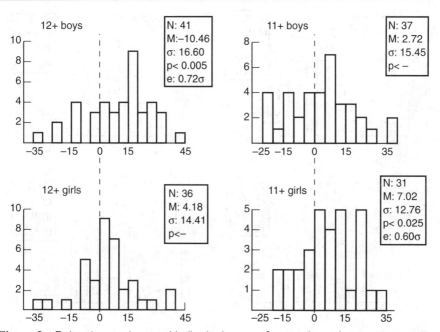

Figure 9 Delayed post-science residualized gain scores for experimental groups: means, etc., and distribution

end of the CASE intervention programme. The 11+ group of three classes took their GCSE in 1990, three years after the end of the intervention programme. We analysed GCSE results for science (amalgamated results for whichever combination of chemistry, physics, biology, and integrated science papers an individual took), mathematics, and English. Results for science are shown in Figure 10.

The effect on the boys 12+ group is even stronger than in delayed test results reported above. This group averages one grade higher than controls, after individual pre-test differences are taken into account. This represents an effect size of 1 standard deviation, achieved two years after the end of the CASE intervention programme. The 11+ boys and the 12+ girls show no significant effects. On the other hand, the girls who started the experiment aged 11+ do show a significant effect. Their science grades have been enhanced, compared with controls, by two-thirds of a standard deviation. Thus the hints from data reported above that there was some effect with the 11+ girls have finally shown up strongly in externally set and marked national examinations of science achievement, *three* years after the end of the intervention. By any standards this must be counted as a long-term effect. In both of the groups which showed significant effects, bimodality of distribution is again apparent, indicating that some benefited far more than others from the 'Thinking Science' experience.

So far, the data provide evidence consistent with the hypothesis that the strategies incorporated into the teaching and materials of 'Thinking Science'

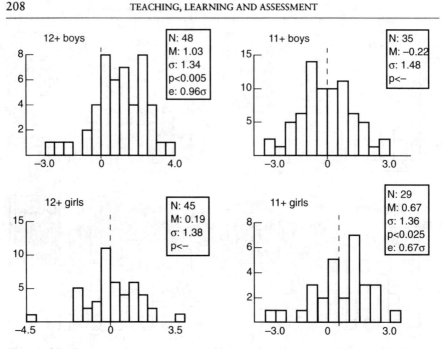

Figure 10 Residualized gain in grades of experimental group on General Certificate of Secondary Education: Science

promote the long-term development of thinking skills general within the domain of science, which can be applied to a wide variety of new learning within that domain. Even allowing for the inconsistency of the effect across different individuals, this already provides substantial support for a particular approach to the long-term improvement of learning in science through the development of general science thinking skills. We will discuss the age and gender differences further below, after results for other subjects have been presented.

Results from the other domains throw more light on the underlying psychological model. Figure 11 shows the results for GCSE mathematics.

Results follow a similar pattern to those in science, with significant effects achieved in the 12+ boys' and 11+ girls' groups. The former result is weaker than that for science and is consistent with a possible 'knock-on' effect of the mathematical nature of many of the 'Thinking Science' activities on achievement in mathematics itself, although the longevity is again remarkable. For the 11+ girls, the effect is stronger than for science (over 0.7 of a standard deviation), as well as being longer lasting even than for the 12+ group. This could be taken as evidence for the effect of the intervention on general underlying cognition. We will return to this discussion below. For both groups there is again evidence of bimodality of distribution of gains.

For a completely different domain, we turn to CGSE English data. Before presenting results, it is worth looking at some tasks typical of a GCSE English examination:

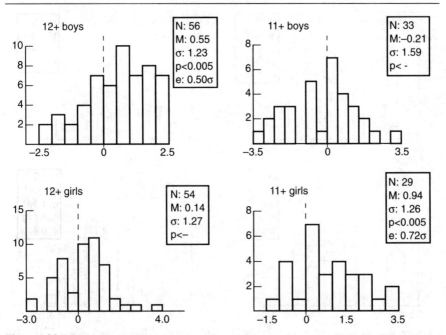

Figure 11 Residualized gain in grades of experimental group on General Certificate of Secondary Education: Mathematics

(1) A tape recording of some dialogue is played twice and a transcript provided. Students are given fifty minutes to write assessments of some of the characters portrayed, to describe the views of one of them on a particular issue discussed in the dialogue, and to write their own response to these views.

(2) Three extracts from guide books describing the same place, written in very different styles, are presented. The student is given forty-five minutes to write two pieces: one describing the place from an historical perspective, and one providing technical information useful for a group making a school visit to the place.

(3) A free composition of about 600 words, for which one hour is allowed. A choice of one out of five topics is given, and each is stimulated by a title, an opening sentence, a picture, or the topic of one of the earlier questions.

From this brief description, it will be seen that the skills required include analysis and comprehension, as well as imagination, creativity, and style. Enhanced achievement in such an English test following an intervention set in a science context must be described as far-transfer of an effect from one domain to another very different from it.

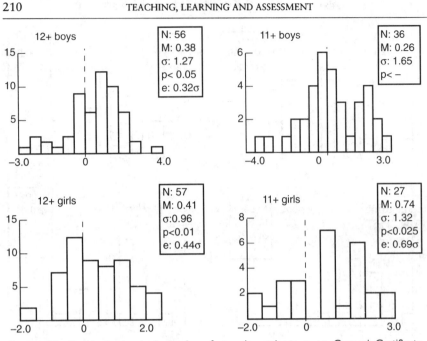

Figure 12　Residualized gain in grades of experimental group on General Certificate of Secondary Education: English

Now, consider the experimental groups' residualized gain in grades on GCSE English shown in Figure 12.

These results show significant effects in three out of the four groups. As before, there are effects in the 12+ boys and the 11+ girls, although rather weak in the former. Additionally, there is an effect in the 12+ girls' group. Even the one group which shows no overall effect, the 11+ boys, shows very marked bimodality of distribution, and would have shown a significant effect if just one of two very low-scoring individuals had scored at the average for the group.

POSSIBLE EXPLANATIONS

Evidence of long-term far-transfer has potential importance for models of cognition, and so it is necessary to explore in more detail possible explanations for these results.

1. Confidence?

The suggestion is sometimes made that the intervention has boosted the confidence of students in their own abilities, and that this in turn improved learning across domains. But it seems unlikely that confidence developed within science would effect performance in other domains (see all the gender-difference work in physical and biological sciences, e.g. Ormerod and Duckworth (1975), Kelly (1981), Hadden and Johnstone (1983)). In any case, a global notion of 'confidence' is vacuous as a causal explanation for improved learning without a mechanism by which confidence influences learning, which brings us back to some sort of cognitive model. At the risk of sounding like behaviourists rejecting mentalistic concepts out of hand, we will not consider this line further.

2. Language training?

An apparently simple explanation of how pupils who followed the 'Thinking Science' programme subsequently performed better in English is that of a direct training effect. This supposes that while the programme was set in a science context, it encouraged reasoned discussion amongst pupils exploring the meaning of new vocabulary in the search for explanations of physical events. This enrichment of language use is then supposed to persist (in memory?) and show up in enhanced performance in general English tests two and three years later. We find it implausible that a language-development effect which is almost incidental to the aims of the programme, and is set in a science context, could be so long-lived and become generalized. A more deep-rooted explanation seems to be necessary.

3. Language develops language?

Perhaps the intervention has enhanced linguistic development so that the new linguistic skills open the way for improved subsequent learning in language. Such a self-promoting system or 'virtuous circle' would be characteristic of development, as contrasted with learning, and as such would be consistent with the hoped-for outcomes of the experiment. Note that this explanation still relates particularly to the development of a domain-specific function, as something that has happened in parallel to but not integral with the development of scientific and mathematical proficiencies.

4. General cognitive development?

Results from the English GCSE are also consistent with the possibility that the CASE intervention, by addressing directly the promotion of the development of underlying cognitive structures, has raised the students' general intellectual processing power and thus enabled them to make better use of all of the learning experiences provided by their schooling. This is the most general level of cognitive explanation and the one for which long-term far-transfer is cited as necessary evidence.

In summary, we consider seriously two explanations at different levels of generality:

   (A) parallel development in linguistic and mathematical-scientific domains, or
   (B) general intellectual development.

We will use differences in effects on different age and gender groups in trying to construct possible explanations, but must admit to some hesitation in this: 11+ and 12+ groups were not different only with respect to starting age. The 11+ group was somewhat more able generally, and many of them were in middle schools which provide a rather different learning milieu from secondary schools. There are thus at least two potentially confounding factors militating against simple 11+ vs. 12+ comparisons.

With this proviso in mind, it is consistent with either hypothesis A or B that it is the girls who make the predominant contribution to the overall gains in language learning. On the first explanation (A), it would be claimed that girls have a greater propensity for language and make the most of the linguistic opportunities within the intervention programme. If general cognitive development (B) is the favoured explanation, the claim would be that students apply their enhanced intellectual power in learning domains which are of greatest intrinsic interest to them, and that the domains of interest tend towards science and mathematics for boys, and language for girls.

The difference in effects with 11+ and 12+ groups is not readily explained on the parallel processing model A. Why should eleven- to thirteen-year-old boys be less susceptible to the development of domain-specific scientific thinking strategies than twelve- to fourteen-year-old boys? Why should eleven- to thirteen-year-old girls be *more* susceptible to the development of domain-specific scientific thinking strategies than twelve- to fourteen-year-old girls? We suggest that only if one uses model B, based on general intellectual enhancement, includes a maturational factor, and adds the long-established evidence on the faster intellectual development of girls over boys at this age, can an adequate explanation be provided. Using model B we can say that at eleven, the intervention struck a chord with the girls' earlier emerging higher-level cognitive processing system, but failed to resonate with the boys, still mostly encased in concrete operational reasoning. Just a year later, the boys have reached the emergent phase that the girls were in previously, and so are ready to make the most of the intervention experiences. Why the twelve-year-old girls seemed to have passed the period of most effective intervention is another question, and we can only speculate that the answer may be found in the evidence on girls' affective disillusion with things which appear scientific when they reach Years 8 and 9 (Grades 7 and 8).

FURTHER ANALYSES

In order to explore the suggested possibilities further, analyses will be centred on the immediate post-test of cognitive development as this is the best measure we have of underlying cognitive structure and the development in that structure that took place during the intervention. Any explanation based on the idea of cognitive structure should be referred back to this measure.

As a preliminary, it is necessary to answer two technical questions:

(a) How widely distributed amongst the experimental classes were pupils who made the greatest gains?

We will consider as 'high gainers' the nineteen 11+ pupils and thirty-one 12+ pupils who showed the highest residualized gains on the PRT post-test, who form the top three bars of the distribution histograms of those scores (see Figure 7). Table 3 shows the percentage of each of the experimental classes who were 'high gainers' thus defined.

The percentage of high gainers in any one class ranges fairly evenly from 15.4 to 45.5, with no outstandingly good or poor results. This argues in favour of the effect being due to the general CASE strategy rather than to its particular expression through one or two exceptional teachers.

Table 3 Distribution of high gainers amongst experimental classes

	11+					12+				
Class identity	51	52	61	91	31	32	71	81	92	111
Per cent high gainers	15.4	42.9	33.3	40.0	18.8	20.0	28.6	19.0	45.5	22.7

(b) Were the high gainers those who either started with a low score (and therefore had much to make up) or with a high score (who might be thought to be 'ready' for the CASE type activities)?

The answer is shown in Figure 13. The individuals who are high gainers highlighted in the distribution of PRT post-test gains are also highlighted in the

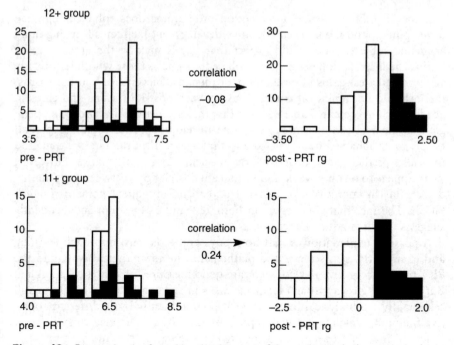

Figure 13 Pre-test levels of cognitive development of those who made the greatest gains to post-test PRT

distribution of PRT pre-test scores. It is clear that high gainers come from a wide range of starting levels, and this is supported by the absence of any correlation between starting level and gain.

Now to three questions which cannot be answered so simply:

(c) Do gains in cognitive development predict gains made in academic achievement?

Table 4 shows the correlations between post-PRT rg scores and the various measures of academic achievement.

Table 4 Correlations between rg scores of PRT post-test, science delayed post-test, and GCSE

		Del. sci. rg	GCSE rg scores		
			Science	Maths	English
Post-PRT rg	11+ boys	0.52	0.47	0.41	0.45
	11+ girls	0.62	0.73	0.61	(0.22)
	12+ boys	0.39	0.33	0.67	0.38
	12+ girls	0.32	0.28	0.30	(0.24)

Figures in brackets do not reach a significance of < .05.

If the 'Thinking Science' intervention programme does enhance cognitive development, and if enhanced cognitive development facilitates learning in all academic subjects, one would expect that pupils making the greatest gains during the intervention programme will be the same as those who subsequently show the greatest gains in measures of academic achievement. In other words, there should be significant correlations between post-PRT gains and gains in academic achievement. Table 4 shows that this is generally the case: immediate gains in the post-test measure of cognitive development successfully predict all GCSE gains achieved by boys two and three years after the intervention, and they also predict gains made by girls in science and mathematics. However, there appear to be only weak non-significant correlations between girls' immediate gains in cognitive development and their subsequent gains in English GCSE. The fact that this occurs in both 11+ and 12+ groups independently suggests that it is not a chance effect.

A possible explanation is that both boys and girls must approach learning and examinations in science and mathematics in an analytical way, and the PRT tests of cognitive development are good measures of analytical thinking. But boys and girls approach language tasks in different ways: while boys still rely mainly on analytical methods, girls predominantly use a different cognitive function, which is not well tapped by the PRTs. Whatever this 'different function' may be, it seems to be positively affected by the intervention since girls who have experienced 'Thinking Science' do in fact make gains in English scores. But our cognitive instruments are less useful for detecting growth of this function.

(d) What happened to the gains in cognitive development during the year following the intervention?

If we use the word 'development' to indicate a non-reversible change which provides the potential to improve further learning, then the hypothesis of enhanced underlying cognitive development is not served by data which seem to show that gains made are not maintained (Figure 8).

Table 5 shows the correlations between delayed PRT rg scores and immediate post-PRT rg scores, and the measures of academic achievement. There is little untoward about the data for the 12+ boys or girls. Correlation coefficients are generally higher than the corresponding values for the immediate post-PRT gains, as one would expect for tests taken one year nearer to the academic achievement measures. Correlations with English GCSE are low, as we found with the post-PRT gains and for which we offered a possible explanation above. In the 12+ groups, only the low correlation with the delayed science gains is at variance with expectation.

For the 11+ groups the data are distinctly odd. Correlation values for delayed PRT gains are *not* higher than they were for post-PRT gains, and in the case of the girls there are no significant correlations between delayed PRT gains and GCSE gains. In reviewing this element in the whole story some years after these delayed PRTs were administered, it is worth noting that three out of four 11+ classes were in middle schools. This meant that the 'Thinking Science' intervention programme was completed at the end of the pupils' sojourn in those schools, and the delayed tests were given after the pupils had spent one year in new (to them) high schools. It is possible that the change in school and the matter of becoming accustomed to new friends, new teachers, and new working methods would have caused a hiatus in the normal progress of cognitive development. If this is the case then, for the 11+ group, we can set aside the apparently aberrant delayed PRT gain scores and point to the ultimate long-

Table 5 Correlations between rg scores of PRT delayed post-test, PRT post-test, science delayed post-test, and GCSE

				GCSE rg scores		
		Post-PRT rg	Del. sci. rg	Science	Maths	English
Del. PRT rg	11+ boys	0.49	0.36	0.44	0.46	0.45
	11+ girls	(0.27)	0.34	(0.28)	(0.25)	(0.24)
	12+ boys	0.65	0.63	0.40	0.64	0.45
	12+ girls	0.40	(0.29)	0.53	0.47	0.29

Figures in brackets do not reach a significance of < .05.

term success in GCSE gains as the most important evidence for the eventual real effect of the intervention programme on academic achievement.

For the 12+ group this explanation is not available, but here, with the one exception of the absence of difference between the experimental and control groups' delayed PRT gain scores, the pattern of correlations is consistent with the view that: (1) the intervention has caused an enhanced development of cognitive operations, and (2) this enhanced development has improved academic achievement in a range of domains. We believe that explanation of the aberrant result would require a further longitudinal study in which the same measures of cognitive development were administered each year for at least three years, and related with academic achievement.

(e) How can we explain the bimodality in many of the distributions?

It seems clear from the distributions of gain scores that some pupils from the 11+ and 12+ groups, boys and girls, have made great gains in achievement compared with controls, while others have made little or no gain. Even in those tests where the greatest mean gains have been achieved, this can often be interpreted in terms of two subgroups: one, consisting of perhaps one-third of the group, making gains of 2 standard deviations or more while the remainder make little or no greater gain than the controls.

We strongly suspect that this effect can be explained in terms of learning styles: the whole 'Thinking Science' approach suited some students better than it did others. Unfortunately the design of the experiment, including limitations of time and money, did not allow us to carry out the in-depth classroom observations and interviews with pupils that might have elucidated this suggestion further. We recognize this as a limitation of the study.

CONCLUSION

Evidence has been presented of substantial and long-lasting effect on general academic achievement of a cognitive acceleration programme which concentrates on cognitive conflict, metacognition, and bridging and which uses the schemata of formal operations as a framework for the development of activities. In particular, boys starting at twelve-plus and girls starting at eleven-plus showed strong, and actually increasing, effects over the period following the intervention programme. There is the possibility that the gender differences observed are due to the different conjunction of the intervention programme with critical periods for girls' and boys' cognitive development.

Two hypotheses, rooted respectively in domain-specific and in general models of cognition, have been explored: that the intervention programme influenced one underlying general cognitive structure, the enhanced development of which permitted improved learning in all academic domains; or, that the intervention acted independently on two intellectual structures (say, a spatial-numerical one and a linguistic one), each of which in turn led to improved performance in its own domain. The evidence does not allow one to choose with a high degree of confidence between these two, and the apparent loss of cognitive advantage by the experimental group one year after the intervention is a puzzling feature. Nevertheless the gains in English remain a reality in need of explanation, and to science teachers-turned-psychologists who in this project worked through science teachers and the science curriculum, it seems unlikely that our intervention directly influenced language behaviour more effectively than language teachers and language curricula did.

Which of the results presented do we expect to be replicable? Firstly we must report that new work in Korea and in England, currently in preparation for publication, provides replication of the immediate gains in cognitive development following a CASE intervention. Further than this we are confident that CASE or similar work in ordinary public (in the US sense) high schools can bring about a long-term gain in academic achievement across a range of subject areas. We are less confident about the apparent age and gender differences in the point at which the intervention is most effective. This, and a careful longitudinal tracking of cognitive development using measures consistent from year to year, remain areas in need of further investigation.

It seems to us that we have responded to Alan Clarke's challenge. An intervention heavily dependent upon Piaget's account of operational thinking has produced large effects on theory-independent national school examinations. We believe that the strongest contender for an explanation for these results is that of a general cognitive processor which has been positively influenced by the CASE intervention. If we have succeeded in raising the head of such a contender an inch above the parapet without it being blown off, we hope that will be sufficient encouragement for others to investigate its viability further. Come back Piaget: much (but not all) is forgiven.

REFERENCES

Adey, P. S. (1988) Cognitive acceleration – review and prospects, *International Journal of Science Education*, 10, (2), pp. 121–34.

Adey, P. S. and Shayer, M. (1990) Accelerating the development of formal thinking in middle and high school students, *J. Res. Science Teaching*, 27, (3), pp. 267–85.

Adey, P. S., Shayer, M. and Yates, C. (1989) *Thinking Science: the Curriculum Materials of the CASE Project*, London: Thomas Nelson & Sons.

Brainerd, C. J. (1978) *Piaget's Theory of Intelligence*, New York, Prentice Hall.

Brown, G. and Desforges, C. (1979) *Piaget's Theory: A Psychological Critique*. London; Routledge & Kegan Paul.

Brown, G. and Desforges, C. (1987) Piagetian psychology and education: time for revision, *British Journal of Educational Psychology*, 47, pp. 7–17.

Case, R. (1974) Structures and strictures: some functional limits to cognitive growth, *Cognitive Psychology*, 6, pp. 544–74.

Clarke, A. M. and Clarke, A. D. B. (1976) *Early Experience: Myth and Evidence*, London: Open Books.

CLISP (Children's Learning in Science Project) (1987) *CLIS in the Classroom*, Leeds, University of Leeds Centre for Studies in Science and Maths Education.

Cronbach, L. and Furby, L. (1970) How should we measure change, or should we? *Psychological Bulletin*, Vol. 74, pp. 68–80.

Desforges, C. and Brown, G. (1979) The educational utility of Piaget: a reply to Shayer (with final comment by Shayer), *British Journal of Educational Psychology*, 49, pp. 277–81.

Feuerstein, R., Rand, Y., Hoffman, M. and Miller, M. (1980) *Instrumental Enrichment: An Intervention Programme for Cognitive Modifiability*, Baltimore, University Park Press.

Fusco, E. T. (1983) The relationship between children's cognitive level of development and their responses to literature. Unpublished Ph.D. thesis, University of Hofstra.

Goossens, L. (1989) Training scientific reasoning in children and adolescents: a critical review and quantitative integration. Paper presented at Third European Conference for Research on Learning and Instruction, Madrid.

Hadden, R. A. and Johnstone, A. H. (1983) Secondary school pupils' attitudes to science: the year of erosion, *European Journal of Science Education*, 5, (3), pp. 309–18.

Hallam, R. N. (1967) Logical thinking in history, *Educational Review*, 119, pp. 182–202.

Inhelder, B. and Piaget, J. (1958) *The Growth of Logical Thinking from Childhood to Adolescence*, London; Routledge & Kegan Paul.

Jurd, M. (1973) Adolescent thinking in history-type material, *Australian Journal of Education*, 17, (1), pp. 2–17.

Karplus, R. (1979) Teaching for the development of reasoning, in A. E. Lawson (ed.) *The Psychology of Teaching for Thinking and Creativity*, Columbus Ohio, ERIC-SMEAC.

Kelly, A. (1981) Science achievement as an aspect of sex roles, in A. Kelly (ed.) *The Missing Half: Girls and Science Education*, Manchester University Press.

Kuhn, D. and Angelev, J. (1976) An experimental study of the development of formal operational thought, *Child Development*, 47, pp. 697–706.

Kuhn, D., Amsel, E. and O'Loughlin, M. (1988) *The Development of Scientific Thinking Skills*, San Diego, Academic Press.

Lawson, A. E., Blake, A. J. D. and Nordland, F. (1975) Training effects and generalisation of the ability to control variables in high school biology students, *Science Education*, 59, (3), pp. 387–96.

Lawson, A. E. and Snitgen, D. A. (1982) Teaching formal reasoning in a college biology course for preservice teachers, *Journal of Research in Science Teaching*, 19, pp. 233–48.

Nickerson, R. S., Perkins, D. N. and Smith, E. E. (1985) *The Teaching of Thinking*, Hillsdale New Jersey: Lawrence Erlbaum Associates.

Niemark, E. (1975) Longitudinal development of formal operations thought, *Genetic Psychology Monographs*, 91, pp. 171–225.

Ormerod, M. B. and Duckworth, D. (1975) *Pupils' Attitudes to Science: a Review of Research*. Slough, National Foundation for Educational Research in England and Wales.

Papert, S. (1961) *The growth of logical thinking: a Piagetian viewpoint*. Unpublished manuscript, Archives Jean Piaget, Genève.

Parsons, C. (1960) Critical notice, *British Journal of Psychology*, Vol. 51, pp. 75–84.

Perkins, D. N. and Salomon, G. (1989) Are cognitive skills context-bound *Educational Researcher*, 18, (1), pp. 16–25.

Renner, J. W., Stafford, D. G., Lawson, A. E. (1976) *Research Teaching, and Learning with the Piaget Model*, University of Oklahoma Press, Norman.

Resnick, L. B. (1987) *Education and Learning to Think*, Washington D.C.: National Academy Press.

Rosenthal, D. A. (1979) The acquisition of formal operations: the effect of two training procedures, *Journal of Genetic Psychology*, 134, pp. 125–140.

Shayer, M. (1978) Nuffield Combined Science: Do the pupils understand it? *School Science Review*, December, no. 211, 210–23.

Shayer, M. (1979) Has Piaget's construct of formal operational thinking any utility? *British Journal of Educational Psychology*, 49, pp. 265–7.

Shayer, M. (1987) Neo-Piagetian theories and educational practice, *International Journal of Psychology*, 22, no. 5/6, pp. 751–77.

Shayer, M. and Adey, P. S. (1981) *Towards a Science of Science Teaching*. London: Heinemann Educational.

Shayer, M. and Adey, P. S. (1992a) Accelerating the development of formal thinking in middle and high school students II: post-project effects on science achievement, *Journal of Research in Science Teaching*, 30, (4), pp. 351–66.

Shayer, M. and Adey, P. S. (1992b) Accelerating the development of formal operational thinking in high school pupils, III: testing the permanency of the effects, *Journal of Research in Science Teaching*, 29, (10), pp. 1,101–15.

Shayer, M. and Adey, P. S. (1993) Accelerating the development of formal operational thinking in high school pupils, IV: three years on after a two year intervention, *Journal of Research in Science Teaching*, 30, (4), pp. 351–66.

Shayer, M., Adey, P. S. and Wylam, H. (1981) Group tests of cognitive development – ideals and a realisation, *Journal of Research in Science Teaching*, 1980, pp. 157–68.

Shayer, M. and Beasley, F. (1987) Does instrumental enrichment work? *British Educational Research Journal*, 13, (2), pp. 101–19.

Shayer, M., Küchemann, D. E. and Wylam, H. (1976) The distribution of Piagetian stages of thinking in British middle and secondary school children, *British Journal of Educational Psychology*, 46, pp. 164–73.

Shayer, M. and Wylam, H. (1978) The distribution of Piagetian stages of thinking in British middle and secondary school children. II – 14- to 16-year-olds and sex differentials, *British Journal of Educational Psychology*, 48, pp. 62–70.

Shayer, M., Wylam, H., Küchemann, D. E. and Adey, P. S. (1978) *Science Reasoning Tasks*, Slough: National Foundation for Educational Research. (Now available from Science Reasoning, 16 Fen End, Over, Cambs., CB4 5NE, UK).

Vygotsky, L. S. (1978) *Mind in Society*, Cambridge, Mass. Harvard University Press.

NOTES

1. Although Kuhn, Amsel and O'Loughlin (1988) are critical of Piaget's logical explanation of formal operations, they do accept that (a) there is a developmental aspect in the growth of scientific thinking, and (b) that the Inhelder/Piaget schemata have provided a rich source for a broadly consistent body of empirical studies into the development of thinking.

2. A typical, but by no means universal, pattern for a six- or seven-form entry comprehensive high school in Britain is to assign children with learning difficulties to a remedial group, and sometimes to select especially able children into a second group, and form four or five equivalent mixed-ability groups from the remainder.

Part 3: Issues in Assessment

Introduction

Dick West

The assessment of learning outcomes has always been a key aspect of good science teaching. Formative assessment provides essential feedback to pupils and teachers as to where they are starting from and the progress they have made towards attaining specified teaching and learning goals. Summative assessment provides evidence as to what has been achieved at the end of a teaching unit: a term, year or course. With the advent of the National Curriculum in England and Wales and the public reporting test and examination results, assessment has taken on a new dimension that of accountability. These readings assume as a starting point the personal nature of assessment and, in particular, the issue of self-assessment – an area not explored as such in the articles included in the Reader. Here the starting point is an important paper by Mary Simpson on 'Diagnostic assessment and its contribution to pupils' learning'.

In this article, which is set in the context of the Dunning Report (Scottish Education Department, 1977), Simpson presents a strong case for the use of diagnostic assessment as an integral part of the teaching and learning process for pupils of all abilities and not just those who have been 'diagnosed' as having learning problems. She argues strongly that failure to achieve is too often blamed on deficiencies in pupils, rather than inadequacies in teaching and learning strategies which 'clearly contribute to many of the common learning difficulties'.

The second article, by Bob Fairbrother, shifts attention to the specific problems of assessing scientific skills. It has long been accepted that the effective teaching of science involves more than the development of a knowledge and understanding of the subject. Good schemes of work have always emphasized the development of essential manipulative (motor) skills associated with the practical aspects of experimentation – the handling of equipment, measurement, the ability to observe and record phenomena, and safety. More recently attention has been drawn to intellectual skills and processes, such as designing experiments, problem-solving, communication and reporting. A key issue Fairbrother seeks to address is that of creating and describing a hierarchy of skills and processes and the problems of reporting on them with both reliability and validity.

The third article – 'Reflections: accountability, the pressures and the opportunities' by Neill Patterson and George Walker – moves us into the issue of accountability as seen by two headteachers. They explore, in a transcript of a public conversation, most of the complexities of accountability yet seek to relate these to science-specific issues – not least the relationship between the science taught by non-specialists in primary schools and its standing as a preparation for secondary science.

3.1

Diagnostic assessment and its contribution to pupils' learning

Mary Simpson

INTRODUCTION

The Dunning Report (Scottish Education Department (SED), 1977) viewed diagnostic assessment and assessment for certification purposes as being intrinsically different processes, and stressed the importance of diagnostic assessment for education in its unequivocal assertion that 'it is insufficient to devise curricular objectives and to find out whether they have been attained by each pupil; for those who are not successful the reasons for misunderstandings require to be identified and alternative methods adopted'. In this chapter I shall argue that pupil learning difficulties are commonly the result of unrecognized inadequacies in instructional strategies and practices, that these can indeed be identified by diagnostic testing and that significant advances in educational practice are likely to be critically dependent on the use in schools of genuinely diagnostic assessment procedures. Many of these ideas were developed in the course of studies of the difficulties encountered by 'O' grade pupils in understanding particular topics in biology. The discovery of serious learning problems among pupils who are not normally regarded as requiring remedial attention suggests that they are likely to be even more widespread and intense among the slower learners who nowadays would be selected for courses at less demanding levels of certification. Although the studies were confined to biology, they have their counterparts in other science subjects and I consider their conclusions to be generalizable across much of the curriculum.

In education, a pervasive myth is that pupil attainment is only to a limited extent affected by changes in teaching strategies and is almost wholly determined by factors which are intrinsic to the pupils: their intelligence, application and motivation. The power of this myth is shown by the extent to which major educational innovations are reinterpreted in terms of its 'explanatory' framework. There are now clear signs that the concept of diagnostic assessment is being revised in this way. Thus, many of the 'diagnostic' tests which have been produced following publication of the report, consist of no more

From: Brown, S. and Munn, P. (eds.) (1985) *The Changing Face of Education 14–16: Curriculum and Assessment*, NFER-Nelson, pp. 69–81.

than assessments referenced to course objectives. As such, they serve to identify the topic areas in which learning failure may have occurred but do not illuminate the reasons underlying failure. Their limitations as diagnostic instruments are revealed by the forms of remediation to which they point. Advice is directed towards the pupil and is of the form 'you should revise', 'read your book at home more often', 'do the remedial worksheets', the latter amounting to little more than a different presentation of substantially similar course material. Any claim that tests referenced to course objectives are inherently diagnostic rests on the assumptions that learning difficulties are defined by the topic area in which they occur and they only arise from the pupils' own deficiencies (Simpson and Arnold, 1983). I shall argue that neither of these assumptions is valid and shall reserve the term diagnostic for those activities designed to discover the underlying reasons for pupil failure.

The view that it is deficiencies in the pupil which set the current limits to learning and are responsible for failure would be difficult to sustain if it were shown that under different conditions of instruction pupils learn much more than they presently do, and that traditional teaching practices create difficulties for all but a minority. Under conditions of conventional classroom instruction, a clear relationship exists between attainment and the personal and social characteristics of the pupil. However, this relationship is not maintained in certain qualitatively different, novel teaching schemes devised to take account of well-established principles of learning. In these, about 80 per cent of pupils attain levels normally reached by only 20 per cent of pupils receiving conventional instruction (Bloom, 1976; Nordin, 1980; Case, 1980; Anania, 1983). Moreover, Johnstone and Kellett (1980, chemistry), Dow *et al.* (1978, physics) and Arnold and Simpson (1980, 1982) and Simpson and Arnold (1982a, 1982b) (biology) have identified serious deficiencies in teaching strategies which clearly contribute to many of the common learning difficulties.

INVESTIGATIONS OF PUPIL LEARNING DIFFICULTIES

During the last few years our work, based in the biology department at Aberdeen College of Education, has investigated the difficulties encountered by secondary pupils in understanding such topics as photosynthesis, osmosis and digestion. These difficulties were puzzling since they were displayed by even 'O' grade pupils, commonly regarded as comparatively able and motivated, and the topics appeared not to demand unreasonably sophisticated levels of reasoning. Our investigations started with open-ended discussions with individuals or pairs of pupils from which emerged hypotheses about the sources of difficulty. These were then checked by objective tests extended by semi-structured interviews in which pupils amplified and gave reasons for their answers. Our methods were designed to find out not how much the pupils could remember of what they had been taught, but *what they actually knew*. Because we wished to chart the development of the pupils' knowledge and ideas these were assessed among pupils from late primary and the first four years of secondary school (S1 to S4). These diagnostic assessments of pupil learning were paralleled by detailed examinations of the topic content and of the teaching material used in the schools.

In all our studies there was clear evidence that the pupils had resorted to rote learning in an attempt to compensate for failure to gain understanding. Correct answers to familiar questions were abandoned when the context of the question was changed and even those pupils whose scores on the more conventional test items would have been regarded as entirely adequate, showed by their answers to further questions a basic lack of understanding of the topics. Moreover, the answers to questions which examined the pupils' possession of 'wrong' knowledge revealed a widespread acceptance of 'explanations' and 'facts' which were wholly incompatible with the material they had been taught.

BARRIERS TO LEARNING

In discussions with pupils it became apparent that they valued the 'O' grade certificate and were prepared to work for it, but interest in *understanding* science had been lost by all but a minority. Their concern in tests and in homework was with the overall mark and not in the test items which they had failed and which could have served to pin-point where their understanding was inadequate. Some were clearly bored, particularly with laboratory practicals, others were lost and felt themselves to be stupid; the majority seemed to feel considerable frustration in their attempts to understand much of the material presented. All appeared to regard the subject as a series of disconnected topics and none had perceived its central themes, e.g. energy flow in living systems.

Pupils entered S3 classes with unknown and widely different levels of concept attainment, different misconceptions, different learning strategies and perceptions of which strategies were useful, and with different histories of exposure to the many styles of teaching. They were nevertheless subsequently taught by lock-step procedures as if they were homogeneous groups. Some were clearly not extended and others were left floundering, either because the teacher had not detected their difficulties or had been unable, due to the constraints of time and syllabus, to do more than recommend the usual revision exercises.

Our studies showed that not only were pupils restricted in their learning by the impersonal class-based instruction, but were also obstructed by difficulties arising out of deficiencies in the teaching of the course content. Two sources of learning difficulty which are of critical importance are inadequate concept development and the possession of wrong information.

Inadequate concept development

In all our studies we found that pupils who had been taught, and were therefore expected to understand, the mechanisms underlying important but complex biological processes had such a poorly developed understanding of the simpler concepts on which the given explanations were based that comprehension was denied to all but a minority. In order to understand the topics of photosynthesis and respiration at 'O' grade, for example, it was essential that they had gained from earlier courses robust concepts of living things, gases, food and energy. They had not. Pupils at the end of S2 had not significantly developed beyond the Primary 7 level in their ability to classify items as living or non-living; 30 per cent of S4 pupils used words and images to describe a gas which were equivalent to those used by primary pupils; 51 per cent and 35 per cent respectively of S3 pupils were unable to classify correctly as solid, liquid or gas, two materials most pertinent to the photosynthesis story, *viz.* carbon and carbohydrate (Simpson and Arnold, 1982a). Further, in order to make any sense out of the proffered explanations of the mechanisms involved in osmosis, pupils must have accurate concepts of a solution. We found few who had. For example, 44 per cent of the pupils believed that if a solution was allowed to stand, the solute molecules would settle out in the bottom of the container. Our findings confirmed Dow *et al.*'s (1978) report that many learning difficulties encountered in some topics in chemistry and physics are attributable to the pupils' failure to gain the necessary basic concepts of solids, liquids and gases.

It was surprising to find that the teachers who participated in our studies were previously unaware of the extent to which their pupils were ignorant of the basic knowledge of these concepts which were necessary for meaningful learning. A detailed scrutiny of the teaching material of the S1 to S4 courses helped to explain the pupils' ignorance. Despite the concern of the course planners that concept acquisition should be of prime importance in science education (SED, 1969), the teaching material used dealt with a wide range of topics but left pupils to guess at the characteristics of the underlying concepts. Concept recognition and discrimination exercises were conspicuously absent and teachers had neither monitored the acquisition of concepts throughout S1 and S2 nor checked for their attainment in any effective way on the pupils' entry to S3.

It is to be expected that pupils who have received such inadequate instruction in concepts should develop for themselves faulty rules of classification. Nevertheless we and the teachers were surprised to discover just how widely such faulty rules were to be found (Simpson, 1983). More than 70 per cent of certificate biology pupils thought that a worm, a human being and a tree were not made of atoms and molecules and a similar proportion thought that energy, heat and light were. These pupils appear to have derived, undetected by their teachers, a simple classification rule: 'if it is in biology, it is made of cells; if it is in chemistry and physics, it is atoms and molecules'! This must provide the shakiest of foundations on which to build any further knowledge of science.

Possession of wrong information

Pupils learn by a process which involves the interaction of new information with their existing cognitive structures. If what they already know is inaccurate and is not specifically corrected, what they subsequently learn, even from well-presented teaching material, is likely also to be incorrect, or acquired merely by rote. In our studies we found that incorrect ideas were widespread among the pupils. Because these ideas had not been revealed by the usual form of classroom tests, whether norm- or criterion-referenced, many teachers were either unaware of their presence or thought them unimportant and had therefore not attempted any remediation. Two types of wrong information may be distinguished: misconceptions which are errors of fact occurring in relative isolation from other facts; and alternative frameworks (Driver and Easley, 1978), which are more elaborate constructions and explanations developed by the learner in an attempt to make sense of his or her life experiences.

One example of the host of learning difficulties caused by undetected misconceptions is drawn from our study of osmosis. The pupils were taught that 'the smaller water molecules pass through the membrane, while the larger sucrose molecules do not' and were expected to learn that *all* the water molecules, being small, can pass through the semi-permeable membrane, and that *none* of the sucrose molecules, being large, can pass. However, approximately half of the pupils believed that water and sucrose molecules each exist in a variety of sizes. Clearly it was possible for these pupils to deduce, erroneously, that some sucrose molecules are small enough to pass, while some water molecules are large enough to be retained. The resulting confusion of pupils and frustration of teachers could perhaps have been avoided if the latter had been aware of the underlying error.

Science teaching normally involves the presentation of facts and experimental observations, and the use of these to construct the theories which explain and unite them. However, what pupils learn can be unexpectedly different from what is taught (Simpson and Arnold, 1982b). It is not uncommon for pupils to select from the facts offered and to construct from them simpler, more concrete, though less comprehensive theories (alternative frameworks) which are extremely resistant to correction. We found evidence of the presence and influence of alternative frameworks in all the biology topics which we examined. For example, when digestion and respiration were taught, pupils were expected to extend their existing simple knowledge of the breakdown of food, of food as a source of energy and of how food is 'burned up' in the body. In every class we examined we found that many pupils had learned not the intended explanations, but instead that the energy releasing process is digestion (not respiration), it therefore occurs in the stomach (not the cells), breakdown is achieved by the acid (not the enzymes), respiration is about CO_2 release (not energy release) and therefore occurs in the lungs (not the cells). Other alternative frameworks have been identified which interfere with learning in physics (Viennot, 1979; Driver, 1983) and in other topics in biology (Brumby, 1979; Deadman and Kelly, 1978) and will undoubtedly be found elsewhere. Their presence and influence on learning are not revealed by normal classroom tests and they tend not to be detected unless the teacher is actively looking for them.

DIAGNOSIS

In their relationships with adults, children are often treated as merely the passive receivers of adult knowledge rather than as active processors of information and producers of ideas. The more formalized the relationship, the more likely this is to occur. The immediate responses of the teachers to the results of our assessments which showed that pupils had not gained the expected knowledge were ones of disbelief – 'But they should have known that!' When shown that pupils had gained incorrect knowledge, they were indignant – 'But I never taught them *that*!' It was as if their pupils had been expected to learn the greater part of what they had been taught, and to learn *only* what they had been taught. If this model of pupil learning were true then diagnosis of pupil learning difficulties could be restricted to the identification of those items of information which have not been acquired. However, learning in children is not an occasional activity; it is a natural and continuous process, and what they have been taught in school amounts to no more than one input of information among many. The process of making sense·of information and of achieving meaningful as opposed to rote learning, is one of establishing relationships between the new experience or information offered and what the pupil already knows. Failure to learn will result if that experience or information is not accurately perceived by the pupil, if the pupil has inadequacies in prerequisite concepts or deficiencies in knowledge which preclude any connection with the new information, or if the pupil possesses knowledge which has incorrect elements, derived from previous experiences, which result in the wrong connections being made. Learning difficulties are thus likely to be highly idiosyncratic.

Diagnosis should, therefore, involve the following questions:

- What does the pupil 'know' when a particular wrong answer is given to a test question?
- Why does that particular answer make more sense to the pupil than the correct answer?
- What does the pupil need to know to answer the question correctly?
- Did the learning experience offered in class make it clear to the pupil what was to be learned?
- Was the information given unambiguous, were the critical ideas salient, and were there inherent possibilities of confusion?
- What did the pupil need to know to understand the taught material?
- Was that prior knowledge made available in previous courses?

Some of these questions require of the teachers a critical evaluation of the standard teaching practices of their subject specialty; others require the teacher to consider how and what the pupils learn from those practices. These are difficult and demanding requirements. Many teachers see the constraints under which they teach as tending to make them examine their teaching more in managerial than in educational terms and they clearly valued the contribution of the analytical 'outsider' (the researcher) in helping them to reconsider their teaching strategies in the light of the actual learning outcomes.

Some diagnostic information can undoubtedly be derived from criterion-referenced assessments conventionally used to see whether pupils have gained the right information or objectives. When the purpose is diagnosis, however, it is the wrong or inconsistent answers and the analysis of their characteristics which are important. Our diagnostic investigations were more detailed. They covered not only the topic area but also its prerequisite concepts and examined the same aspects of the topic several times, using test items in which there was a change of context or emphasis, to check the robustness of the pupils' knowledge; they also included items which specifically examined the pupils' possession of wrong information and faulty concepts.

The main difficulty in setting up diagnostic tests of this type lies in discovering the kinds of wrong information and faulty concepts which should be examined. Teachers were not only unaware of the source of their pupils' difficulties but their rating of parts of the topic as 'easy' or 'difficult' occasionally bore little relationship to our actual findings. They were experienced, committed and enthusiastic, but the perceptual framework within which they operated was one in which the course objectives, the right information and well-organized teaching were paramount; they were unaccustomed and were indeed not trained to think of their work in the radically different framework of the cognitive processes which are involved when pupils are trying to learn a specialist subject and of the ways in which learning can go wrong despite the genuine efforts of pupils to learn.

We used semi-structured interviews with open-ended questions to probe the pupils' knowledge and the concepts on which it was based. Since our concern was to discover rather than evaluate what pupils knew, we took particular care to avoid hints to the pupils that their answers were to be judged as right or wrong. These discussions provided much clearer clues to the sources of learning difficulties than were given by class test results or the information supplied by teachers and we were left in no doubt that listening to pupil talk should be regarded as the most important single diagnostic activity of the teacher. It is an illusion to think that pupil learning difficulties can be detected and defined by 'diagnostic tests' alone and it is inevitable that difficulties will continue to remain undiagnosed until listening to pupils plays a much larger role in classroom activities. If listening is to be diagnostic, the teacher must encourage the fullest exposition of the pupil's knowledge, right or wrong, in the pupil's own words. This activity is only possible if teachers are prepared to move away from their secure roles as experts and examiners and towards the less certain role of advisers and learning specialists. Such a form of diagnosis may be difficult to incorporate into classrooms where the 'discussion' between pupils and the teacher is governed by rigid conventions and in which, by tradition, it is the teachers who talk and it is the pupils who listen. Possible procedures for encouraging pupil talk have been described by Francis (1982) and by Hornsey and Horsfield (1982).

The longer that cognitive difficulties remain undiagnosed, the greater will be the damage to learning and the more difficult will be remediation. Diagnosis should therefore be a continuous process. This does not imply that formal diagnostic tests should be continually applied, but rather that the normal classroom teaching should be informed by diagnostic principles. To permit this, there needs to be a deliberate shift of attention from the subject and the course objectives to the learning processes of the pupils.

When tests are applied it is strongly recommended that pupils should mark their own answers and that they should discuss these answers with their teachers (Black and Dockrell, 1980; Arnold and Simpson, 1981). Since it is important that pupils recognize that diagnostic tests are designed to help rather than judge them, the results of diagnostic tests should not be incorporated into summative assessments and this distinctive function of diagnostic tests should be made clear to pupils.

REMEDIATION AND PREVENTION OF LEARNING DIFFICULTIES

Once the source of learning failure has been diagnosed (Simpson and Arnold, 1984), the form of appropriate remediation may become clear: misconceptions may be removed by discussions with the teacher; difficulties arising from inadequacies in earlier courses may be dealt with by, for example, selected concept recognition and discrimination exercises; problems of handling large amounts of information may be eased by showing pupils how these can be classified into smaller more manageable units by 'chunking' (Johnstone and Kellett, 1980). Difficulties arising from the pupils' possession of alternative frameworks however are much more resistant to direct remediation. These explanations are based on erroneous but mutually supportive ideas which have been derived from the pupils' own interpretation of events, are commonly at a lower level of abstraction and therefore simpler and more attractive to the pupil than the prescribed theories, and are commonly reinforced by popular opinion. Their displacement by the approved theories is extremely difficult and seldom occurs merely as a result of the formal presentation of new conflicting information (Driver and Easley, 1978; Brumby, 1979). Nussbaum and Novick (1981) have reported encouraging results from a structured approach in which the pupils explain and explore their own ideas, are confronted with conflicting evidence, discover the inadequacies of their own explanations and are assisted to reinvent or explore for themselves the more powerful, approved theories.

In the long term, it is likely to prove more cost-effective and certainly better for the self-esteem of the pupil to prevent than to remediate pupil learning difficulties. Criterion-referenced assessment, as currently practised, directs attention to curricular goals and to the action to be taken by the pupils for their attainment. The diagnostic approach will direct some of that attention to the learning needs of the pupils and the remediation which it suggests is likely to take the form: 'the teacher should devise teaching strategies which are appropriate to those needs'.

Many learning difficulties could be prevented if certain inadequacies in course content and presentation were to be remedied. Two of the many areas in which improvement is necessary are discussed below.

Concepts are not fixed items of information which can be straightforwardly taught. They are ways of classifying which enable some events and processes to be related to or distinguished from other events and processes; they are constantly developing in the pupils' minds and can go awry unless much greater care is taken than at present. The key concepts which are necessary to the understanding of subject topics in the years S1 to S4 should be identified and a strategy of concept development agreed in the school which will ensure that pupils arrive at the various stages of their courses with appropriate preparation. Much more attention must be paid to their formal teaching, testing and revision and course material must contain identification and discrimination exercises (Markle, 1975; Merrill and Tennyson, 1977; Herron *et al.*, 1977). Ideally, the attainment of these concepts should be made 'intended learning outcomes' as was done by Black and Goring (1983) in geography. At present, the constraints of the syllabus deny the necessary time for adequate instruction in concepts. But if pupils are to understand more than they now do, time must be made available, even though this may have to be at the expense of a contraction of the syllabus.

A second, preventable, cause of learning difficulties results from an inadequate consideration of *why* pupils should be expected to gain particular knowledge at specific stages in their education and of what level of abstraction is appropriate. The present syllabus appears to suggest that most topics, regardless of their complexity, should be taught at the explanatory level. This commonly results in the use of teaching strategies which are not matched to the learning needs of pupils (Simpson and Arnold, 1984) and often requires the use of simplifications and 'fictionalizations' which are a source of ambiguity and confusion, and which have to be unlearned at a later stage (Dow *et al.*, 1978; Simpson and Arnold, 1982a, 1982b). Reconsideration might suggest a less stringent requirement, that pupils be able to understand certain topics at the descriptive level and to use their knowledge predictively, i.e. to know that 'X will occur' rather than to know why and how.

IMPLICATIONS

Pupils' learning failures have always been a central preoccupation of teachers and education administrators. But the focus of concern has been the assessment of differences in the incidence of failure among pupils to select them for various types of instruction and to grade them according to levels of attainment for the convenience of employers or of other educationalists.

The Dunning Committee took the wider view of assessment: that it should not merely be concerned with certification, but should make a positive contribution to teaching and learning by identifying the reasons underlying failure and by prescribing remedies. It may appear paradoxical to predict that the net result of a move from 'assessment as sorting' to 'assessment as diagnosis' is likely to be a decrease in the emphasis placed on remediation. This follows because research on pupil learning difficulties seems certain to confirm that many of these may be prevented by changes in teaching practice, so that remediation becomes unnecessary.

Many of the necessary changes outlined in this chapter can be incorporated into current educational procedures; others are more radical. What is required is that educational methods should be developed which take full account of the psychological processes involved when pupils learn. There is now a growing body of evidence which suggests that two of the determinants of Piagetian levels of reasoning, the size of the working memory available for a task and the selection of appropriate information processing strategies, can be improved by particular forms of teaching (see Case, 1980, for a review). These methods have yet to be extended to the teaching of specialist subjects and would un-doubtedly be difficult to implement in the context of class instruction. What is certain is that 'individualized learning' and 'resource-based learning' schemes will amount to no more than a repackaging of the old materials and will be equally limited in their effectiveness if they are not informed by more accurate theories of pupil learning.

The myth of pupil deficiencies as the source of learning failure survives because it does not tell people what they do not wish to hear. It absolves teachers and curriculum planners from anything more than token respon-sibility for pupil learning; it removes the need for administrators to consider the findings of the growing body of educational research which suggests, for example, that the price of an extensive syllabus has been paid at the expense of poorer learning for all, and that all pupils may have the potential to achieve, though at different ages, learning goals which are presently obtained by only a minority.

We should not expect the myth to be exploded by the 'big bang' of the curriculum development which is now in progress; it is more likely to be eroded by the small but steady stream of local innovation resulting from the classroom activities of practising teachers.

REFERENCES

Anania, J. (1983) The influence of instructional conditions on student learning and achievement, *Evolution in Education: An International Review Series*, 7, 1, 1–81.

Arnold, B. and Simpson, M. (1980) *An Investigation of the Development of the Concept Photosynthesis to S.C.E. 'O' Grade*. Aberdeen: Aberdeen College of Education.

Arnold, B. and Simpson, M. (1981) *Diagnostic Testing for Pupil Difficulties in Osmosis. A Teachers' Handbook*. Aberdeen: Aberdeen College of Education.

Arnold, B. and Simpson, M. (1982) *Concept Development and Diagnostic Testing–Osmosis in 'O' Grade Biology*. Aberdeen: Aberdeen College of Education.

Black, H. D. and Dockrell, W. B. (1980) *Diagnostic Assessment: A Teachers' Handbook*. Edinburgh: Scottish Council for Research in Education.

Black, H. and Goring, R. (1983) *A Diagnostic Resource in Geography*. Edinburgh: Scottish Council for Research in Education.

Bloom, B. S. (1976) *Human Characteristics and School Learning*. New York: McGraw-Hill.

Brumby, M. (1979) Problems in learning the concept of natural selection. *Journal of Biological Education*, 13, 2, 119–22.

Case, R. (1980) Implications of neo-Piagetian theory for improving the design of instruction. In: Kirby and Biggs (1980), *infra*.

Deadman, J. A. and Kelly, P. S. (1978) What do secondary school boys understand about evolution and heredity before they are taught the topics? *Journal of Biological Education*, 12, 1, 7–15.

Dow, W. M., Auld, J. and Wilson, D. (1978) *Pupils' Concepts of Gases, Liquids and Solids*. Dundee: Dundee College of Education.

Driver, R. (1983) *The Pupil as Scientist?* Milton Keynes: The Open University Press.

Driver, R. and Easley, J. (1978) Pupils and paradigms: a review of literature related to concept development in adolescent science students. *Studies in Science Education*, 5, 61–84.

Francis, E. (1982) *Learning to Discuss: a Report of the Moray House Discussion Skills Project*. Edinburgh: Moray House College of Education.

Herron, J. D., Cantu, L. L., Ward, R. and Sprinivasan, V. (1977) Problems associated with concept analysis. *Science Education*, 61, 2, 185–99.

Hornsey, M. and Horsfield, J. (1982) Pupils' discussion in science: a stratagem to enhance quantity and quality. *School Science Review*, 63, 225, 763–7.

Johnstone, A. H. and Kellett, N. C. (1980) Learning difficulties in school science – towards a working hypothesis. *European Journal of Science Education*, 2, 2, 175–181.

Kirby, J. R. and Biggs, J. B. (eds.) (1980) *Cognition, Development, and Instruction*. London: Academic Press.

Markle, S. M. (1975) They teach concepts, don't they? *Educational Researcher*, 4, 3–9.

Merrill, M. P. and Tennyson, R. D. (1977) *Teaching Concepts: An Instructional Design Guide*. Englewood Cliffs, N.J.: Educational Technology Publications.

Nordin, A. B. (1980) Improving learning: An experiment in rural primary schools in Malaysia, *Evolution in Education: An International Review Series*, 4, 2, 143–263.

Nussbaum, J. and Novick, S. (1981) Brainstorming in the classroom to invent a model: a case study. *School Science Review*, 62, 221, 771–8.

Scottish Education Department (1969) *Curriculum Paper 7: Science for General Education*. Edinburgh: HMSO.

Scottish Education Department (1977) *Assessment for All: Report of the Committee to Review Assessment in the Third and Fourth Years of Secondary Education in Scotland*. (The Dunning Report). Edinburgh: HMSO.

Simpson, M. (1983) The molecell rules – O.K.? *Biology Newsletter*, 42, 7–11. Aberdeen: Aberdeen College of Education.

Simpson, M. and Arnold, B. (1982a) Availability of prerequisite concepts for learning biology at certificate level. *Journal of Biological Education*, 16, 1, 65–72.

Simpson, M. and Arnold, B. (1982b) The inappropriate use of subsumers in biology learning, *European Journal of Science Education*, 4, 2, 173–82.

Simpson, M. and Arnold, B. (1983) Diagnostic tests and criterion-referenced assessment; their contribution to the resolution of pupil learning difficulties, *Programmed Learning and Educational Technology*, 20, 1, 36–42.

Simpson, M. and Arnold, B. (1984) *Diagnosis in Action*. Occasional Paper No. 1. Aberdeen: Aberdeen College of Education.

Viennot, L. (1979) Spontaneous reasoning in elementary dynamics, *European Journal of Science Education*, 1, 2, 205–21.

3.2

Problems in the assessment of scientific skills

Bob Fairbrother

WHAT DO WE MEAN BY SKILLS?

There is a variety of scientific skills; a variety which is made large by uncertainty over what exactly is meant by a skill. The Secondary Science Curriculum Review (SSCR, 1984) identifies skills as being separate from processes. A skill is seen as 'a specific activity which a student can be trained to do'; a process is seen as 'a rational activity involving the application of a range of skills'.

Which, then, of the following are skills and which are processes?

listening, searching, measuring, numeracy,
thinking, negotiating, selecting, drawing conclusions,
predicting, inferring, modelling, assessing

According to the SSCR the first four are skills and the others are processes. If you tried to do the classification using these definitions, you will almost certainly have disagreed with the SSCR, and with anyone else who tried to do it. Rather than enter into the controversy I think one should bypass the terminology argument and just decide that there are certain things we want students to do; call them skills if you like but make it clear that the word embraces broad actions as well as specific ones, macro-skills as well as micro-skills. One should note, though, that scientific skills are not confined just to practical work.

Following on from this, two further things emerge. The first is perhaps rather pedantic but it is necessary to deal with it in order to remove confusion. We are dealing with *actions*; I call them '*ings*'. All of the above are 'ings' except numeracy. Adding, substracting, multiplying, and dividing are actions, but numeracy is not and so does not belong in the list. If you can put 'ing' on the end of the word, you are talking about something you may want students to do.

The second thing to emerge is the existence of visible 'ings' and invisible 'ings'. Measuring is visible because you can see someone doing it and there is something happening which is assessable; thinking is invisible because you

From: Wellington, J. (ed.) (1989) *Skills and Processes in Science Education*, Routledge, London, pp. 99–115.

cannot see anything tangible. There is no doubt that we want students to think, but the evidence of the thinking is inevitably indirect and must be inferred from some other action. The solution of a problem must involve thought. (If it does not, there was not a problem in the first place.) The solution may have been arrived at but it has to be conveyed through writing, speaking, or some other action, and then the quality of the thinking is 'contaminated' by the writing, speaking, and so on. Similar problems exist with other skills such as listening and, to a lesser extent, reading. One does not know what is going on in another person's mind. This is the major difficulty with using Bloom's classification of educational objectives (Bloom *et al.*, 1956). The categorization by teachers of questions into knowledge, comprehension, application, and so on, involves the teachers making judgements about the way students are likely to find the answer to a question. However, one student's comprehension can be another student's application.

We should be clear what it is we are trying to do. We are trying to assess the performance of individual students in a range of skills, and then we want to make use of that information in some way. In general there are two main uses; one is formative in which we feed back the information in order to improve future performance, the others is summative in which we use the information in order to make judgements. Most of the difficulties we have in the assessment of skills arise from the interaction between the measurement and the use, and from the conflict between formative use and summative use.

FORMATIVE ASSESSMENT AND SUMMATIVE ASSESSMENT

Formative assessment is an integral part of teaching, it is ongoing and is used for diagnostic purposes to provide feedback to both students and teachers to improve the learning and teaching process. Summative assessment tends to be one-off and final, and concerned with achievement. It is strongly associated with sitting in judgement and awarding grades. Two major conflicts occur in continuous teacher assessment. The first is that of needing to use the information on student performance for two different purposes, that is, to indicate achievement for the award of a final grade and also to provide feedback to improve performance. Information about earlier performance ought to become redundant as performance improves; and performance will fluctuate anyway, being influenced by a variety of factors, such that numbers alone do not give a proper reflection of ability. An assessment scheme which allows teachers to collect data for formative purposes but is then flexible (for example permits some teacher judgement) in the way these data are used for summative purposes helps to overcome this conflict. [. . .]

The second conflict occurs because the teacher has to fill two different roles, that of helper and that of judge. Students will reveal their deficiencies to someone who is genuinely helping them to overcome the deficiencies, but they will be reluctant to reveal their weaknesses if the revelation might count against them. Many people believe that this conflict cannot be overcome with the present examining system. However, I think it can be reduced through a proper realization by students and teachers of the aims and objectives of assessment, and by having an organization which enables assignments to be discussed and developed together. It will also be reduced as the ethos of the GCSE moves away from the old teacher-controlled approach of the GCE and, to a lesser extent, the CSE, and moves more towards a participative model involving both students and teachers in making decisions. This is reflected in the work of the TVEI and the CPVE. The problem will also be reduced as the GCSE evolves away from the single grade reporting of results and towards a more descriptive, profile report. This move will be influenced by the various Records of Achievement projects and by the many Graded Assessment schemes which are being developed. These latter have a major aim of giving credit to students in stages throughout their period of compulsory education, and have the potential for providing more information at more convenient times than can the GCSE as it is at the moment.

SETTING STANDARDS – THE PROBLEM OF DIFFERENTIATION

There is another range of problems arising out of the need to allow everyone to show what they know, understand, and can do. This phrase has become well known through its use in connection with the GCSE, but it applies at all stages of education. However, the end of the period of compulsory education is a particularly important stage so it is right to emphasize the need at that stage. When they are able to leave school, all students can do more than when they started. The principle of differentiation which is enshrined in the GCSE is to find out what students can do and make some positive statement about it. This is distinct from discrimination in which we try to separate students without being positive about the achievement of all of them. Differentiation is closely bound up with criterion referencing in which we try to find out what students can do by making reference to the skills themselves and not by making comparisons with what other students can do, that is, norm referencing. Indeed, the movement towards identifying and measuring student performance in skills inevitably takes us away from norm referencing into criterion referencing.

However, where does one start? What is the bottom line for reporting performance? If the interest is with the students, the bottom line is what the least able student can do. If you set a task and some students cannot do it, the task is too hard and you must find an easier one. For example suppose you think students should be able to recall some common temperatures. You might, then, ask the following set of questions:

(1) At what temperature does water boil?
(2) What is the temperature of a healthy person?
(3) At what temperature does water freeze?
(4) What is the approximate temperature in the laboratory?

These seem to be fairly simple questions capable of being answered correctly by most secondary school students who have gone through a unit of work involving this information. (This is not necessarily a GCSE situation; it might be a unit of work done in the first or second form and you want to make a report about positive achievement.) If, however, you find that there are some students who get the questions wrong, you have not found out what this group of students know. They might be able to answer a simpler set of questions, for example:

Use the temperatures in the box to answer questions 1 to 4.

> 0°C   20°C   37°C   100°C

(1) The boiling point of water is ———
(2) A healthy person has a temperature of ———
(3) The freezing point of water is ———
(4) The temperature of the laboratory is about ———

There will always be at least one student who gets at least one question wrong. In the search for increasingly simpler questions a decision eventually has to be made when to stop. This is an arbitrary decision, and in recent years we have been hearing of eighty–eighty tests in which at least 80 per cent of the students get at least 80 per cent of the marks.

This 'bottom-up' approach was adopted by the ILEA Graded Assessments in Science Project (GASP) based at King's College, London. The problem about it is that the bottom line may be very trivial and do damage to the image of the subject. In an internal, formative situation this is not too serious, but in an external, summative situation it may be. Should one be true to the students or true to the subject? In a criterion-referenced situation in which it is clear to everyone what is wanted we might be able to avoid this problem by raising the level of the lowest performance. As yet we do not have enough experience of the effect of making clear to students just what it is they have to do. The findings of, for example, the APU are based on the way students have been taught and assessed in the past; it remains to be seen what the effect is of having clearly defined goals, and of teaching and assessing students in different ways. [. . .]

HIERARCHIES: ACROSS SKILLS AND WITHIN SKILLS

The determination of usable hierarchies is one of the biggest problems in the GCSE, not only in the teacher assessment of practical skills, but also in written papers. Differentiation demands a hierarchy of some kind. Is the hierarchy to be achieved by placing skills in some kind of rank order in which the lower ones are achievable by everyone but the higher ones are achievable only by the best students? Or is the hierarchy a more sophisticated one in which there may be a rank order of skills but students develop the easier ones to a greater extent than the harder ones? Some of the early submissions to the GCSE Science Committee of the SEC took the simpler view and identified higher order skills (assessment objectives) which would be tested only in the extension papers. The committee took the more sophisticated view and was of the opinion that all the assessment objectives should be open to all students, otherwise how would we know what the students know, understand, and can do?

The draft proposals for the criteria for the award of grades appear to take a similar sophisticated view. Recognizing is seen to be easier than recalling. When linked with the content by identifying foundation material and extension material, different levels of performance are then proposed:

LOW LEVEL	Recognizing from the foundation material
	Recalling from the foundation material
	Recognizing from the extension material
HIGH LEVEL	Recalling from the extension material

This is a theoretical hierarchy which has to be put to the test; and the notion of easy (foundation) material and harder (extension) material is difficult to sustain at the level of the GCSE. For example, it is repeatedly said that the concept of the mole (not the biological version) is difficult. In what sense is it more difficult than dozen, score, or ream as measures of a quantity of things? Much of the difficulty comes from what we ask students to do with the concept. A ream might be just as difficult if we asked students to balance equations using reams of atoms instead of moles of atoms. There is not room here to argue this fully, but the main message is that content (concepts) and processes cannot be separated when making judgements about difficulty.

Nevertheless, if one subscribes to the differentiation philosophy, one needs a model of assessment which matches the philosophy. (The differentiation-by-alternative-components model which is so much favoured in the GCSE brings with it as many problems as it solves, not least of which are how to make decisions as to who should sit which alternative, and how to deal with the results for the award of a grade. In addition it does not easily fit with the dictum that all students should be enabled to show what they know, understand, and can do; if there is a component which you have not tackled, you have been denied the opportunity to show your full worth.)

The measurement of performance in a skill depends upon one's view of how skills develop. Most people take a developmental view in which students are positioned somewhere in the continuum of increasing competence in the skill (see Fairbrother, 1986). The dichotomous view in which students either possess the skill or do not possess it (see the NEA GCSE Biology scheme) takes a point in the continuum as the reference point (the criterion) for making judgements. The problems with the continuum view are identifying the path of progress and determining whether it is a straight path with no side turnings or plateaux. There are two basic approaches to solving these problems. One is simply that of describing what a student has done without attempting to assign some kind of hierarchy of progress. (This leads to another problem when it is necessary to add together in some way the separate performances so as to make a decision about the award of an overall mark or grade; descriptions are not additive.) The absence of a hierarchy of progress, however, implies a lack of teaching strategy designed to give a progressive development of the skill, and hence removes one of the main planks of formative assessment.

There is a great need to bring together theories of child development, models of learning and methods of assessment. Behaviourism, for example the work of Skinner, operant conditioning, and programmed learning, seems to have lost favour. Developmentalism, for example as propounded by Piaget (see Shayer and Adey, 1981), seems to be riding high and tends to govern the models of teacher assessment of practical work in the GCSE. Constructivism, for example as discussed by Brook, Driver, Gilbert, and Watts (see for example Brook and Driver, 1984; Driver et al., 1985; Gilbert and Watts, 1983), is seductive but has not yet found its way into the classroom, the laboratory, and the expertise of the examiner. It seems to lend itself only to descriptive reporting of student performance and not to numerical or alphabetical grades. We are not short of books about learning strategies (see for example Nisbet and Shucksmith, 1986), but these seem only to add to the skills which students need. Learning to learn is a particularly important one. However, they do not suggest a coherent approach to the three educational activities of teaching, learning, and assessing.

The second basic approach, and the one which is particularly prevalent at the moment, is to try to use experience and research to identify a usable hierarchy. If this can be done, one can still give a description but at the same time numbers can be assigned to different stages in the hierarchy and so help to solve the problem of determining an overall grade. These stages then become criteria of performance for the award of a particular mark. One must realize, though, that the use of numbers not only implies a precision which is usually not justified, but also implies, wrongly, a ratio scale in which a mark of 4 indicates a position which is twice as far along the path of progress as a mark of 2. Despite its widespread use, this approach is still in only a rudimentary stage of development and presents many problems. We can see some of these problems when we look at some of the proposals that have been put forward for the GCSE by the various examining groups.

HIERARCHIES AND CRITERIA

In all the proposals we can see the examining groups struggling to cope with the problems of finding a hierarchy of performance, of trying to describe the hierarchy in criterion-referenced terms and of awarding marks to different stages in the hierarchy. Finding a perfect criterion-referenced hierarchy will be impossible because students do not behave like this. The NEA's attempt to use grade descriptors at this stage in the proceedings highlights this problem, and it is faced by all the groups when they try to apply the grade descriptors to help determine the award of grades at the end of the whole examination. In Reporting Experimental Work in Block A (Investigating) of the NEA Science (Dual) Award, a Grade F candidate is supposed to be able to 'describe in discussion during experimental work the main stages of a procedure'.

Examiners are free to make this kind of decision provided it is consistent with the overall grade descriptors given in the National Criteria and with similar decisions made by other examiners in other groups. However, it ought also to be consistent with the next description for Grade F performance in Reporting Experimental Work, that is, 'Can report in non-scientific language, the more striking parts of a procedure, even if out of sequence. Often begins a report with observations and measurements.'

In addition it ought to be consistent with all the other thirty-five descriptions of Grade F performance which are contained in Blocks A and D of the NEA scheme. However, consistency across thirty or forty descriptors is impossible. Candidates will always exhibit characteristics, some of which fall into one grade and some of which fall into other grades. The fault does not lie with the NEA, or any other examining group, of course. The fundamental problem is that criterion-referencing is incompatible with single-grade reporting of results. Teachers using the NEA scheme are thus required to use their judgement as best they can and assign students to the grade which most closely matches their behaviour. Examiners have to make similar judgements when using the grade descriptors to award grades at the end of the examination. However, one should note the warning given to teachers by the MEG in their Combined Science Syllabus: 'It is strongly emphasised that an overall impression mark awarded at the end of each year is not normally regarded as a satisfactory form of assessment.' It would be better if the MEG modified this warning to take into account what teachers, and examiners, actually have to do.

This difficulty in following the rules is further evident when one looks at the detail of what is involved. For example, the LEAG Physics Syllabus A requires *manipulative skills*, among other things, to be assessed as a part of coursework. Manipulative skills in the LEAG scheme involve four aspects: *safety, selection, assembly,* and *use* of apparatus, for which a total of five marks is available. When planning and organizing a teaching scheme it is not always possible to include all of these four aspects in a single lesson; for example *safety, assembly,* and *use* may be involved but not *selection*. Information about the ability to select apparatus may have to be obtained in another lesson. So one has to store information obtained at different times, and use one's judgement to combine it together at a later stage in order to give the assessment that is needed.

WORK-LOAD VS RELIABILITY

The amount of work involved in making these assessments is quite large. The LEAG Science (Syllabus M) requires five abilities to be assessed on three occasions for a single certificate (fifteen assessments), and five occasions for a double certificate (twenty-five assessments) for each candidate. With a class of twenty-five pupils this makes a total of 375 and 625 assessments respectively. These can be spread over the two years prior to the final examination, but they still represent an average of nearly two assessments per lesson. The twenty-four assessments per candidate for the SEG Integrated Science (Single Certificate) were originally expected to be done in only the two *terms* prior to the written examination. This was eventually changed to give teachers more time.

Multiple measurements of the same skill increase the reliability of the measurement compared with a single measurement, and hence can help to improve the validity of the examination. It makes statistical sense, if not logistical sense, to ask for several measurements, and is fairer for the candidates, any one of whom could have an off-day on the occasion of a single assessment. The logistics can be improved if there is a good choice of scale for the measurements. A scale which has just two points (yes–no, or right–wrong) leaves teachers in an agony of indecision because the statements of behaviour on which they have to pass judgement are never sufficiently precise for this kind of judgement to be made. (See the examples given above.) On the other hand a scale with many points on it can leave the teachers with too many decisions to make and gives a false sense of precision. Armitage (1986) sees another danger in using a large number of points, that it can too easily lead to a reversion to norm-referencing. I think that his argument is based upon a misunderstanding of what is meant by norm-referencing (see Fairbrother, 1986, for a fuller discussion). However, he supports the idea which many groups have adopted of having a four-point scale (3–2–1–0) and has found that teachers find it useful to assume all pupils start with a score of 3 and to deduct marks depending on the level of help offered during the course of the work.

The logistics can also be improved if there is more time in which to make the assessments. The National Criteria do not require them to take place in the final two terms, nor in the final two years. The only requirement is that 'The standards applied in the assessment of course work must always be those which apply for the final examination, irrespective of when the course work was actually completed or the assessment made' (DES, 1985a, p. 6). This brings with it other problems such as the meaning of the standard for the final examination, and, as discussed above, what one does with the earlier assessments when the later ones show an improvement. (The NEA scheme, which requires teachers to collect evidence over a period of time and then to use that evidence to arrive at a final judgement, goes some way towards solving this problem but puts a great responsibility on the teachers to make the right judgement.)

NORMS, CRITERIA, AND STANDARDS

In a strict criterion-referenced examination many of the above problems disappear because one is looking for clearly defined levels of performance, and a student is credited with the highest level reached. However, arriving at the right standard is an example of the way in which norms have to be used in order to decide upon reasonable criteria. This was discussed earlier when we were trying to decide what might be the bottom line in assessing students. An example from athletics illustrates the point further and exposes further problems.

We know it is unreasonable to ask 16-year-old students to run 100 metres in 10 seconds because our experience tells us so, that is we know the norm for 16-year-olds in this event. Knowing what 16-year-olds are capable of doing we can use our professional judgements to decide upon standards. For example we might decide that a gold award will be given to anyone who can run 100 metres in 15 seconds, a silver to anyone who can do it in 17 seconds, and a bronze for 19 seconds. Having made this decision, we can now have a criterion-referenced assessment system in which anyone who reaches the right standard will be given the award for that standard without reference to anyone else who may have reached it. What is more, there is nothing to prevent a 13-year-old being given an award if he or she merits it: once the standard is decided, anyone and everyone has the opportunity to try for it. We can now see how confusing is the advice given by one GCSE examining group when it says that teachers should 'make full use of the scale in order to credit candidates' positive performance'. If teachers interpret this as meaning that they must award the full range of marks available, it would be valid in the GCSE only if there happened to be in the class students at all levels of achievement.

We can extend the sporting analogy by requiring students to attempt a variety of events taken from the field and the track in order to get a measure of general athletic prowess. We can see that someone who can get a gold award in the 100 metres may fail to get even a bronze award in the shot-putting event. Adding together these separate performances in order to award some kind of final overall grade is permissible using certain arbitrary rules, as in the decathlon, but reporting only the final points total represents a loss of quite a lot of information.

The problem of a student who obtains a gold award in the 100 metres at the age of 14 and then puts on weight such that the performance is less at the age of 16 is not so easy to resolve. Returning to the GCSE, if the award is supposed to represent what it is that a student can do on some particular date (the day of the final written examination?), then continuous assessment as is required for the assessment of coursework becomes impossible. Such decisions would make a nonsense of the GCSE, so we must allow evidence to be admissible whenever it is obtained, understanding when we do so that the student has at least achieved the required standard at some stage. In addition, having achieved the standard at an earlier age, we know that the student does not give up science and 'grow fat through lack of exercise' because the study of science continues at least until the age of 16. Acceptance of this argument opens the GCSE door to the various graded assessments projects, most of which currently aim to assess throughout the period of compulsory secondary education and hence obtain information about student performance over a period of at least five

is not sufficiently flexible to cope with this kind of situation,
xtinct along with the dinosaurs. The GCSE cannot stand still; it
in ten years' time it will be different from what it is now in just the
that it is now different from what it (the GCE and the CSE) was ten
o.

PLANNING FOR COURSEWORK ASSESSMENT

A major problem for teachers is to make sure that they provide their students with sufficient opportunities to develop the necessary skills and so show what they can do so that assessments can be made. This entails planning ahead. Basically what is necessary is to set the skills involved against the intended lesson plans in order to ensure that the required skills can be developed in the lessons and can be assessed. If 'Assessing evidence and evaluating arguments' is one of the skills, lessons must be devised so that students are given an opportunity to show how well they can do this. If it is considered that only one-third of the students can be assessed in this skill in any one lesson, three lessons must be planned. If each student has to be assessed in this skill three times, nine lessons must be planned. In addition, as explained above, it may not be possible in one lesson to assess all of the aspects involved in any skill or objective, which adds further to the planning required. Finally the students must be given the opportunity to develop and practice the skill before any final judgement is made. It is obvious that this kind of planning needs to be done well in advance. Skills and abilities which teachers have normally developed in their lessons in the past are easier to accommodate. Others require teaching methods to change and they present problems not only of knowing what to do but also of overcoming the natural conservatism associated with any kind of curriculum development.

It is important to identify those activities which produce a permanent assessable *product*, and those which do not. Skills connected with, say, recording and reporting are likely to produce permanent evidence which can be evaluated after the event. Those connected with, say, manipulative skills involve *processes*, are more ephemeral, and need to be assessed as they occur. For these good planning, organization, and record-keeping are essential. For example, it may be necessary to concentrate on certain selected students in any one lesson knowing that the evidence needed is going to be apparent only in the first twenty minutes of the lesson. Subsequent lessons enable a different set of students to be assessed, so good record-keeping is necessary in order to know what has been done and what needs to be done. These are 'internal' records which go into each lesson and are probably kept on a clip-board. In addition there are 'external' records which must eventually be sent to the examination group. The form of the internal records needs to be planned with the external records in mind in order eventually to reduce the amount of work involved in transferring the information.

Some examination groups are quite clear about what information they need, others are less so. Some require quite a lot of information, others require relatively little. As an example, the NEA Science (Modular) scheme is very thorough and requires two kinds of information:

(1) an assignment Record Sheet listing the assignments which have been used and the skills which are assessable in each assignment;
(2) an Individual Record Card for each pupil which gives the marks awarded for each skill and the assignment which was used to obtain the marks.

So, not only must the mark needed for each skill be recorded, something which all examination groups obviously need, but also a description of the work that the student did when the skill was assessed must also be given, and not all groups need this.

The NEA says that fuller details must also be available for the purposes of moderation. This is a requirement for all groups, whether they say so or not, since the National Criteria say that there must be provision for samples of any end-product or other tangible form of evidence of candidates' work to be submitted for inspection. Thus, adding to the problems of keeping records are those of keeping samples of students' work. However, this is rather important if one is to be as fair as possible to students because, not only can this work be made available to moderators if necessary, but also it can be used within a school to help in arriving at common standards among several teachers, and in ensuring consistent standards from one teacher over the assessment period. This need arises because there are problems associated with assessing different students on the same skill in different activities. One of the problems is that the nature of the activities will be different and so may not present situations of equal difficulty. For example, being able to follow instructions given in a work-sheet is as much influenced by the nature of the work-sheet as it is by the ability of the student. Another is that students who are assessed later have had more opportunity to practise the skill which is being assessed.

It is necessary to be aware of these problems and try to reduce their effect or remove them. One can reduce their effect by sensitive choice of work and by judicious comparison with earlier tasks; hence the need to save samples of students' work. One can also reduce the problem by using different kinds of lesson plan. For example, a class of twenty-seven students can be organized into three groups of nine. The three groups can circulate round three activities, one of the activities being designed to give the required information for all the students in the course of one lesson. It might also be possible to make inferences from indirect evidence, for example it may be possible to say that a student has used a piece of apparatus properly because a particular result has been obtained – the correct diameter of a piece of wire is evidence that a micrometer screw gauge has been used correctly; accurate counting of the number of minibeasts on a slide is evidence that a hand lens or a microscope has been focused properly. Copying can be avoided by having a number of different samples.

The need to obtain information about individual students is a big problem. Normally grouping into pairs and trios is necessary because there are not enough facilities to do otherwise. It will be necessary sometimes to ask individuals who are working in groups to show what they can do. This is particularly important if there is a rather dominant student in a group. An organization of four groups of six students circulating around four different activities, one practical, the others non-practical, in the course of two or three lessons allows individuals to work on their own. It might even be possible to arrange for two teachers to be timetabled together for a limited number of periods.

None of the above suggestions will be easy to organize; some will be impossible for some classes. Neither teachers nor students can get used to different ways of working overnight, but the situation will get easier with familiarity and practice and as ideas get spread around. It will be found that more than just the planned objectives can be assessed in any one lesson; an occasional rather formal practical test may be used, but it will be unfortunate if this is done too often since it is not in the spirit of what is intended by coursework assessment in the GCSE. It is important to make sure that there is not too much assessment and too little teaching.

REFERENCES

Armitage, P. (1986) Coursework assessment: a powerful weapon, *Times Educational Supplement*, 12 September.

Bloom, B. S., Englehart, M. D., Furil, E. J., Hill, W. H. and Kreithwohl, D. R. (eds.) (1956) *Taxonomy of Educational Objectives: Handbook 1, The Cognitive Domain*, London: Longman.

Brook, A. and Driver, R. (1984) *Aspects of Secondary Students' Understanding of Energy: Full Report*, Leeds: Children's Learning in Science Project.

DES (1985a) *GCSE: The National Criteria – Science*, London: HMSO.

DES (1985b) *GCSE: General Criteria*, London: HMSO.

Driver, R., Guesne, E., and Tiberghien, A. (1985) *Children's Ideas in Science*, Milton Keynes: Open University Press.

Fairbrother, B. (1986) How is science teaching evaluated, assessed and examined?, in J. Nellist and B. Nicholl (eds.) *ASE Science Teacher's Handbook*, London: Hutchinson/Association for Science Education.

Gilbert, J. K. and Watts, D. M. (1983) Concepts, misconceptions and alternative conceptions: changing perspectives in science education, *Studies in Science Education* 10: 61–90.

Nisbet, J. and Shucksmith, J. (1986) *Learning Strategies*, London: Routledge & Kegan Paul.

SEC (1985a) *Coursework Assessment in GCSE: Working Paper 2*, London: SEC.

SEC (1985b) *Differentiated Assessment in GCSE: Working Paper 1*, London: SEC.

SEC (1986) *Draft Grade Criteria: Science*, Report of Working Party, London: SEC.

Shayer, M. and Adey, P. S. (1981) *Towards a Science of Science Teaching*, London: Heinemann Educational.

Skevington, J. H. (1986) Internal assessment of practical coursework in the GCSE, *Physics Education* 21, 4: 204–11.

SSCR (1984) *Towards the Specification of Minimum Entitlement: Brenda and Friends*, London: Schools Council Publications.

Reflections: accountability, the pressures and the opportunities

Neill Patterson and George Walker

Neill: Good morning ladies and gentlemen. My name is Neill Patterson. I am Head of Boxmoor Primary School in Hemel Hempstead. Boxmoor is a popular school of some 200 children, situated in an affluent commuter zone and close to Boxmoor Station. Boxmoor is also one of George's thirty feeder schools and our children have traditionally gone to Cavendish and another local school on a fifty/fifty split.

George: I'm George Walker, the Head of The Cavendish School, an 11–18 comprehensive school in Hemel Hempstead, with about 1,100 pupils. Our annual intake, which is somewhere between 180 and 190 youngsters, comes from over thirty different primary feeder schools, of which Neill's is one and ten schools in the immediate vicinity of the school that supply the majority of our youngsters.

Neill: Pupils will transfer to secondary schools with carefully differentiated National Curriculum assessments. How will the secondary schools build on this?

George: For me this is one of the biggest problems. I think that of all the different areas of accountability that we are concerned about and which we will be discussing today, the educational accountability to our pupils is the most important. We have the responsibility for their learning in science, but we also have a much wider responsibility for their growing up, their increasing maturity, their self-image, their development as a whole pupil, and I would suggest to you that whatever else we do in assessment, it must not damage this overall process. So I am concerned to know that increasingly, youngsters will be coming to our school with a series of labels attached and we will be challenged – perhaps provoked might be a better word – to take this into account in the organization of the school. I think we need to be very honest about this,

From: *Assessment and Accountability* Fairbrother, B., Foden, West, D. and Wilson (eds.) (1990) ASE Occasional Papers, pp. 57–71.

and professionally more honest than we have been, because I don't think there is a simple answer. I think there is an element of dishonesty in what secondary schools, and ours is no exception, have tended to do in the past, which is to advertise the merits of a fresh start. In other words, to ignore everything that has gone on previously and start again – very convenient, but no longer acceptable. Let's not, however, dismiss the merits of that, of giving youngsters an opportunity to show in a different environment and different circumstances, the very positive things that they are capable of.

I reject the notion totally, of setting pupils according to their National Curriculum assessments at eleven or twelve, and I think we face an enormous challenge of reconciling the need to keep youngsters' learning buoyant, positive and encouraging, particularly at that age, with the need to recognize that they will be at different stages of it. As I said earlier, I don't think anybody has got simple answers to it and the challenge of differentiated learning within a mixed-ability context is the one that certainly we will be trying to answer. I think that is very difficult, but we are going to get better at it slowly. We have got an awful lot to learn and an awful lot to teach each other.

I want to come back to you with a question, which relates to the fact that the youngsters coming to us, as I said earlier from those thirty different schools in a typical year, have a lot of differences, but they have, I think, one thing in common. They have on the whole an enormous enthusiasm for learning. We may complain, and we do, about what they know and what they don't know and what they can do well. Some schools have done this and some schools haven't done the other, but I don't think we're complaining about the fact that they are coming to us highly motivated, particularly in terms of science, wanting to learn and being very positive about their learning. I think that is an enormous credit to the primary schools, and something we and, I am sure, you want to retain. I therefore wonder how you are going to avoid switching pupils off at an earlier stage, so that they come to us feeling that they have already reached some kind of point of no return in their learning.

Neill: Thank you for the credit, George, and there is fairly ominous warning in what you say there. I would like to look at one of the principal purposes of assessment. Assessment is intended to bring about a closer match between the pupil and the programme and to that extent, if that does come about and we get a personalized and tailored programme, assessment could be viewed as stress relieving. I say that somewhat tongue in cheek, because quite genuinely most teachers do have very real concerns, i.e. the side-effects of assessment *per se*. We will be assessing children from seven years old through to eleven years old. Now to make sure that children are on stream at seven, we will also be taking a very critical look at them from six years old. So from six years old right the way through to eleven, we will be taking a much sharper focus on the activities and progress of our children.

That in itself may upset some children, whether they are able or less able, some children won't appreciate that detailed focus. That may be a fact of life.

We are under time pressures, for science is only one aspect of the curriculum. We have a very detailed geography syllabus, we have a history syllabus and maths and we have got to shoe-horn all of this into a week. Now we don't know whether it is going to go. Certainly one thing it is going to do is to make teachers very much more conscious of time, and so children are also going to encounter time pressures. We are going to have to guillotine activities and say we have got to stop here, we have to get on.

That sort of constraint has not really been part of the primary school environment, but certainly it is here and it is growing. We have also got the individual pressure on the teacher. Nobody wants to be seen as a failing teacher who didn't get the class up to standard, and this terrific pressure on the teachers to be seen to succeed, will inevitably lead them to turn the screw. Now to an extent, pressure is a necessary and vital part of life. It is what motivates people, it is what pushes people on to succeed. But we have thirty individual little engines in our class, each like a delicately balanced carburettor and we have got to make the adjustment carefully. It isn't insensitive teachers, who will cause their children anxiety. It is just the fact that we have this relationship of one to thirty, and with the best will in the world, you can't make those adjustments as sensitively as you might like to do. So there are some of the side-effects which will be consequent upon things which the teachers have to do.

Now we also have what I would like to call third-party effects. The parents, legitimately so, will become part of this. They will have access to the results. Some of you, I am sure, will have been along to a primary school football match after school and you will have seen the visiting team come in, and if you don't watch the children sometimes you will find the spectators much more interesting. You will listen to the language, the aggression coming from parents, and you can see this can be translated by parents into classroom activity. We are actually giving parents a handle on an issue, with fairly crude labels. Some of those parents will use those labels to put more pressure on their children to achieve. That's fine if it's a legitimate and realistic objective, but where the child can't achieve or is doing his or her best, then it becomes unwarranted pressure. So I do have some concerns about what parents will do with these results and how that will interact in the classroom.

We have always exercised a degree of confidentiality when we have tested our children, whenever we have gone through an assessment procedure. We don't read out a register and say John – Level 2, Mary – Level 2, Wayne – Level 1, Josiah – Level 3, because we know the consequences of this. Some children will feel deeply hurt and yet because the parents have access to the results, what they do with those results is beyond our control. I know quite well, that many children will come into school and they will tell their peer group what level they are on and are going to get disappointment, frustration and pressure arising from that context as well.

How do we overcome this? I think there are two things open to us on this question. One, we are going to have to counsel parents. We are going to have to explain what the results mean and how to handle them and trust their judgement. Secondly, as the teacher did who trialled the seven-year-olds SATs this summer, if we find this pressure in the classroom is unwarranted, then we are going to take a stand. We have a duty of care to our pupils, we are responsible not only for their academic developments, but also for their moral well-being and if we find those pressures become unacceptable then we have to make that statement, explain this to our governors and to our parents, and carry the situation with us in the interest of our children.

Now George, our parents come to school each day, we see them at the end of the day and they frequently bring their children along in the morning. So establishing a contact with them for us is relatively easy. We never have any difficulty in attracting parents to come into the school, so we can explain more easily to them what assessments mean. How in your larger and more complex context will you be able to handle this issue of contact?

George: A fair question. Clearly the whole area of accountability to parents, as we saw in the earlier sketch, is an enormously important one. I must say I have enormous faith in the parents; they take education on the whole very seriously indeed and anybody who would suggest differently would do well to come to Hemel Hempstead at the moment. They should see the degree of care and trouble that is taken over the finding out about what secondary schools are offering, as we are now in the business of secondary transfer for next year. Talking only yesterday to a rather irate parent, to have quoted back to me, things that I had promised that parent three or four years earlier, was a salutory experience and not a bad one for me to have to listen to. I think we do well to take very seriously what parents are saying, thinking and doing in connection with education. We in turn, and this is my experience, not just in our school but the vast majority I know, take our contact with parents very seriously and go to all kinds of lengths to see that it is done well and done properly. Over the last year we have completely rethought our pattern of reporting and meetings with parents and matching the two up much more coherently, and I think parents, if they are involved in the process of education, can understand very well what's going on. For example, at Cavendish we have been teaching integrated science for a dozen years I suppose, and a dozen years ago it was quite a controversial issue that we didn't do physics, chemistry and biology up to what was then GCE O-level and CSE. That required a lot of explanation and we took time explaining it. We won over parents who were very satisfied and very pleased with the scientific experience their youngsters had. If one takes time and trouble then it can be done.

As another example, we have had on the go a fairly extensive profiling exercise now for a couple of years. That has culminated this year in the changes I mentioned earlier, and we involved our parents in giving us very informal feedback on that. No other issue since I have been at Cavendish, now nearly ten years, has created more extensive, useful, helpful feedback than that particular one. Virtually every parent responded to us. Some critically, some supportively, but the critical ones were almost invariably helpful, and as a result of that we modified quite extensively what we were going to do and the approach we adopted. I think right across the range of parents (and we have a very wide and interesting cross-section of parents) they have got something helpful to say about how to go about it. So I think the challenge for us is to put National Curriculum assessment into context of the courses we are teaching, the way we are teaching it and how that fits the philosophy of the school that we are talking to parents about, right from the moment of secondary transfer.

Also, if I may suggest, not to take it too seriously. I think this is very important indeed. There is more to life than the National Curriculum, there is more to the National Curriculum than National Curriculum assessment, and I think it is important that parents realize that. I think they are shrewd enough to do so, because in my experience they are taking a large number of different factors about a school into account in their judgement and their ultimate support of it.

I think I would like to come back to you Neill, on a slightly more focused aspect of this because I think many secondary school teachers, perhaps, unkindly and wrongly, would say that in the past, teachers in primary schools haven't been sufficiently honest with parents, haven't faced up to the truth with parents about their youngsters and are going to have a difficult time doing that in the next few years as the National Curriculum assessment comes on stream. Fair comment or a stereotype view?

Neill: I'll take issue with you on that one. This is a reflection of a comment which is written in one of the industrialist's papers, that teachers should say the bad as well as the good. First of all the parents will all get a written report and that is their entitlement, but I think that report is actually going to be a blander sort of document than parents perhaps think at this point in time. Precisely what sort of truth is going to be revealed in their National Curriculum reports? We are going to get aggregated levels which will blur distinctions rather than show differentiation. You take fourteen levels and aggregate them and what do you get? The differentiation certainly doesn't come through. We have also got some very broad levels in the National Curriculum. I know it is a science conference, but let me just point out English writing Level 2. A child who is functionally able to write in sentences isn't differentiated from a child who has a flair or an aptitude for language. It just doesn't come across. That is going to be a little upsetting for the parent of the child who has the flair being lumped together with a child who has just a mechanical ability. Dick West also made the point that 'progress particularly in oral developments isn't a linear thing'. George will know this too well, and we have experience of this too. We have the infants who come into school, reticent on the first few days, then you can't shut them up. They are talking all the way through their primary school days until they get to about the third year junior stage, then it peaks, then it goes down again. Now we are using oral development to try and assess the practical activities which the children are doing. So what do we make of an assessment when we can't get the child to speak? How do we actually get into it and how does this reflect in National Curriculum documents? So the cur-vilinear effect is also problematic in the actual recorded result.

We also have the problem of group-administered tests. We have the helpful child and the forward child who we can't shut up, so the other four or five children in the group all have the same result. So what sort of truth does that bring over to the parents when they look at their National Curriculum record? I wouldn't like to say to what effect, but we will also find teachers who are concerned and anxious who will say these children should aspire to Level 2, that being the norm in this class. 'I'm going to go SAT spotting, and I'm going to make sure that they all reach Level 2. I am going to construct a situation so that they all reach Level 2.' These are some of the problems in the actual record which we give to parents.

George has mentioned that there is an educational policy not to say the unfortunate things about a child's progress. In my whole experience, this has never actually been a problem in primary school. When I first started teaching, the great problem was that teachers were too ready to say all of the negative things, and to outline all of the weaknesses in a child's progress and they weren't sufficiently willing to indicate the successes. Now we have got a bal-anced record on children. It has never been a difficulty with teachers to report weakness. The difficult area has been, I think, to put a format upon that and to say to the parents, here are the problems associated with your child, here are the areas that we need to pay particular attention to, and here is the con-structive way forward. You need to do this and this, and here are the areas where we can help. I think, we as a professional body, are much better geared up to making that response today, than perhaps we were in the past. So really, to go back to your original question, George, I don't honestly think it is true of teachers to say that there is any danger of them not facing up to telling unpalatable truths. What we need to see is that when they say, or highlight areas of weakness, that they put the constructive situation forward to the parents. I am sure when we all do this, then we are going to have a much better partnership with our parents.

Now pupils will transfer to secondary schools with our carefully prepared records of progress in science. These will be carefully differentiated, carefully made out on a matrix. How will your secondary school teachers actually be able to use these results, which we hand over to you?

George: Well, here comes another enormous challenge of course, because as I was trying to indicate earlier, the principle of the fresh start, i.e. that pupils haven't existed before the age of eleven years, and come in fresh at eleven-plus to secondary schools, simply won't do in future. I think we are on a third area of accountability here. We have talked about the teachers being accountable to their pupils, accountable to their parents and also I think they are accountable to each other. I feel, certainly at Cavendish, very much part of a team of twelve science teachers. That's part of my job, as well as being Head. I am part of a science team, and I am accountable to members of that team, depending on what year or years I am teaching in, and what sub-team I'm a member of and who is leading that team and so on. What I do in my science teaching, undoubtedly effects the rest of the team. The records that I produce, the information that I have and passed on, is a very important area of accountability. I take that very seriously and only the other week I was being torn off a strip by a much younger, less experienced teacher, for having left a lab in the state which she didn't appreciate, when she took her class in the next lesson, and quite right too. I think therefore that we are getting better in terms of accountability between each other in the profession within a school. There is a much greater emphasis nowadays on team work, and the future of the National Curriculum and the development of the National Curriculum depend critically upon team work, within subject areas and across subject areas as well. Where I think we are professionally hopeless, is between phases, and somehow, I'm not sure how we are going to do it when, as I indicated earlier, we are actually responsible for youngsters coming from well over thirty different schools, albeit the majority from say ten. Somehow we are going to have to create cross-phase teams and feel that there is a sense of team work, a sense of accountability and a sense of obligation across the phases, and that's going to need an awful lot of thought.

I think there are two problems here that have to be overcome. One is quite simply trust. On the whole we don't trust what other people are saying or doing, I think, as a profession. We are not prepared on the whole to take information, opinions, views and data from other people, and accept it as being accurate, true and a good basis to build upon. Now that may upset you when I say that, but in my experience that is true of the teaching profession. We are not at all good at trusting one another and saying 'Well, that is what Neill and his colleagues have said about these youngsters, that is the information they have given us. I think that is right, I think I can trust that, I can use that and I can build on that.' That is related to the second problem, which is the eternal one and I don't have to tell you this, of reinventing the wheel, of feeling that we can't own something, we can't internalize something, we can't personalize it and make it part of our own experience without actually having to construct it in the first place. Certainly, when I was involved in teacher education, as I was for five years, I look back on some of that period with great criticism, because I think a lot of it was concerned with the students there reinventing the whole time, as though nobody had done anything before. As though they were never going to be challenged in their life, as they will on the whole be challenged, to take on other people's ideas, take on other people's materials and use that as a basis for their programmes of work. So I think those two areas, which clearly go hand in hand, of trust and feeling that we are going increasingly to have to take on board what other people have done and build upon that as a foundation, are very important indeed. I think that comes with working with one another, obviously. I trust my other eleven colleagues at Cavendish in the Science Faculty, because we work with each other regularly.

We know each other, we know our strengths, we know our weaknesses. We can say quite openly what we think, so that young teachers can come along and say, 'Look I'm not putting up with this any more. What are you going to do about it next lesson?' That kind of openness is very important and I think the challenge to create that sort of work cross-phase is a very difficult one indeed and we can only go about it in a small but realistic way and not try and erect grand structures which will fall down, frustrate people and turn them off.

Having said all that which is very positive, let me be very cynical, because I think cynicism or suspicion, and lack of trust, lie at the basis of some of these problems. It might go something like this. I very much hope it doesn't reflect my colleagues' views, but it might do. There are twelve of us, all highly qualified, experienced science teachers. At least half of our Science Faculty has worked in industry and with that experience as well, we think we know pretty well what science is about. We have done a lot of science, we have been at it in aggregate for quite a long time. There's not much you lot can tell us about science teaching! But you lot, as we know, don't actually know much about science at all. Thus when we get these records that you are talking about, which you know are going to be in an enormous amount of detail, superficially very helpful indeed, we don't believe a word of it! Why should we?

Neill: I have to concede some little bits of George's question, because we had a researcher come from Oxford to talk to us about forces and he gave us all a little test in the staff room. I won't reveal quite what the results were, but I think we are still very much at an Archimedean level of understanding. I make some concession your way, but we are very good at process skills in primary school, we always have been, the exploration, the enquiry and so on. I think actually, George, we have been able to teach you one or two things there. I am thinking of one particular example which one used to see in a secondary science book, of a candle burning inside a jar and when the flame went out, it went out because all of the oxygen was gone. Now we in primary school actually knew, I think, a lot sooner than your secondary colleagues that there was actually plenty of air inside that jar to support a whole host of small creatures, including a mouse, for some considerable time afterwards. We have encountered this type of thing and made our own private discoveries, because using a genuine enquiry-based investigational set-up, we have, as I say, not been hindered by the artifices of your own specialisms. So to some extent we have had a much clearer and incisive insight into real science, George.

I would confess, however, when one looks at electricity and forces at the higher National Curriculum levels that our understanding of logic gates is perhaps not what it should be. Nevertheless, when I reflect on my own education in maths, long, long ago, when I had to learn all about cosines and tangents and so on, I can't think of one single context where I have had to use a cosine in my entire life. I think it is also quite possible that there may not be a single occurrence in my life when I have to use knowledge about a logic gate either. So I am not too worried about those little difficult areas, George, that some of your colleagues think we should understand to a deeper degree than we actually do.

I do concede that there is a greater need for INSET in primary school. We enjoyed having two teachers go on the ESG course for science, that was very beneficial to us. They spent a year with a considerable amount of time out of school, and that was very profitable for us all. They have since left and got jobs elsewhere and now we are back to square one. I really don't think I can find much to say about the cascade system of INSET. One person selectively goes along to a course or seminar about which the rest of us know nothing and they come back and speciously shower us with what they have decided to pass on and the rest of the staff are sitting there with their umbrellas up in the staff room, not wishing to be cascaded upon. So I think we have got to get INSET right. There are more funds for INSET readily available today than there have been, but we need considerably more for all of us, not just for one of us.

I have to go along with you, George, and say that there is something the matter with these transfer records, but it's not really our fault. You spoke about us reinventing the wheel, well this year we have got 430 schools in Hertfordshire and we have probably got 430 different transfer records, because the County hasn't espoused one standard format, nor has the Government. So we have got square formats, rectangular formats, circular formats, nor do we have any standard convention for marking these things in, so some will have checks on them, some will be coloured with fluorescent pens, some will have alphabetical levels written on them and that's obviously going to be very difficult for you to interpret if you have got thirty of these different formats coming in to you. It's rather as though we have all been given a quick introduction to shorthand, but our reports all come out in thirty different languages. So that's the sort of context which George faces.

Again, the other problem with these records, is that they don't often reveal the context in which the concept has been learnt. So the teachers at George's school won't understand the topic in which the material has been presented. Worse still, they will not know which particular exemplar we have used in the classroom. All I can say to George, with a certain degree of a smile, is that we will have used the best illustrative exemplar that we can find, the most graphically exciting ones which we have been able to lay our hands on, and I know that will cause George's teachers a certain degree of frustration when they get our children and they set up some little exposition and our children shout out 'We've seen that Sir, we did that last year!'

George: As I was saying earlier, Neill, I think the most important aspect of accountability is between that responsibility of the teacher for the pupil, the pupil's learning and the pupil's whole learning. I think I want to modify that slightly now and suggest that there is another kind of accountability that we are trying to develop, particularly during the secondary years. That is self-accountability. The pupils should feel accountable to themselves as individuals for their learning, their progress, their attitudes, and their behaviour as they grow older. I think a crucial part of that is the whole development of self-assessment, and I was very pleased to see that feature in the David Hargreaves paper and also in the paper written by Dick West and Cathy Wilson. I think of all the things that we have tried to do in developing assessment at Cavendish over the last few years, the one I would put my money on as being the most significant is the one of self assessment. I am enormously impressed with the care that youngsters take, the coherence and the honesty with which they write when they come to talk about themselves, about where they have been and where they hope they are going. I just wonder whether that figures at all in primary schools and whether in any way you think it is appropriate that you should be preparing them for that sort of process?

Neill: Well, the answer is yes, George. It certainly figures in primary schools. It is an in-built part of the National Curriculum in a general sense that children have to take on the editorial process and differentiate between one of two levels. It may be that a child is capable of producing a piece of work and redrafting it with the help of the teacher. The next level is that the child produces a draft of work on his or her own initiative. To a lesser extent, and I'm not pushing this one, primary schools have always made books, and undertaken projects and the children have had to select work carefully. This has been part of an editorial process whether it is one of single or multiple authorship.

At my own school, we instituted quite specifically, a records of achievement programme and essentially what we did was buy each child a hard-backed folder and in those folders we have something like fifteen plastic inserts. So a folder is able to take about thirty pieces of work. Now the children self-select pieces of work to go into this folder. When they have selected a piece of work, they must also pop a little insert on the back of that work and explain why it has been selected – what their criteria are for having selected that work. When the folders become full, it does not mean that they stop collecting work. What it does mean is that they have to take a piece of work out and replace it with another. That means that they have to be able to discriminate between two pieces of work, and when they put in the new piece of work, they again have to put in a slip and explain on what criteria they have put in the new one. So they are taking on board the evaluative process. Instead of this being external to the individual, it is becoming internalized and we find that this is very, very valuable. It is not something extra or particularly difficult for the teacher to have to do in the classroom because it is based on ongoing work. We find that very valuable. Now how widely spread is this in the primary sector? Well I would have to say that it is probably not very widely spread and it's not widely spread for several reasons. One is ambivalence at County level. The process is 'desirable'. You read in County papers, and in Government papers too – 'This is desirable', not 'this is a necessity'. We know why these words have been chosen – because the process costs money! When you institute a programme like this, your photocopying bill goes up. We had to add about another £80 per year on for that. You have to have a camera, you have to buy film and pay for processing because you can't put a three-dimensional model into a folder – you have to photograph it. You have got to buy the files and the inserts themselves. Our initiation costs were in excess of £300. To some of you that might be an absolute trifling sum of money, but if you have got £4,700 per year and you find that perhaps £3,500 of this has gone on the telephone, the photocopier, the consumable goods, the first aid and so on, you only have a small capital sum for investment. So £350 is a significant investment to make to establish such a programme. So because of the cost concomitants and the ambivalence, I don't think these schemes are as widespread as they might well be.

When I look at our children's record of achievement files, I am very pleased with them. They belong to the children and we pass them on to George. But I have the suspicion that as these children leave your school, the employer is not going to want to see a whole collection of eccentric-looking material in a ring-back folder. He is going to be considerably more interested in levels of attainment in National Curriculum terms. So, down what route does this lead you?

George: Yes, the levels! I may have told some of you the story about when I was part of the National Curriculum Science Working Group. One evening, quite late into the night, we were working on part of the Earth Science material. There weren't many of us left at that stage. Most people had departed for the North, but we were stuck in the basement in some hotel in Kensington working away quietly, when John Holman looked up and said 'Origin of Universe – Level 8, do you think?' That kind of summed it up! I was also reminded of that lovely book by Raymond Briggs – *Gentleman Jim*. I don't know if you know it, but do read it if you can. The chap is a lavatory attendant and this lovely man is always going on to his equally lovely wife about how he never got any further in life. He never really progressed, because he never 'got the levels', so I think we need to be rather careful of 'the levels'! I think this kind of ambivalence that Neill drew to our attention between 'assessment for development' and 'assessment for selection' is interestingly present in both the background papers that you have from the employers. Of course it is extremely important that we have an accountability to the users of the system, whether they are employers, whether they are further education or higher education or whatever, that is extremely important. Let us recognize that some of the enlightened developments in assessment (I am thinking in terms of record of achievement; I am thinking in terms of some of the work done by the Royal Society of Arts Education for Capability movement) have had a very strong industrial thrust behind them, a very strong industrial thrust indeed, and we would be very foolish to ignore that. But of course there is an enormous range in the degree of enlightenment across the spectrum of employers and no such things as 'an employer's view'. The more work I do, for example with ICI, which I am quite involved with at the moment, the more I realize that it is very difficult to get an 'ICI view' on any aspect of education. There isn't one. There are a whole range of different views that hopefully can be distilled into some kind of acceptable statement. Again, I think we get better at it. We are improving, we learn from each other. One thing I learn from my increasing contacts with industry is that teachers, and education in general, do not have the monopoly of caring and concerned views about life. There are just as many deeply committed people who care working in industry as there are in schools, and we need to recognize that. If they are saying different things then that is the start of a dialogue and not an opportunity to ignore one another and switch off. So I think we need to be grateful to a large number of people in the sphere of employment, for the advice and thrust that they have given to developments in assessment. At the same time there is a great deal of work to do and I think the whole area of records of achievement is an enormously important one and will come to its climax, hopefully at the end of Key Stage 4. Hopefully, it will go on way beyond that. As we get the idea that the majority of youngsters might actually be capable of learning even after the age of 16 years – a strange concept in this country, but its one that is slowly beginning to permeate I think! – that sort of development will be even more important.

Let me switch focus, perhaps finally Neill, and say that I am about to introduce a rather old-fashioned concept of the 'educational community'. Your school is in Boxmoor which is located in a pretty plush area of Hemel Hempstead. I don't know whether Neill can afford to live there; I don't think he can – and I certainly can't. Between us we might afford a garage in Boxmoor, so it is a pretty plush area of a pretty plush authority, because Hertfordshire is still quite well off in national terms. Your school, one could say, is in a favoured social area and therefore, by definition, your youngsters are going to do rather well. When the time comes to publish, as alas it will, the aggregated results at the end of Key Stage 2, you are going to feel rather smug about it, I should think. Your governors and your parents too, because I reckon Boxmoor JMI will be doing rather well.

I think there is actually a wider community of education, and it now sounds rather old-fashioned to say this, because the Government would have us believe otherwise, that there are actually individual schools and nothing else matters very much. I don't believe that. I think that what happens at Neill's school and what happens at our school, does actually have a profound effect upon other schools. It can be for the good and it can be very much for the worse. What sort of responsibility are you going to have in terms of your published results and is it going to make any difference in your relationship with other schools in the area?

Neill: Well basically, I don't see any divorce at all between our school and other schools in less well-off parts of the town or county. We all share common problems, though perhaps to a lesser and different degree. We have neglected children. Affluence can cause neglected children, where you have two parents who select as their first goal the setting up of the family business. We have professionals who work long hours, come back late from London and haven't time to spend with their children. So we have children who suffer lack of time, not lack of care, lack of time. We also have a different problem, we have overindulged children, where everything is done for them and we have to try and teach them some sort of independence. We have also got more single-parent families. They seem to grow in proportion each year. Four years ago, we had nobody on free school meals. Now I can't number them on both hands and there is an obvious upward trend. The economy has taken its toll on the neighbourhood. So we do have a perception of the same problems, but as I say the degree is in the quantity.

We are very fortunate that we have an active School Association which buys us books, maths and science equipment, and pays our repair bills on things like the duplicator. It buys us paint for the school. It is a terrific asset. This golden goose is being viciously squeezed – the more so each year – as we need a bigger egg, and obviously this thing is not going to be able to produce the size of egg that we are going to demand from it. One day it may just roll over and be dead. So although we are comfortable right now, we can't rely on this private source of funding to be the mainstay of the school. It depends on the personalities of the Fundraising Committee and the amount of vigour and effort they are prepared to put into it, at any one point in time. It is also subject to certain vagaries in the market, like newspapers. We used to collect and recycle news-papers, but the bottom has dropped out of the newspaper market, so we have a slump at the moment. These are the sort of problems that we have here. So, how do we feel about our colleagues in other schools. Well, we admire their grit and determination in moving their children the same amount forward or even more, as we do with our own. Our starting points are different, we know that, we recognize that and we are also prepared to explain that to anybody who queries that of us.

Now I think I can extend our concern, George, even one step further, and not just take it and leave it with our colleagues. Let's take it to the children. I feel a great shame that in this country we have not got equality of provision or equality of access to opportunity for our children. That, I think, is appalling. We have failed to recognize our principal national asset, our children. I also find it very difficult to take on board, this constant denigration of the teaching profession, which we have had in the last decade. Nor can I, for the life of me, understand how anybody can construct a scenario in which we are leading our primary and secondary schools to the brink of material bankruptcy. So to come back to you, George, we are all part of the educational community and, yes, we do show a great concern for the direction that our education generally has taken and we hope for better things to come in the future.

I appreciate George's great dilemma over the publication of results and one of the questions that we will get asked at the end of the autumn term in a year's time will relate to interpretation. Parents will come to us and say 'Cavendish has published its results and Hemel School has published its results. How shall we interpret them?' That is going to pose something of a dilemma to us, and rather than my just giving my own opinion on that, I would like to come to George and say 'What advice would you give us when parents ask how they should interpret the secondary school results?'

George: Well, I think with a large pinch of salt probably. I do find myself being increasingly sucked into this competitive scenario that we now operate within. An increasing amount of my time as a Head, is spent in the presentation of the school, in winning not just material resources, but ensuring that the human resources for our next year's youngsters are going to come our way rather than somebody else's way. And that, under Local Management of Schools (LMS), is going to be even more acute in the future.

Just to give you two small examples. We are obviously obliged by law to publish our public exam results and I don't resist that, but I have always kept them fairly low key. I find myself for the first time this year, giving them out to everybody coming to our open evenings for prospective parents. So instead of doing what I have done in the past and that is handing them out in an un-marked brown envelope to those who are bold enough to ask for them, I am actually thrusting them into everybody's hands and saying 'Look at these!' I also find myself giving out this year, and I have never done this before, where our Upper Sixth leavers went to last year, because they did rather well. I wonder whether I should be doing that. I find myself giving more time to all that kind of thing and I worry; I am concerned about it. But we are in that sort of environment. At the same time I try very hard to support other secondary colleagues and not to be cutting the ground from under their feet. I take your point entirely about the Parent Teachers' Association that we are relying on to raise, not just hundreds of pounds as you are, but thousands of pounds and that is worrying. So it is a difficult area this one, a very difficult area indeed. But I come back to the point I made and perhaps I will finish with this, saying that in the final analysis, I actually have great respect for, and great trust of, parental views about schools. I think if we are open and honest to parents, we have got little to fear even if the media distort and mislead. I think parents are pretty shrewd in looking for a range of different qualities in a school for their children and if we are prepared to meet them more than half way in our honesty, I don't think we have got a great deal to fear.

Now what we have tried to do in the last three-quarters of an hour – look at that Neill, isn't it brilliant timing? – the BBC would be proud of us! What we have tried to do and I wish we had more time to do this, week in and week out, as part of our professional lives – is to raise for you, and I hope it will be part of your discussion during the day, the areas of accountability that seem to us important in terms of assessment in the National Curriculum.

To sum these up, we have talked about accountability towards our pupils, we have talked about accountability towards their parents, accountability be-tween teachers, between colleagues and particularly cross-phase. Account-ability towards employers, and (I hate this word) the users of our 'product'. There is not a product of education and wherever you see that word in a paper, you should cross it out, cut it out, get the scissors to it; it's awful. We have, I think, a profound accountability towards the rest of the educational com-munity because I think there *is* something called the educational community and the parts of it add up to a whole and they influence that whole. Perhaps what we have not talked about enough is our accountability towards our governors, our governing body and their accountability in turn towards all the groups that I have mentioned. Neill has mentioned it, but I have hardly mentioned it at all and it is increasingly important. So clearly that should feature in your discussions as well.

I hope you have found this exchange – which is a very genuine exchange between two colleagues whose schools are very much enmeshed and who get on very well, not just on the platform, but in the reality of our professional lives – of some use. Thank you Neill.

Author Index

Adey, P. S. 113, 190–220, 242
Aikenhead, G. S. 25
Aldrich, M. 52
Aldridge, W. G. 49
Allsop, T. 24
Alport, J. M. 45
American Association for the
   Advancement of Science (AAAS) 49, 52
American Chemical Society 49
Amsel, E. 195
Anania, J. 226
Anderson, J. R. 156
Anderson, O. R. 82
Angelev, J. 191
Archibald, D. A. 48
Armitage, P. 244
Armstrong, J. 49
Arnold, B. 226, 229, 232, 233
Askew, J. M. 52, 128
Atlay, M. 3, 79–97
Auld, J. 226, 228, 233

Baird, J. 13
Baird, J. R. 133
Baldwin, J. M. 146
Baron, B. 48
Barrows, H. S. 82
Bawden, R. J. 82
Bealer, J. M. 58
Beane, D. 52
Beasley, F. 191
Bell, B. 23
Bennett, S. N. 135
Benson, A. 5
Benson, G. D. 24
Bereiter, C. 155
Bestor, A. 38

Black, H. 233
Black, H. D. 232
Black, P. J. 84
Blake, A. J. D. 190
Bloom, B. S. 226, 238
Bonnstetter, R. J. 99
Boud, D. J. 80–9
Boyd, S. E. 52
Boyer, E. L. 46
Brainerd, C. J. 190
Brandt, D. 88
Bridgham, P. W. 14
Brook, A. 242
Brophy, J. E. 144
Brown, A. L. 147, 155, 157
Brown, D. E. 143, 157, 173
Brown, E. 3, 66–78
Brown, G. 190
Brown, J. S. 139, 155, 164
Brumby, M. 229, 232
Bruner, J. S. 147
Brush, S. G. 24
Brusic, S. A. 25
Buchwald, C. E. 52
Burbules, N. C. 151
Burdett, P. 24
Bush, V. 39
Byard, M. 171–89
Bybee, R. W. 24, 52

Caillot, M. 25
California Department of Education 49
Calinger, B. J. 52
Campione, J. C. 147, 155, 157
Cantu, L. L. 233
Carey, S. 6, 142, 147, 149, 156
Carre, C. G. 135

Carter, D. S. 135
Case, R. 139, 156, 158, 191, 226, 234
Cassels, J. R. T. 120
Chambers, R. G. 89
Champagne, A. B. 48, 52, 147
Chase, N. 139
Children's Learning in Science Project
    (CLISP) 132
Clancy, M. J. 155
Clarke, A. D. B. 191
Clarke, A. M. 191
Clement, C. 142
Clement, J. 143, 147, 157, 173
Clough, E. E. 13, 24, 153
Clune, W. H. 47
Coble, C. R. 58, 60
Cognition and Technology Group at
    Vanderbilt 155
Cohen, D. K. 49
Coleman, J. S. 144, 159
Coley, R. J. 47
College Board, 52
Collins, A. 139, 155, 164
Comber, L. C. 128
Committee on Education and Labor 46
Committee on Science and
    Technology 40, 43, 44
Conant, J. 127
Corbett, R. 135
Crane, L. L. 139, 142
Cremin, L. A. 36, 37
Crissman, S. 52
Cronbach, L. 203
Cryer, N. 88

Darling-Hammond, L. 48
Davies, I. K. 88
Davis, A. 49
Deadman, J. A. 229
Department of Education and Science
    (DES) 129, 244
DES/WO/DENI 127, 130–1
DES/WO 124
Desautels, J. 7, 25
Desforges, C. 190
Dewey, J. 144, 159
DeWitt, N. 40
di Sessa, A. 147
Dibbs, D. R. 6
Dixon, B. 17
Dockrell, W. B. 232
Doise, W. 156
Doran, R. L. 67
Dorr-Bremme, D. W. 48

Dow, W. M. 226, 228, 233
Downs, R. M. 155
Draper, S. 171–89
Driver, R. 13, 23, 122, 131, 153,
    171–89, 229, 232, 242
Duckworth, D. 210
Duguid, P. 139
Duhem, P. 16
Dumas-Carre, A. 25
Dunn, J. 80–9
Duschl, R. A. 5, 13
Duveen, J. 24

Easley, J. 229, 232
Easley, J. A. 45, 98
Eccles, J. S. 144, 160
Eckert, P. 144, 159
Educational Policies Committee 59
Edwards, D. 79–87
Elkind, D. 160
Ellis, J. D. 24
England, J. M. 39
Englehart, M. D. 238
Erickson, F. 100
Erickson, G. L. 133
Evans, R. 6, 24
Eylon, B. 140, 149

Fairbrother, R. 223, 237–49
Farmer, B. 15, 25
Feistritzer, E. 48
Fensham, P. J. 13, 133
Ferrara, R. A. 147, 155, 157
Feuerstein, R. 191
Feyerabend, P. K. 9, 14, 16
Firestone, W. A. 47, 48
Francis, E. 231
Fraser, B. J. 101
Frederiksen, J. R. 154
Freyberg, P. 131
Friedler, Y. 25, 147
Friot 190
Fuhrman, S. H. 47, 48
Furby, L. 203
Furil, E. J. 238
Fusco, E. T. 193

Gabb, R. G. 84
Gakuseisha, R. 61
Gallagher, J. 49
Gallagher, J. J. 98, 99, 102
Gardner, P. L. 8, 85
Garnett, P. 4, 98–109
Garrard, J. 133

Gennema, E. 144, 160, 161
Gentner, D. 147
Gerrans, G. C. 84, 89
Giere, R. N. 18
Gil-Perez, D. 25
Gilbert, J. 131
Gilbert, J. K. 242
Gilbert, S. W. 13
Gilligan, C. 144
Glaser, R. 140
Goertz, M. E. 47
Good, T. L. 144
Goodlad, J. I. 46
Goodrum, D. 100, 101
Goossens, L. 191, 193
Goring, R. 233
Gott, R. 126
Grandy, R. E. 13
Greene, J. 121
Greeno, J. G. 156
Grissmer, D. W. 48
Grubb, W. N. 37
Guesne, E. 13, 122, 173, 242
Gunstone, R. F. 13, 147, 174, 182

Hacking, I. 21
Hadden, R. A. 210
Haertal, E. 48
Hafner, R. 23
Haggstrom, G. W. 48
Hall, P. 52
Hallam, R. N. 193
Halloun, I. 174
Hamilton, R. 13
Hanifen, E. 15, 25
Happs, J. 106
Harlen, 114, 124-38
Hartley, R. 171-89
Hawking, S. W. 127
Head, J. J. 13
Hegarty-Hazel, E. 80-9
Heil, D. R. 52
Hein, G. 48
Heller, J. 173
Hellingman, C. 85
Hennessy, S. 171-89
Herman, J. L. 48
Herron, J. D. 233
Hestenes, D. 174
Hewson, M. 173
Hewson, P. 173
Hickman, F. M. 52
Hicks, C. 121
Hill, W. H. 238

Hioki, M. 58
Hodgkinson, H. L. 52
Hodson, D. 3, 5-32, 128
Hoffman, M. 191
Hofstein, A. 82
Holton, G. 18, 41
Honda, M. 6, 24
Hornsey, M. 231
Horsfield, J. 231
Hudson, L. 48
Hughes, A. 16
Hungate, H. 173
Hyde, J. S. 144, 160, 161

Inhelder, B. 139, 140, 156, 157, 193
International Association for the
    Evaluation of Educational
    Achievement 52, 68, 69, 70, 71,
    72, 73

Jacobson, W. J. 67
Jacoby, B. 12
Jay, E. 6, 24
Jegede, O. 18
Jehng, J. C. 155
Jelly, S. J. 134
Jenkins, L. B. 52
Johnson, L. M. 47
Johnstone, A. H. 113, 115-23, 131, 210,
    226, 232
Jurd, M. 193

Kadaya, S. 58
Karplus, R. 190
Kass, H. 5, 133
Keating, D. P. 139, 142
Keeves, J. P. 66, 73, 128
Kellett, N. C. 226, 232
Kelly, A. 210
Kelly, P. S. 229
Keys, W. 66-7, 74, 75, 76, 77
Kirscher, P. A. 16, 20, 24
Kirst, M. W. 47, 48
Klopfer, L. E. 25, 64, 79, 83, 147
Knorr-Cetina, K. D. 17
Koertge, N. 16
Kreighbaum, H. 40
Kreithwohl, D. R. 238
Kruger, C. 134
Kuchemann, D. E. 190, 202
Kuerbis, P. J. 52
Kuhn, D. 191, 195
Kuhn, T. S. 10, 16, 22, 127, 156
Kyle, W. C. 45

Lambert, D. M. 16
Lamon, S. J. 144, 160, 161
Lantz, O. 5
LaPointe, A. E. 52, 128
Larochelle, M. 25
Latour B. 17
Laudan, L. 19
Lawson, A. E. 3, 58–65, 190, 191
Lederman, N. G. 5
Lee, Shin-Ying 60
Letton, K. M. 120
Lewis, E. L. 145, 150, 151, 152
Liben, L. S. 155, 157
Library of Congress 39, 40
Linder, C. J. 26
Linn, M. C. 25, 113, 139–70
Loving, C. C. 24
Lovitts, B. E. 52
Lucas, A. M. 83
Lucker, G. W. 60
Lunetta, V. N. 82, 99
Lynch, P. P. 22, 84, 89
Lynd, A. 38

Macadam, R. D. 82
Maccoby, E. E. 160
Macdonald, J. J. 131
Macdonald-Ross, M. 86, 87
McCarthy, S. 24
McDermott, L. C. 174
McInerney, J. D. 52
McKinnon 190
Madaus, C. F. 135
Makayama, G. 58
Malcolm, S. M. 52
Mallen, C. 171–89
Mander, A. H. 84
Marchman, V. A. 98
Markle, S. M. 233
Marsh, P. E. 45
Martinez-Torregrosa, J. 25
Mashiter, J. 126
Mason, R. O. 17
Matsubara, V. U. 58
Matsumoto, C. 52
Matsumoto, K. 58
Matsumoto, S. 58
Matthes, F. 58, 60
Maxwell, N. 11
Mead, N. A. 52, 128
Medawar, P. B. 19, 20, 21
Mergandoller, J. R. 98
Merrill, M. P. 233
Millar, C. D. 16

Millar, R. 16, 25
Miller, M. 191
Minstrell, 143, 157
Mitchell, I. 133
Mitman, A. L. 98
Mitroff, I. I. 17
Mohamed, G. 171–89
Morris, R. 124
Mugny, G. 156
Mullis, V. S. 48, 52

Nachmias, R. 25, 147
Nadeau, R. 7
Nakayama, H. 58
National Academy of Sciences 46
National Assessment of Educational
    Progress 46, 161
National Center for Education
    Statistics 44
National Commission on Excellence in
    Education 46, 47
National Governors' Association 46
National Science Board 46
National Science Foundation (NSF) 33,
    41–2, 50, 51
Neame, R. L. B. 82
Nersessian, N. J. 13
Newman, S. E. 155, 164
Newmann, F. M. 48
Newton-Smith, W. H. 14
Nickerson, R. S. 191, 198
Niemark, E. 190
Nisbet, J. 242
Nolan, L. M. 151–2
Nordin, A. B. 226
Novak, J. 127
Novick, S. 133, 232
Nunan, E. E. 10
Nussbaum, J. 133, 232

Oakes, J. 48, 53
Odden, A. 49
Ogborn, J. 84
O'Loughlin, M. 195
O'Malley, C. E. 171–89
Ormerod, M. B. 210
Orpwood, G. 124, 125
Osborne, R. 131
O'Shea, T. 113, 171–89

Packer, M. J. 98
Packham, P. J. 82
Palincsar, A. C. 147, 155, 157
Papert, S. 192

Parsons, C. 192
Patrick, J. J. 52
Patterson, N. 224, 250–64
Penick, J. E. 99
Perkins, D. N. 191, 198
Perret-Clermont, A. 156
Phillips, G. 128
Physical Sciences Study Committee
    (PSSC) 41
Piaget, J. 139, 140, 146, 147, 156, 157,
    193
Polanyi, M. 14
Popper, K. 127
Postlethwaite, T. N. 66, 67, 68, 70, 71,
    72, 76
Powell, J. C. 24
Price, R. M. 88
Pulos, S. 142, 149

Qualter, A. 24
Quick, B. 52

Raghavan, K. 25
Raizen, S. A. 3, 33–57
Ranbon, S. 61, 62
Rand, Y. 191
Ravetz, J. R. 19, 25
Ravitch, D. 38
Rawson, H. 40
Reeve, R. 147, 155, 157
Reid, D. J. 22
Renner, J. W. 190
Resnick, D. P. 45
Resnick, L. B. 45, 191
Rider, J. G. 88
Rosenthal, D. A. 191
Rosier, M. J. 66, 73
Rothkopf, E. 89
Russell, B. 33
Russell, T. 127, 132
Rutherford, F. J. 41

Salomon, G. 198
Sarason, S. B. 45
Sardar, Z. 18
Saruta, Y. 58
Scanlon, E. 171–89
Scardamalia, M. 155
Schauble, L. 6
Schibeci, R. A. 6
Schlechty, P. 48
Schoenfeld, A. H. 142, 155
Schon, D. A. 107
Schwartz, J. L. 48

Science Processes and Concepts
    Exploration (SPACE) 132–3
Scot, L. 24
Scottish Education Department
    (SED) 223, 225
Scottish Examination Board (SEB) 122
Secondary Science Curriculum Review
    (SSCR) 237
Shamos, M. H. 52
Shapiro, B. 133
Shayer, M. 113, 190–220, 242
Shucksmith, J. 242
Shulman, L. S. 107
Shymansky, J. A. 45
Siegel, H. 22
Simon, H. A. 139, 156
Simpson, M. 133
Simpson, M. 223, 225–36
Sizer, T. 46
Smith, E. E. 191, 198
Smith, R. B. 172
Smolicz, J. J. 10, 22
Snitgen, D. A. 191
Soloman, J. 133
Solomon, J. 13, 24
Songer, N. B. 113, 139–70
Spargo, P. 12
Spensley, F. 173, 182, 186
Spiro, R. J. 155
Spooner, W. E. 58, 60
Sprinivasan, V. 233
Stafford 190
Stake, R. E. 45, 98
Stern, V. 52
Stern, J. 145, 150
Sternberg, R. J. 139
Stevens, A. L. 147
Stevenson, H. W. 60
Stewart, J. 23
Stiger, J. W. 60
Strang, J. 24
Strube, P. 24
Summers, M. 134
Swatton, P. 24

Tadokoro, Y. 58
Takemura, S. 58, 62
Tamblyn, R. M. 82
Task Force on Education for Economic
    Growth 46
Taylor, R. 24
Tennyson, R. D. 233
Tiberghien, A. 13, 122, 147, 173, 242
Tobin, K. 4, 98–109

Toulmin, S. 127
Tucker, W. 151–2
Twentieth Century Fund Task Force 46
Twigger, D. 171–89
Tyler, R. W. 6

Unger, C. 6, 24

Valentine, J. 82
Van der Valk, T. 24
Vance, V. 48
Viator, K. A. 48
Viennot, L. 173, 229
Villani, A. 13
Vygotsky, L. S. 140, 144, 147, 164, 195, 199

Walker, G. 224, 250–64
Wandersee, J. H. 24
Ward, R. 233
Watson, F. G. 41
Watt, D. 132
Watts, D. M. 174, 242
Webb, G. 131
Weiss, I. R. 45, 52
Welch, W. W. 43
Werdelin, I. 124, 125
West, L. 133

Wham, A. J. B. 120, 122
White, B. Y. 154
White, F. C. 14
White, R. 13
Whitehead, A. N. 33
Wiggins, G. 48
Wiley, D. E. 66, 67, 68, 70, 71, 72, 76
Wilson, B. 135
Wilson, D. 226, 228, 233
Wiser, M. 142, 147
Wolf, R. M. 46
Wolfe, L. F. 5
Wood-Robinson, C. 13
Woodring, P. 38
Woolgar, S. 17
Woolnough, B. 24
Wooton, W. 39
Wragg, E. C. 135
Wylam, H. 190, 202

Yager, R. E. 99
Yates, C. 193
Yoshida, A. 58
Young, R. M. 17

Zeidler, D. L. 5
Zietsman, A. 143, 157
Ziman, J. M. 21

Subject Index

accountability, pressures and
    opportunities 250–64
  cross-phase 256–8
  opportunities 260–1
  to other teachers 255–6
  to parents 252, 253–5
  problems 261–3
  to pupils 250–3
  pupils' self- 258–60
adolescence *see* cognitive and conceptual
    change . . . ; conceptual change . . .
alternative frameworks 229
alternative realities kit (ARK) 172
assessment 15–17
  see also diagnostic . . . ; formative . . . ;
    skills . . . tests, international
    comparisons;
  of learning failures 233–4
  of pupils 135, 136, 251, 260
  records 246
  scales 244
Assessment of Performance Unit (Science)
  (APU(S)) 74
  surveys 127, 128–31, 240

bridging to other contexts 193, 200
Business and Technology Education
  Council (BTEC) 80
  Higher National awards 90
  science unit 92–5

Children's Learning in Science Project
  (CLISP) 131–2
classroom
  practice
    see also EPSME
    teachers' emphasis 98–9
  problems 10

cognitive and conceptual change
  in adolescents 139–70
    case study 145–55
    conclusions 163–5
    mechanisms of 156–9
    research conclusions 165
    research theories 139
    social context 159–62
    theoretical perspective 140–5
cognitive
  conflict 193, 195–8
  development 211–16
  difficulties 232
  learning 98–9
  outcomes 99
Computer-as-Lab-Partner (CLP)
  see also curriculum
  principles 166
concepts 117–18, 121
  inadequate development 227–8
conceptual change
  in science project (CCIS)
    171–89
  in adolescents 141–2, 156–7
    curriculum design 176–82
    evaluation 182–5
    features of 171
    overview 173
    purpose 172
    results 185–7
    software design 182
    students' prior conceptions
      174–6
conceptual readiness 193, 193–5
constructive process 163
course content
  inadequacies 233

course design
  behavioural 80–9
    aims and objectives 84–5
    formulation 85–8
    goals 81–2
    scientific inquiry 82–4
    student guidance 88–9
  non-behavioural 89–95
    BTEC schemes 89–91
    BTEC science unit 92–5
  computer-based curriculum 171–8
coursework
  planning of assessment 246–8
criteria and hierarchies 242
curriculum
  see also hidden . . .
  activities 5
  CLP 145, 147–9, 157, 162
  computer-based experiment 171–87
  consequence of 152
  development in USA 41–4, 45, 48–9
  image of science 7
  indices for international tests 73–4
  planning 6–7
  rational planning 6–7

degree programme
  aims and objectives 81–2
design of computer curriculum 173
development
  see also cognitive . . . ; curriculum
    . . . ; method . . . ; research . . .
  concept 127
  of ideas 126–7
  scientific 18
  theoretical 10
diagnostic assessment
  pupils' learning 225–36, 238
    barriers to 227–9
    diagnosis 230–2
    difficulties 226–7
    remediation 232–3
direct manipulation of mechanical
    microworlds (DM3) 182
differentiation 250
discipline-centred approach 81
domain differentiation 143, 164

Exemplary Practice in Science and
    Mathematics project (EPSME) 98–109
  case studies 101–4
  comparison of case studies 104–8
  overview 99–100
  purpose 100–1

experiments 118–20
  see also intervention programme . . .

formal science 116–17
formative assessment 238–8

gender differentiation 160–2
government
  association with 34–6

hidden curriculum 5
higher and further education
  practical and lab work 79–97
hierarchies 240–3
holistic approach 22–5
hypothetico-deductive approach 6

inductivist approach 6
information processing 158
inquiry
  scientific 82–4
INSET
  need for, in primary schools 258
integrated education 26
International Association for the
    Evaluation of Educational
    Achievement (IEA) survey 128
international comparisons 66–78
  analysis of English data 75–7
  curriculum indices 73–4
  data collected 67–8
  national objectives 74–5
  Second International Science
    Study 66–7
  tests 68–71
  test data 71–3
intervention programme ('Thinking
    Science')
  in secondary school 190–220
    activities 193–200
    background 190–2
    context 192–3
    experiment and tests 200–3
    immediate results 204–5
    delayed results 205–6
    long-term results 206–10
    results analysis 210–17
intuitive conceptions 146–9, 150–1

Japanese science education see USA . . .

knowledge 125
  acquisition by students 141–2
  action 145–6

knowledge (cont.)
  boundaries and principles 153–5
  descriptive 8, 11
  differentiation and integration 142–4
  explanatory 8, 11
  pursuit of 8, 11
  teachers' 134–5
  theory and model 11–12

laboratory practice
  in further and higher education 79–97
    aims and key factors 79–80
    behavioural course design 80–9
    non-behavioural course design 89–95
    purposes 82
    training and skills 211
  in schools 103–4, 118–9
language 123
  barrier 120–1
  confusion 149–50
  instrumentalist 5
  observation 9
  realist 5
learning difficulties 115–23, 226–7
  see also diagnostic assessment
  conflicting message 121–3
  layperson's view 116–17
  social context of 144–5
  teaching in schools 117–21
  prevention of 232
long term far-transfer
  see intervention programme

metacognition 193, 198–9
method
  development of 14–15
misconceptions 229
model 13
  creative phase 19
  experimental phase 20–1
  inductivist 8
  learning 121–3
  objectives 6
  Piagetian 190, 192
  recording and reporting phase 21–1
  theoretical 12–13
multilevel thought 118, 122

National Academy of Science (US) 34
National Curriculum (US) 251, 254
National Science Foundation 34–6, 39, 46
  funding 40, 41, 42, 43–4, 44, 46
  programmes in the 1980s 49–51
norms and standards 244–5

objectives see also course design
behavioural and non-behavioural (in lab
  work) 80–9
objectivity and rationality 18
opportunities see accountability

peer groups (USA) 159–60
performance hierarchies 240–3
  criterion referenced 242
philosophy and sociology 5–32
  assessment and evaluation 15–17
  cultural phenomenon 17–18
  holistice and integrated education
    22–5
  knowledge 11–13
  messages 6
  method 13–15
  model 19–22
  purposes of science 8–11
  underlying philosophies 6–8
practical work 79–87, 122
practice see classroom . . . ; laboratory . . .
pressures 252
  see also accountability
primary teaching
  see also research and development
  case study 101–2, 104–8
principles 151–5
prior conceptions 174
process
  definition 237–8
  skills 127
progressive education in the USA 37–8
purposes of science 8–11

rationality see objectivity
reasoning ability, a comparison 58
reform in the USA see USA
research and development
  see also cognitive and conceptual
    change . . .
  in primary school 124–38
    achievements 128–31
    developing ideas and skills 131–4
    future implications 134–6
    teaching goals and
      expectations 125–7
  in secondary school 187
    see also conceptual change,
      adolescents . . .

schools
  see also primary, secondary
  expansion in the USA 36–8

science (as a cultural phenomenon)
  concepts in schools 17, 117
  principles 151
science Processes and Concepts
  Exploration (SPACE) 132–4, 134
scientific knowledge 11–13
scientific method 13–15
scientism 7
Search for Excellence project 99
Second International Science study
  (SISS) 66–7, 74, 75–7
secondary school
  see also intervention programme
  Computer as Lab Partner Project
    (CLP) 139–70
  Conceptual Change in Science Project
    (CCIS) 171–89
  teaching case study 102–8
Secondary Science Curriculum
  Review 74
skills 125
  see also development . . . ; laboratory
    practice . . . ; learning difficulties . . .
  definition 237–8
  inquiry 82–4
  problems in assessment of 237–49
    in primary school 131
    formative and summative
      assessment 238–9
    hierarchies of performance 240–3
    planning coursework 246–8
    practical work 80
    setting standards 239–40
    standards' norms and criteria 244–6
    workload and reliability 243–4
sociology see philosophy . . .
Standard Grade Chemistry
  programme 122
standards
  assessment 239–40, 244–6
summative assessment 238–9
survey
  international 128–31
    SISS 66–77
  national
    APU 128–31
    CLISP 131–2
    SPACE 132–3
  techniques 131–4

teacher
  and assessment 250–64
  and assessment of skills 238–49
  and computer 171–87
  and philosophy and sociology of
    science 5–32
  and thinking skills 190–220
  exemplary practice 98–108
  institutes in the USA 39–41
  role change 134
  shortage in the USA 48
teaching
  goals and expectations 125–7
  and learning
    philosophy and sociology 5–32
tests
  see also assessment
  diagnostic 232
  international 68–73
  student intelligence (USA) 38, 47–8
theories 11–13
  assessment and evaluation of 15–17
  research 139
'Thinking Science' see intervention
  programme

USA
  and Japanese science education
    58–65
    causes of difference 59–63
    comparison of reasoning
      abilities 58–9
  science and education reform 33–57
    as taught in schools 117–21
    the future 51–3
    growth of science and
      education 34–9
    original vision 33–4
    1960s and 1970s 39–45
    1980s 45–51

verification approach 6
vocational education in the USA
  36–7

working memory 158–9, 234
workload of skills assessment
  243–4
wrong information 228–9, 231